Philosophical Theories of Political Cinema

This book utilizes philosophical tools to build up a framework for the classification, analysis and assessment of political cinema. The author first maps the category of political cinema, clarifying what it means for a film to be 'political', and then analyzes the relation between the value of a film as a political film and its value as art.

Through philosophical enquiry, Angelo Emanuele Cioffi builds up a framework that could be of use in art-critical practice and that can help with the classification and assessment of political films. Grounded in analytic philosophy of art and cognitivist film theory, with insights from political science, political philosophy, epistemology and cognitive science, the book presents a unique analysis of the relation between films and the 'political'. This theory is tested with detailed case studies, and the author uses specific films as examples of the applicability and explanatory power of this theoretical framework.

As such, this book will be of interest not just to film studies, film theory and political philosophy scholars, but to anyone with an interest in political film, aesthetic practice and philosophy of art.

Angelo Emanuele Cioffi studied Political Theory and Cultural Policies at the Universities of Pavia and Warwick and received his PhD in History and Philosophy of Art from the University of Kent. He teaches 'English for the Arts' at 'LABA' Fine Arts Academy and Literature at a high school in Brescia.

Routledge Advances in Film Studies

Why We Remake
The Politics, Economics and Emotions of Remaking
Lauren Rosewarne

Hollywood Remembrance and American War
Edited by Andrew Rayment and Paul Nadasdy

Film Noir and Los Angeles
Urban history and the Dark Imaginary
Sean W. Maher

Australian Genre Film
Edited by Kelly McWilliam and Mark David Ryan

Flashbacks in Film
A Cognitive and Multimodal Analysis
Adriana Gordejuela

Trans New Wave Cinema
Akkadia Ford

Love in Contemporary Cinema
Audiences and Representations of Romance
Benjamín de la Pava Vélez

Horror Franchise Cinema
Edited by Mark McKenna and William Proctor

Philosophical Theories of Political Cinema
Angelo Emanuele Cioffi

For more information about this series, please visit: www.routledge.com

Philosophical Theories of Political Cinema

Angelo Emanuele Cioffi

Routledge
Taylor & Francis Group
LONDON AND NEW YORK

First published 2022
by Routledge
2 Park Square, Milton Park, Abingdon, Oxon OX14 4RN

and by Routledge
605 Third Avenue, New York, NY 10158

Routledge is an imprint of the Taylor & Francis Group, an informa business

British Library Cataloguing-in-Publication Data
A catalogue record for this book is available from the British Library

Library of Congress Cataloging-in-Publication Data
A catalog record for this book has been requested

ISBN: 978-0-367-41924-0 (hbk)
ISBN: 978-1-032-04622-8 (pbk)
ISBN: 978-0-367-81687-2 (ebk)

DOI: 10.4324/9780367816872

Typeset in Sabon
by Apex CoVantage, LLC

A mia Madre e Luigi

Contents

Introduction

In this book, I develop a theory of political cinema. I use philosophical tools in order to build up a framework for the classification, analysis and assessment of political cinema. I define the category of political cinema, and to do that, I also tackle the problem of what it means to be 'political'; then I analyze the relation between the value of a film as a political film and its value *qua* art. I move from two hypotheses: (1) the purpose of a political film can differentiate it from other kinds of films, and (2) this very purpose can affect our aesthetic appraisal of political films. Hence, my aim is twofold. I aim to map the category of political cinema and to identify analytical tools that could be used to assess the value of political films. This means that, through philosophical enquiry, I aim to construct a framework that could be of use in art-critical practice and that can help with the classification and assessment of political films.

I aim to provide a theory of political cinema because I am dissatisfied with the terminological inaccuracy and lack of systematization that characterizes the relation between art and the 'political'. In art-critical practices and film criticism, the label 'political' is often used to describe 'something' about the artwork, but there is no clarity around the definition of the 'political' and the role of such a political dimension in the assessment of films, and artworks more generally, is left unclear. The problems around the interrelation between art and the 'political' are left unsystematized in both the analytic philosophy of art and the cognitivist tradition of film studies. In the analytic tradition of the philosophy of art, there are open debates on the normative problems about the value of art. In particular, I think of the debate on the possibility of valuing art for the purposes it may serve, for instance because it teaches a moral lesson, or of the debate on the interrelation between aesthetic value and other values.[1] Nonetheless, there is no systematic account of the possible interrelation between the political and the art's value.

Cognitivism, as an approach to film theory, has established itself in opposition to what has been labeled the 'Grand Theory' of film studies (Allen & Smith, 1997; Bordwell & Carroll, 1996; Plantinga & Smith, 1999). This was not actually a single theory but rather an aggregate of doctrines derived from Lacanian psychoanalysis, structural semiotics, post-structuralist

DOI: 10.4324/9780367816872-1

literary theory and variants of Althusserian Marxism. Such Grand Theory was conceived as an indispensable frame of reference to understand all filmic phenomena, as the study of films was subsumed under generally encompassing schemes that were developed to explain society, language and psychology. Grand Theory viewed films as being deeply bound up with the political. Within this framework, films are all politically connoted simply because they are cultural artifacts and, as such, their production and consumption are taken to be politically or ideologically determined. Carroll notes how proponents of theory focused their analyses on the unconscious processes that they took to be the core of spectator's response to films, and more specifically, they endorsed psychoanalysis because they thought ideology worked through unconscious processes (Carroll, 1996a).

If, for proponents of theory, considerations on political and ideological dimensions were an integral part of the very study of films, cognitivists brought a piecemeal approach to film theory: they focused on a number of middle-range questions to study films, questions that do not need to depend on political and ideological considerations (Carroll, 1996a). Within the cognitivist tradition of film theory, there are works inquiring into the rhetorical and ideological dimensions of films (Carroll, 1996a; Plantinga, 1997a) and there are theorists who have dealt with issues of gender and race (Flory, 2000, 2008; Freeland, 1996), which are clearly political or politically relevant. However, we lack a systematic reorganization of the relation between films and the political, which seems to remain a prerogative of Grand Theory. This is where my work wants to make a contribution. In contrast to the 'Grand Theory' approach to the study of films and cultural artifacts, I aim to provide a value-neutral theory of political cinema, that is, a theory that does not depend on any previous endorsement of any specific ideological doctrine; a theory of political cinema that could clearly differentiate between political films and films that are not political and that explores the role of cognitive processes at play in the spectator's responses to film. In particular, I argue that the spectator's cognitive capacities are crucial for the assessment of a film's epistemic dimensions and, therefore, for the overall analysis of political films.

The methodology of my investigation is to be framed within the analytic tradition of philosophy, even though I also take into account standpoints that stem from the continental tradition of philosophy; in particular, I consider at length the Brechtian conception of political theater. I agree with Gregory Currie (2004) when he says that analytic philosophy is a natural ally of a cognitivist approach to film studies, as it is committed to clarity of exposition and the power of argument, it is science oriented, and, importantly, it aims to 'unpack' complex issues, so as to focus on particular problems rather than promote an overarching Grand Theory. The leading questions that guide my enquiry are further unpacked into sub-questions that are tackled in each chapter of the book and whose interrelation is central if we are to provide a coherent approach to the analysis of political films. To proceed in my investigation, I use tools of analytic philosophy of art and film theory but also import insights from cognate disciplines that can help us develop a more accurate analysis of the relation between films and the 'political'. In particular, I import tools from political science, political philosophy, epistemology and cognitive science. Moreover, I take it that the theoretical effort needs to be tested with specific case studies, so I also use specific films as examples of the applicability and explanatory power of the theoretical framework I propose.

The relationship between the 'political' and films could be analyzed from a variety of angles. If we think of art more generally, we say that there is a perennial relation between art and the political dimension, a relation that we can trace back to Plato's *Republic*. Nonetheless, as I remarked previously, in the field of analytic philosophy of art the relationship between the 'political' and art has hardly been analyzed. Conolly and Haydar (2001, 2007, 2008) have presented some interesting insights into the possible role that the political dimension may play in our aesthetic appraisal of artworks, in particular of narratives. Noël Carroll has a chapter in a book (2010a) where he discusses the possible interrelations between aesthetics and politics. He identifies four main categories that are organized around the relation of support and opposition: art can support or oppose politics, and politics can support or oppose arts. This is a good starting point, but the analysis of the relation between art and politics requires more details and precision. For instance, Carroll does not distinguish between politics, polity and policies, and we may say that there can be policies, rather than politics, that promote artistic production, or that some artworks may support or legitimize a polity, rather than politics.

However, I take it that Carroll moves from the right starting point. That is, the arts both influence and are influenced by the political dimension. I propose to think of such relation in terms of the 'active' or 'passive' role of artworks. Artworks can be passive in the relationship, that is, they may be influenced by the 'political'. A policy may influence artistic production in different ways; it can promote artistic production or it can oppose it. Moreover, artworks, as cultural artifacts, are necessarily influenced by their cultural environment. This is to say, artworks may mirror the social organization from which they originate. If such social organization is characterized by politically relevant inequalities, the artistic production may, symptomatically, mirror such inequalities. For instance, if a society is characterized by a lack of gender equality, a film may mirror this social organization – so we can say that artistic production is influenced by the political dimension, and more specifically it is a symptom of the social organization from which it arises.

Artworks can also have a more active role. As noted by Carroll, they may serve as symbols to legitimize political regimes, or they may try to persuade or influence people. Here we can distinguish between artworks that are intended to have a political purpose and those that are simply used for political purposes. That is, an artist may create an artwork with a specific purpose in mind, and yet, say decades after its creation, the artwork may be used for entirely different purposes (see Parsons & Carlson, 2008, discussing functional beauty). Moreover, we have seen that artworks are necessarily influenced by the politically relevant social relations that form the milieu from which they originated. In the same fashion, artworks may also influence their receptive environment, for instance, by reinforcing the same politically relevant social relations of which they are a symptom. This kind of 'reinforcing' action is to be conceived of as a subtle force, often operating at the subconscious level.[2]

Summarizing, we can categorize the relation between the political dimension and art depending on art's role in the relationship. If artworks are the passive element in the relationship, it means that (1) there are policies that can influence the artistic production or, more generally, (2) the artistic production is a symptom of a specific cultural milieu, hence it reproduces the politically relevant social relations of its environment. When artworks are the active element, it means that they (3) serve a political purpose, either because they are intended to serve this purpose or because they are used to serve it; or (4) they reinforce the politically relevant social organization of which they are a symptom.

Here I do not analyze how art is influenced by political phenomena, for I only focus on art's capacity to play a political role. This means that I only investigate if and how art can have an impact or influence on the domain of the 'political'.

More specifically, considering the field of film studies, we see that Grand Theory provided a conceptual framework to study artistic production as symptomatic of a given society, and how it subconsciously reinforces that very social organization of which it is a symptom (points 2 and 4 of the previous list). However, to inquire into the relation between the political dimension and films, proponents of Grand Theory developed overarching theoretical commitments, inscribing the study of films within a more general study of society, language and psychology.

In this book, I focus exclusively on films that are intended to have a political purpose. This means that I also aim to differentiate between films that have a political purpose and those that do not have such a purpose. My investigation narrows down the body of the research, for I aim to identify the category of political films and then I analyze the features that are characteristic of these films, developing a framework that could facilitate their appraisal and assessment.

The first three chapters are devoted to definitional problems and setting out the theoretical framework I use to analyze political films. In Chapters 4, 5 and 6, I focus on the analyses of the kinds of epistemic gains that political films may afford, and in Chapter 7, I argue against the possibility that some kinds of imagining, in particular empathic imagining, may impair films' capacity to afford epistemic gains.

In Chapters 1 and 2, I aim to define political cinema, and I propose considering the category of political cinema as a genre. Hence, I clarify these two concepts: 'genre' and 'political'. I hold that genres can be distinguished according to the functions they aim to serve, so I identify the two main functions of political cinema. A film is political when its intended aim is to (1) persuade the audience about the validity of a political standpoint or (2) elicit reflection around a political issue. A political issue is an issue that shapes social conflict and grouping along the friend/enemy distinction, and a political standpoint is a specific position within the debate shaping the social conflict. The first function is a 'rhetorical' function and the second is an 'explorational' function. I then analyze these functions in depth and set out a theoretical framework for analyzing political films. I suggest that in order to classify and assess political films, we ought to analyze three epistemic dimensions: (1) epistemic voice, (2) epistemic merit and (3) pedagogical method.

In Chapter 3, I introduce and define the category of propaganda and I argue that propaganda films are a subcategory of political films. More specifically, I aim to understand what it means for a political film to be successful, and I analyze the interrelations between the rhetorical function of political films and their epistemic merits.

The first three chapters of the book show that in order to analyze and assess political films we need to investigate films' epistemic dimensions, for political films aim to have an impact on the audience's system of beliefs. But can films actually afford epistemic gains? This is a central question in the subsequent chapters, for if we cannot show that films can afford epistemic gains, then political films are doomed to fail. So, the aim of Chapters 4, 5 and 6 is to show that political films can be epistemically valuable. However, demonstrating that political films are epistemically valuable is only a partial achievement, for it does not suffice to say that such epistemic value contributes to the value of the film *qua* art. Some epistemic contributions can be aesthetically relevant (they can contribute to the value of the work *qua* art) and some others cannot. If epistemic contributions are never relevant, then the category of political films loses its relevance as it does not provide adequate tools to assess political films for their value *qua* art. But I will argue that political films' epistemic contributions can be aesthetically relevant, for they can play a role in our appreciation of the film. In particular, I hold that epistemic gains tend to be aesthetically relevant when they are expressed by artistic means, so that it is the way or mode in which epistemic gains are afforded that makes them of aesthetic relevance.

In Chapter 4, I analyze more closely the relation between epistemic value and aesthetic value. I open the chapter with an overview of the debate on the distinction between aesthetic value and artistic value. I endorse Berys Gaut's artistic theory of the aesthetic value (2007), and I use it as a framework for my enquiry on the relation between epistemic value and aesthetic value. In this chapter, I argue that art, and films in particular, can convey empirical knowledge through testimony. Testimony is a reliable source of knowledge, so it can justify the beliefs we acquire from our engagement with artworks. Nonetheless, I also want to highlight what I take to be the limits of testimonial transmission. Testimony is entirely dependent on the trustworthiness of the author and it bypasses the artwork. When the belief conveyed is exclusively justified by testimony, as in the case of the empirical knowledge conveyed by *Leviathan*, this epistemic gain is not aesthetically valuable for it is not expressed by artistic means.

In Chapter 5, I focus on all the possible epistemic gains political films may afford. I argue that political films can have an *impact* on the audience's system of beliefs. This formulation is intentionally vague, and it is intended to cover all the possible ways that artworks can affect the system of beliefs: they can clarify already-held beliefs or make them more vivid; they can also bring new knowledge that can be articulated in propositional terms; they can foster understanding of specific issues, characters, or situations and they can foster empathic and sympathetic imaginings that are relevant skills for moral reasoning. In particular, in this chapter, I consider Conolly and Haydar's argument about political narratives. The authors hold that while narratives about personal morality can convey propositional knowledge, narratives about political morality can at best clarify already-held beliefs. I take issue with the authors' argument, as I see it as being grounded on an arbitrary and inaccurate distinction between personal and political morality. Moreover, I do not consider epistemic values to be hierarchically ordered. In the second part of the chapter, I emphasize how political films can foster understanding of characters, situations and issues and how they can promote coherence within our system of beliefs. I also show that epistemic values are interrelated, so that understanding and coherence can also lead to new propositional knowledge. This chapter prepares the ground for the one that follows. In Chapter 5, I consider all the possible epistemic gains political cinema may afford, and in Chapter 6, I analyze the possible source of justification for such values.

In Chapter 6, I propose considering films as thought experiments. In the first part of the chapter, I defend the view that imagination can justify our beliefs, in general terms, arguing that we can imagine with constraints and that this kind of imagining is a reliable source of knowledge; I then discuss the epistemic reliability of thought experiments, arguing that they are epistemically valuable as they are capable of activating mental processing mechanisms that are not activated by abstract and general reasoning. The affective mechanisms activated by thought experiments can lead to the formation of beliefs that are in disequilibrium with previously held beliefs and can trigger a process of revision to regain equilibrium within the system of beliefs. In the second part of the chapter, I develop the analogy that films can function as thought experiments. I consider some objections to such an analogy and I argue that films can afford epistemic gains just as thought experiments can, that is, by activating low-level, automatic processing mechanisms that would otherwise be inactivated by abstract reasoning. Moreover, I hold that cinema can afford epistemic gains through typically cinematographic means; that is, as the epistemic contribution depends on the film's capacity to activate affective, noncognitive responses, the only way to elicit such activation is to experience the film. This means that we can paraphrase the film's message and inscribe its contribution within a general *problematique*, but in doing so we encounter a loss in epistemic efficiency, since our paraphrasing does not activate those low-level processing mechanisms that enable the epistemic contribution.

In Chapter 7, I delve into the role of imagination in promoting critical reflection. In the first chapter, I highlight how my definition of political cinema is indebted to the Brechtian conception of political theater, but as I take imagination to be the source of the justification of the epistemic contributions that films can afford, I need to confront a possible Brechtian objection to specific modes of imagination. Brecht held that some artworks – those fostering identification between characters and spectators – systematically 'block' critical thinking. In this chapter, I unpack Brecht's objection by considering two different possibilities: the problem may be that empathic imagining prevents critical thinking or that emotions may 'blind' the spectator's critical capacities. I argue that empathic engagement does not 'block' critical reflection and emotions do not blind our critical capacities. However, emotions can be used for rhetorical purposes, and some texts may try to elicit specific emotional responses that are not warranted by the narrative. I argue that works that aim to elicit 'tender' emotions concealing epistemic defects can be labeled as sentimental, and since sentimentality is related to an epistemic defect, it is also an aesthetic flaw for political films.

I should note in closing that my approach is not exclusively theoretical, as I test the theoretical framework proposed on specific films. In the first chapter, I closely analyze nonfiction films like *California Reich* (Parkes & Critchlow, 1975) and *Mr. Death: The Rise and Fall of Leuchter Jr.* (Morris, 1999). In the second chapter, I argue that *Dead Man Walking* (Robbins, 1995) is an epistemically meritorious film. In the third chapter, I analyze *Leviathan* (Zvyagintsev, 2014), as I claim that the main aim of the film is to convey empirical knowledge about corruption in Russia. The kinds of propositions it aims to convey can only be justified through testimony, so while we can say that the film is epistemically meritorious, I argue that the film's epistemic value is not aesthetically relevant. In Chapters 4 and 5, I provide an in-depth analysis of *The Golden Door* (Crialese, 2006), and in Chapter 6 and 7, I use as examples *The Act of Killing* (Oppenheimer, 2012), *Two Days, One Night* (Dardenne brothers, 2014) and *American Sniper* (Eastwood, 2014). These case studies and the accompanying theoretical reflections all serve to achieve the overall aim of this dissertation: to present a new and compelling theory of political cinema.

As a final note, I should clarify the *modus operandi* of this book. I said previously that there is little if no bibliography at all on the analysis of political films in the fields of aesthetics and cognitive film theory. So, I have been engaged in a conversation with what I take to be relevant debates in cognate disciplines that could have been used to provide useful coordinates to guide my endeavor; I hope to guide the reader through these debates, which I have used to carve out my own view on the subject, and, for this reason, I hope this book could also be useful to the student who is approaching for the first time studies in the fields of film theory and aesthetics and wants to get a taste of these debates.

Before we move on, I just want to thank Hans Maes and Murray Smith for their guidance, help and support. They have been a source of inspiration, as academics and as persons.

Notes

1 For an overview of these debates, see Carroll (2002) and Lopes (2011)
2 I take it that this is a typical standpoint endorsed by proponents of Grand Theory; here I do not want to question the merits of this proposal but merely note this as a conceivable possibility.

1 The 'political' of political cinema

The relation between politics and films has been analyzed from a variety of angles, both in film studies and related disciplines, like media and cultural studies. The bibliographical landscape is quite diverse. There are heterogeneous points of view on what counts as a political film, as some take political films to deal with political institutions, while others may consider a Hollywood comedy or a Hitchcock's film political. In spite of all this talk about political films, very few efforts have been made to sketch at least some guidelines for the definition of the category. There seems to be a tacit agreement between writers and readers about what counts as a political film – of the kind 'I know it when I see it'. Also, scholars have limited their field of analysis to subcategories of political cinema. Some authors have focused their attention on films of emerging countries (the so-called third cinema) in order to investigate the possible interrelation between political change and cinema. Others have focused exclusively on avant-garde and arthouse cinema in order to investigate the value of political cinema. Studies on Hollywood's relation to politics and the political have many different angles of analysis. Some scholars see Hollywood as a capitalist machine that serves the purpose of spreading capitalist's ideology. Other scholars have analyzed Hollywood's films with overt political commitment or the politics of films in the blacklist era (see Humphries, 2008; Krutnik, Neale, Neve, Stanfield, & American Council of Learned Societies, 2007; Langford, 2010; Maltby, 1983; Ryan & Kellner, 1990; Scott, 2000; Smith, 2014). One thing seems to be clear: it is impossible to limit the category of political films to a single time and place. There were political films in the postwar era, as there are now, and these kinds of films seem to be ubiquitous, as every national culture has its own 'flavor' of political cinema.

In this book, I want to propose a theory of political cinema that transcends local foci of attention. This aims to be a theory of what political cinema is and why this is of value. As this aims to be a general theory of what counts as a political film, it should not depend on specific places or production eras.

Do we need a category of 'political cinema'? I think we do. We classify artworks because classification helps with their interpretation and assessment.

DOI: 10.4324/9780367816872-2

That is, our aesthetic judgments depend on categorical classification. Kendall Walton used the famous example of Picasso's 'Guernica', which 'seems violent, dynamic, vital, disturbing to us' (1970, p. 347). Whereas, were we living in a society without an established medium of painting, but rather one that produces a kind of work of art called *guernicas* – variations of Picasso's 'Guernica' done in various bas-relief dimensions – we would perceive Picasso's 'Guernica' 'as cold, stark, lifeless, or serene and restful, or perhaps bland, dull, boring – but in any case *not* violent, dynamic and vital' (p. 347). Something similar happens to artworks about political issues: they are best appreciated if assessed and interpreted in light of the main characteristics of the category to which they belong. So, here I propose considering the category of political cinema as a genre, as I believe that it provides relevant tools for the classification and assessment of films.

When is a film political? What are the functions of political cinema? How do we assess it? These are the questions that guide the investigation of the first three chapters of the book. However, this first chapter is going to be primarily concerned with some theoretical clarification. In order to define what is characteristic of the political genre, these two concepts require clarification: 'genre' and 'political'. I introduce the main theoretical difficulties related to the definition of genre (Section 1), and I stress how the focus of my attention is on problems related to the definition of an individual genre, that of political cinema. I highlight the difficulties in determining clear-cut criteria that could identify political films (Section 2), so I turn to the definition of the concept of the political (Section 3), and I introduce the tripartite distinction between politics, policy and polity (Section 4) as this distinction can help in mapping the concept of the political. The aim of this chapter is to provide an initial sketch of what constitutes political cinema. It will be clear that in classifying political films we cannot rely on formal elements and that an interpretative effort is required for an accurate classification of political films, so in Section 5, I clarify which interpretative practice I take to be most relevant for my purposes.

1 What is a genre?

Brian Laetz and Dominic McIver Lopes advance a proposal for a definition of movie genre:

> Category K is a genre if and only if K has multiple members, which are made by more than one artist (for any given artist role) from any background, and K has features in virtue of which K figures into the appreciation or interpretation of K's audience
>
> (2008, p. 156)

This proposal has the merit of identifying those features that help distinguish a genre from any other category. We can have categories with only a single member. Indeed, every artwork belongs to a category of which it is the only member, like the category of novels that are identical to *To Kill a Mockingbird*. Moreover, there are categories that are made by the artistic production of only a single artist, like the category of films directed by Alfred Hitchcock. Such a category is not a genre – but an *oeuvre* (Laetz & Lopes, 2008, p. 155). Also, artists can hold a variety of roles in the production chain: directors, producers, actors, cinematographers and so forth. No categorization based on a single artist, for any given role, will make up a genre: 'movies-that-star-Jimmy-Stewart' is not a genre and neither is a complex category like 'movies-directed-by-Alfred-Hitchcock-starring-Jimmy-Stewart' (Laetz & Lopes, 2008, p. 155). This is true not just for cinema. We can think of a parallel in literature: novels-written-by-Daniel-Pennac is not a genre, nor is the category of novels-on-Benjamin-Malaussène.

For a category to be a genre it needs to be somehow 'open'; that is, different artists need to have the opportunity to make works in that category. Hence, categories that have clear boundaries in a historical period cannot be genres either. If I were to build a church in the style of Brunelleschi, that would hardly be considered an example of Renaissance architecture. As the category of works belonging to Renaissance architecture is historically confined, no architect can, today, build a church belonging to that category. The closure of such categories (those made by a single artwork, or single artists, or historically confined) seems to be the major difference from those categories that are prototypically called 'genres' like comedy and tragedy.

Laetz and Lopes's proposal, however, also includes categories that we would hardly call 'genres', as the authors themselves acknowledge: 'R-rated movies, movies with happy endings, and movies with foreign dialogue meet all the conditions laid out in the proposed schema, but it is a stretch to think of them as genres' (p. 157). Probably we could gather more examples when exporting this theory of genre outside cinema. The category of artworks painted oil on canvas would be another candidate for being a genre, yet we do not really think of it as such.

Nonetheless, I take Laetz and Lopes's proposal to be a valid starting point of analysis. Indeed, we can actually appreciate the difficulties of formulating a classical definition of genre based on necessary and sufficient conditions if we look at the problems affecting theories of single genres. The problems of 'openness' in Laetz and Lopes's theory of genre mirror problems in the development of theories of *a* genre. The authors correctly argue that theories of each individual genre need to be worked out separately from a general theory of genre as each individual genre will be characterized by different features relevant in the appreciation and interpretation of tokens of its set. Yet, scholars writing about individual genres can hardly agree on what count as necessary and sufficient conditions for belonging to the particular category K. We can see how a problem about the limits of a category reverberates from one theoretical level to the other. At a more abstract level there is the difficulty of tracing the borders of what counts as genre, and theories of individual genres struggle to identify a close set of features capable of classifying all relevant tokens. My book aims at contributing to these kinds of theories, that is, theories of an individual genre.

An example of a debate around the definition of a single genre can prove the complexity I mentioned. Here I want to quote a passage from Rick Altman's reconstruction of the debate around the definition of 'western'. This reconstruction is quite significant and shows the definitional difficulties faced by a theory of a single genre:

> Jean Mitry provides us with a clear example of the most common definition. The western is a 'film whose action, situated in the American West, is consistent with the atmosphere, the values, and the conditions of existence in the Far West between 1840 and 1900'. . . . Marc Vernet's more detailed list is more sensitive to cinematic concerns . . . Vernet outlines general atmosphere ('emphasis on basic elements such as earth, dust, water, and leather'), stock characters ('the tough/soft cowboy, the lonely sheriff, the faithful or treacherous Indian, and the strong but tender woman'), as well as technical elements ('use of fast tracking and crane shots'). . . . For [Jim] Kitses the western grows out of the dialectic between the West as garden and as desert (between culture and nature, community and individual, future and past). John Cawelti attempts to systematise the western in a similar fashion: the western is always set on or near a frontier, where man encounters his uncivilised double. The western thus takes place on the border between two lands, between two eras, and with a hero who remains divided between two value systems (for he combines the town's morals with the outlaw's skills)
>
> (2012, pp. 31–32).

Rick Altman, following Fredric Jameson and Todorov, distinguishes between a semantic and syntactic approach to genres. However, Altman's use of the term 'semantic' is not related to the global meaning of a work (Jameson, probably more pointedly, uses the term in this fashion); instead, semantic, for Altman, refers to 'lexical choices' or semantic units characterizing a text. Hence, the author holds, definitions depending on 'a list of common traits, attitudes, characters, shots, locations, sets, and the like' (2012, p. 31) are semantic definitions, whereas 'definitions that play up . . . certain constitutive relationships between undesignated and variable placeholders' (p. 31) are syntactic definitions. It follows that the first two definitions (Jean Mirty's and Vernet's) are semantic definitions, whereas Kitses and Cawelti use a syntactical approach. I am not convinced that Altman's approach and distinction between semantic and syntactic definitions may actually be illuminating. If anything, Altman's use of the term 'semantic' can be misleading, as the definitions that he labels as 'semantic' have an actual focus on film form: they have an emphasis on mise-en-scène and cinematography, whereas the 'syntactic' definitions are focused on film content or meaning.

However, what this brief survey demonstrates is that genre theory suffers from deep definitional problems that can be traced back to the complex interplay of form and content.

Robert Stam argues that genre analysis is plagued by at least five major problems. The first, and more obvious, relates to the question of ***extension***. Certain labels are too broad, and they end up being unhelpful for critical assessment, like the general label of 'comedy', whereas other labels end up being too restrictive, say 'Biopics on Sigmund Freud' or 'disaster films concerning earthquakes' (Stam, 2000, p. 128). The second problem Stam points to is ***normativism***: 'having a preconceived idea of what a genre film should do, rather than seeing genre merely as trampoline for creativity and innovation' (p. 129). Now, this second problem needs to be further clarified; any theory of genre will imply a certain degree of normativism, as we need a schema of selection of the relevant patterns and conventions that make a work belong to a particular genre. Otherwise we get stuck in a vicious circle in which we try to come up with a descriptive definition via an inductive process, but then we have to ask ourselves how it is we come to know the prototypical examples of a given category in the first place? As Edward Buscombe put it: 'if we want to know what a western is, we must look at certain kinds of films. But how do we know which films to look at until we know what a western is?' (2012, p. 14). So, a certain degree of normativism is necessary to build a theory of genre as long as this leaves the genre sufficiently open to recognize change, innovation, deviations from the norm and overlap with other genres. Third, genres are often imagined to be ***monolithic***, whereas, in reality, even classical Hollywood movies blend genres, and the possibilities of mixing genres are part of the process of innovation and creativity that any theory of genre needs to take into account. The fourth plague is ***biologism***: scholars, like James Naremore, have posited that genres have a 'life cycle' moving from birth to maturity and then parodic decline. Biologism is denied by actual counterexamples: parodies develop quite a lot earlier than the alleged decline of a genre. Stem suggests as examples Richardson's *Pamela* and Fielding's *Shamela* in literature, or Griffith's *Intolerance* and Buster Keaton's *The Three Ages* in film. Also, the idea of a 'life cycle' seems to associate genres to historical periods, turning them into closed categories.[1] Fifth, Stam argues, genres can also be ***submerged***. This happens 'when a film appears on the surface to belong to one genre yet on a deeper level belongs to another, as when analysts argue that *Taxi Driver* is "really" a western, or that *Nashville* is ultimately a reflexive film about Hollywood' (p. 129).

This consideration reveals probably the most important struggle for a theory of genre, that of clarifying the dialectic between classification and interpretation. Some genres can be 'submerged' because interpretation pulls in a different direction from the previous classification. We have seen in the opening of this paragraph, with Laetz and Lopes, that genre classification is important and of value, because it can help us to cast light on problems of interpretation and critical assessment of an artwork. Yet, is it possible to classify without interpreting an artwork? Let me consider Alfonso Cuaròn's *Gravity* by way of example. The film is classified as a science fiction thriller – two different genres are needed for the classification. We can say, quite roughly, that the movie is *about* Dr. Ryan Stone's attempt to get home after an extraordinary incident has left her floating alone in space. Yet, if we were to limit our interpretation to the plain understanding of the story we are told and we were to assess the movie exclusively on this basis, our evaluation and engagement with the work will only be partial. It is true that Cuaròn makes skillful use of cinematographic elements in order to create suspense and keep the audience engaged throughout the film. And this is surely an aesthetic achievement. But this is only a partial assessment of the reasons why *Gravity* is such an accomplished work. Actually, the film is *about* mourning and the elaboration of tragic events in our lives. The lowering of body temperature together with the feeling of dizziness are physiological states that are typical consequences of a shocking event. Hence, right from the beginning, *Gravity* seems to suggest a parallel between Dr. Stone's space odyssey and her personal tragedy – the loss of her daughter. The entire journey, from the initial space accident to her landing on earth, can be seen as a metaphor for her personal journey in the process of mourning. The scene where Kowalsky (George Clooney) 'magically' reappears in the Russian capsule serves as an explanation of her psychological state. In the final scene, when she lands on earth, first she floats in water, then crawls on the land and finally stands up on her feet. The scene is a symbol for a new born, which concludes her journey: the space journey as well as her mourning. Cuaròn himself, in a public interview, suggested this interpretation and, as much as we can find even further messages hidden in the overall narrative, this seems to be the central one. When we are to classify the film, if we simply say that it is a sci-fi thriller, we are not in a better position to assess and appreciate, in full, its aesthetic qualities. When we understand that the film can be seen as a psychological drama, then we are best placed to appreciate it.[2] Indeed, the idea to set the movie in the open space to represent an emotion, that of grief, is in itself an accomplished metaphor – one that we would not value, or even grasp, if we were to think of the film simply as a sci-fi thriller.

I wanted to dwell on this example because it is particularly relevant to what I have to say about political cinema. As I describe later, a political theme may not be immediately evident: interpretation may be required to detect the relevance of the political element of the film. Films like *Two Days, One Night* (Dardenne brothers, 2014) or *American Sniper* (Eastwood, 2014) may not be immediately defined as political, as their plots concern personal dramas, but attentive analysis reveals the political element of these films, which is crucial for their appreciation and assessment. The aim of the first three chapters of this book is to provide a schema through which we might identify artworks belonging to the category of political cinema. And,

I argue, political cinema cannot be identified on the grounds of stylistic and formal elements; rather, we are to look for the work's content and message if we want to draw the boundaries of a category that can actually be helpful for the assessment and evaluation of films.[3] We are to pay attention to the content of a film in order to classify it; however, with the word content I do not just refer to the plot or story of the film but to its semantic implications. My claim is not that in order to classify films we are always to take into account interpretation and that to classify political films interpretations is always required. Sometimes, classification can be straightforward; Oliver Stone's *JFK* is about a real-life politician and it is a political film, but it need not be, as political themes, whose understanding would be crucial for the assessment and appreciation of the film, may be semantically implied.

With this paragraph, I wanted to provide an overview of all the difficulties we face in the process of classifying films. My aim is not to define genre *tout court* but to define *a* genre, the political genre. To do so, I have remarked how we cannot simply classify political films through an analysis of formal elements. In the paragraphs that follow I will expand on this problem and show that we need to look at the authorial semantic intentions to identify political works.

2 The 'political' in films

We have seen how the relation between form and content problematizes the definition of a genre. I hold that a definition based solely on formal properties will not provide a satisfying framework to classify political films. Hence, I need to say something about the content of films that we want to define as political. More specifically I hold that we need to take two steps if we want to clarify what political cinema is. First, we need to clarify what 'political' means, and second, we need to understand how films can articulate political themes in order to actually 'be' political.

The main problem we face is that of the extension of the category. There can be cases where we have no difficulties in saying that some artworks are political, for example, those artworks that are related to actual political happenings (Oliver Stone's *JFK* (1991)) or that clearly reference political institutions (for instance, the Netflix production *House of Cards* (2013–2016) or Elio Petri's *Todo Modo* (1976)). But the label 'political cinema' or 'political art' is not always used coherently, and most importantly, it is not clear which features make an artwork political. There are two problems that can broaden the category of political films to the extent of making it pointless: (i) we can define as 'political' an issue which is not actually political or (ii) we can interpret the work as 'political', when the 'political' element was only meant as background for some other message or the 'political' element may not even be intended to be relevant altogether for the interpretation.[4] First I focus on the clarification of what is 'political' (Sections 3 and 4) and then I turn to the second problem (Section 5).

That 'political artworks' are related to the political is a tautology that does not qualify what political artworks are, unless we spell out the meaning of the term political. We need to clarify 'what' is political, and then we can apply this label to artworks. Clearly, a number of issues are closely related to the political sphere, but that does not justify an indiscriminate use of the term. Nonetheless, in defining the category of political cinema I do believe that we need to accommodate our intuitions about the political, including all the complexities that this will bring. Let me provide a few examples to clarify this point. I hold that we would not have any trouble in considering Oliver Stone's *JFK* as a political artwork. The most obvious characteristic of the movie is that it is about a real-life politician. Hence the clear link with the label 'political'. Marco Bechis's *Garage Olimpo* (1999) is also a political film. Yet again, there is a clear reference to a political regime: the Argentinian dictatorship. I take Roman Polanski's *Death and the Maiden* (1994) to be a political film too. Here the link with the actual political regime (again, Videla's regime) is loose, although still present. Yet I take Polanski's movie to be political not because of its loose thematical connection with the Argentinian military regime, but rather because it poses the problem of how to punish political criminals. Here we can already appreciate a substantial thematical departure: *JFK* is about a real-life politician, whereas *Death and the Maiden* is about fairness of punishment. This leads to an important consideration: we can associate the label 'political' with a given issue or problem that is not necessarily related to an actual politician or a political institution. Indeed, we say that some ethical issues like same-sex marriage, abortion, euthanasia or fairness of punishment are political problems as well. The category of political artworks needs to make sense of all these different examples, and it cannot be limited to artworks referencing political institutions or real-life politicians. The category of political art needs to be wide enough to entail those artworks that we would define as political despite not being about political institutions. At the same time, we need to provide a set of criteria to avoid an unlimited category that would be useless for our purposes.

3 What is 'political'?

I will provide a very broad characterization of the term 'political' borrowing from Carl Schmitt's analysis of the concept. The Schmittian category of the 'political' needs to be understood just as a minimal criterion that is necessary for the instantiation of the concept. Furthermore, I will use the tripartite distinction between politics, policies and polity to identify three declinations of the political. In particular, this tripartite distinction will help us in the classification process, as films with a political content can be about one or more of these declinations.

Carl Schmitt's (1996) analysis of the concept of the political aims to identify what is ultimately distinctive about the category of the political. In his words:

> the political must . . . rest on its own ultimate distinctions, to which all action with a specifically political meaning can be traced. Let us assume that in the realm of morality the final distinctions are between good and evil, in aesthetics beautiful and ugly, in economics profitable and unprofitable. The question then is whether there is also a special distinction which can serve as a simple criterion of the political and of what it consists
>
> (1996, p. 26).

Schmitt then claims that the specific political distinction to which political actions and motives can be reduced is the distinction between friend and enemy.

Friend and enemy are to be understood as the greatest degree of unity and disunity within a given community. As explained by Ernst Wolfgang Böckenförde (2010), this dichotomy identifies only a 'potential' distinction that in practice is to be relativized. Friend and enemy are the poles of a continuum that defines allegiances around public issues. The actual instantiation of the two extremes of the continuum means open conflict and civil war. War, in Schmitt's words, is the negation of the political and, at the same time, is a necessary antecedent and last, potential, resource of any political confrontation. The role of the State is to limit enmity and allow for pacified confrontation. Hence, a political phenomenon involves social groups facing each other within the boundaries of such pacified confrontation. Such confrontation between social groups can reach different degrees of intensity and the friend/enemy distinction denotes the utmost degree of union or separation – which are to remain as potential. 'Political' is any relativized conflict – that is, conflict which is not brought to its extreme manifestation: war – that shapes the public debate along the lines of the friend/enemy divide.

This distinction is essentially public and not private. Of course the individual can have personal friends or enemies, but this is not relevant to the category of the political. Conflict needs to be public, involving social groups. Schmitt understands this distinction as the essence of the political, and it also explains how we can coherently conceive of ethical problems as political. Indeed, any issue that determines social allegiances along the lines of the friend/enemy distinction is political. To say it with Schmitt: 'every religious, moral, economic, ethical or other antithesis transforms into a political one if it is sufficiently strong to group human beings effectively according to friend and enemy' (p. 37).

I take Schmitt's analysis to be particularly useful for our purposes as it aims to clarify what is specific about the political, and it identifies the final criterion to establish what is political and what is not. The main advantage of Schimitt's conception of the political is that it does not try to list the reasons for social conflicts but instead identifies a criterion that is typical of political confrontations.

Let me bring some examples, so we can make sense of a film being 'political' in light of the Schmittian criterion. *Garage Olimpo* is an example of a power struggle between social groups, as is, for example, Spike Lee's *Do the Right Thing* (1989), which also focuses on the power relations between different social groups, where these groups are identified by racial criteria. Polanski's *Death and the Maiden* raises the problem that shapes the public debate of how to punish criminals. A similar theme appears in Tim Robbins's *Dead Man Walking* (1995), where Robbins wants us to reflect upon the death penalty and shows how the issue divides the public, whereas Marco Bellocchio's *La Bella Addormentata* (2012) is about the ethical problem of euthanasia and shows how the public division on the issue enters the parliament, exposing its political relevance. Already among these few examples there are some significant differences. In all of them we can trace the element of social conflict. In *Dead Man Walking*, *La Bella Addormentata* and *Death and the Maiden* the social cleavage is represented by the grouping (friend/enemy) around an ethical problem. Ethical issues are also at stake in the other examples, *Garage Olimpo* or *Do the Right Thing*, but here there is a deeper focus on the actual power relations (suppression of the opposition, racism and submission) between social groups.

4 Mapping the political: politics, policies and polity

From the examples I have been mentioning so far, we can already see a great diversity among political films. Here I suggest a mapping strategy: the 'political' can be declined in the three dimensions of politics, policies and polity. This is a common distinction in political science, one that is never highlighted in discourses around political cinema. These terms are not synonyms and identify different dimensions of the political.

Here I define 'politics' as the power relations between social groups; 'policy' refers to the course of action pursued by a party, administration or political organization; and 'polity' is the boundary of a political community and its form of government.

The term politics refers to what is usually taken to be the typical political action: the power struggle between social groups fighting for the allocation of limited resources -the term 'resources' is to be understood in a broad fashion, not just economic resources, but also authoritative and symbolic resources (Lasswell, 1952; Pareto, 1991). In its typical formulation, we call politics the competition and bargaining process of parties trying to reach positions of power. In an episode of the Netflix series *House of Cards*, Frank

Underwood (Kevin Spacey) explains, suggestively, what politics is. In this episode there is a meeting between Frank (who, at the time, is the vice president of the United States), his wife Claire (Robin Wright), and the House Majority Whip Jackie Sharp (Molly Parker). The president of the United States runs the risk of being impeached, and to her surprise Jackie finds out that instead of protecting the president, Frank wants her to 'whip the votes' to support the impeachment. Jackie seems reluctant. This is how Frank explains the situation to her:

JACKIE SHARP: 'I can't abandon the President'.
FRANK UNDERWOOD: 'If the party rescues him, we will lose fifty seats in the House in the midterms; you will lose your position in the leadership; and it will take us a decade to regain the trust of the electorate'.
CLAIRE UNDERWOOD: 'All we are asking is that you have an open mind'.
F.U.: 'Claire kept an open mind, and you will pass sexual assault reform as a result'.
J.S.: 'You can't possibly compare impeachment. . .'
F.U.: 'It's an illustration, Jackie. Of what the future looks like. What we offer is progress, with a promise of more to come'.
C.U.: 'It's only the beginning, Jackie'.
F.U.: 'Ruthless pragmatism! Remember? That's why I wanted you to be the whip. The three of us are cut from the same cloth'.
J. S.: 'Mr. Vice President, what you are asking is just shy of treason'.
F.U.: 'Just shy, which is politics'.

However, it would be limiting to consider politics as confined within the boundaries of the state or of political institutions. Schmitt's analysis of the concept of the political aimed to prove that politics is also outside the state. Human beings group around the distinction friend/enemy, and these groups compete for the allocation of resources. This competition – power struggle – between social groups is diffused, as it does not take place just through institutions. On the one hand, the friend/enemy criterion helps overcome a problem of 'closure': if we were to understand politics as related to the state and power relations within political institutions, also our consequent characterization of political cinema would have been limited. On the other hand, such a characterization of politics as a diffused phenomenon in society can still produce an excessively broad construction that will not be helpful in any process of classification, interpretation or assessment. To limit the extension of the category, we need to stress the importance of the 'public' dimension of the conflict.

Oliver Conolly and Bashshar Haydar have also faced the problem of defining politics, underlining the same concerns I am pointing to:

> the scope of the political can be conceived more or less broadly. The narrow view is that politics is concerned with the nature and legitimacy of

> the state, government, legal and other coercive institutions. The broad view is that politics is concerned with power relations between social groups that are mediated not through institutions but through attitudes (2008, p. 88).

Moreover, the authors also remark that not every power relation is political, setting a boundary to the extension of political power struggles. They use the example of a love relation where Y has power over X since X loves Y more than Y loves X. This relation would not be political for two reasons. First, Y's power is not dependent upon Y's membership to a group of Ys: recipients of excessive love. Second, there is 'nothing anyone could sensibly do, in terms of proposals for political change, even in the broad sense of a collective change in mentality, to alter the power the Ys have over the Xs' (p. 89). Hence, instead of focusing on all kinds of power relationships, they claim we should consider as 'political' only those power relations taking place between social groups, and such relations need not be mediated through institutions but just through attitudes (2008, p. 88).

A policy is a course of action pursued by an institution. Political discourse revolves around possible courses of action that a government might take. The core of political debates is focused on the rationales of governmental policies. Education reforms, as well as an economic policy, can be guided by different principles and values. Every policy can be analyzed in terms of the values shaping it. A tax reform has serious impact on the citizens' wealth distribution and it can be guided by different conceptions of equality and social distribution that a government may pursue. At the core of the debate around different governmental policies there are relevant moral values. I take it that, due to their relevance in shaping public policies, our definition of the category of political cinema will only be partial if it did not take into account these ethical values. As we have seen previously, ethical values can shape social conflict and group human beings along the friend/enemy distinction. For instance, the ethical problem of euthanasia has repercussions for state policy. Marco Bellocchio's film *La Bella Addormentata* is focused on this moral problem and it clearly intended to elicit reflection on this issue. Moreover, the film was immediately considered political due to the fact that the Italian public sphere was absorbed in the debate around the case of Eluana Englaro, which is overtly mentioned in the film. Clearly, a definition of political cinema needs to accommodate these cases where what is at stake is a moral value that shapes political decisions.

Polity has a double meaning. On the one hand it refers to the form of government or constitution of a political unit, and on the other it refers to the boundaries of the political community. It is this second meaning that is of interest for our purposes. Indeed, collective identities are just as important as moral values in order to shape social conflict. I shall explain my point starting from an example that I borrow from Martha Nussbaum (2013).

This is a stanza from Whitman's poem 'When Lilacs Last in the Dooryard Bloom'd':

> Lo, body and soul – this land,
> My own Manhattan with spires, and the sparkling and hurrying tides, and the ships,
> The varied and ample land, the South and the North in the light,
> Ohio's shores and flashing Missouri,
> And ever the far-spreading prairies cover'd with grass and corn.
> Lo, the most excellent sun so calm and haughty,
> The violet and purple morn with just-felt breezes,
> The gentle soft-born measureless light,
> The miracle spreading bathing all, the fulfill'd noon,
> The coming eve delicious, the welcome night and stars,
> Over my cities shining all, enveloping man and land.

The poem is an elegy written in 1865 to mourn the assassinated President Abraham Lincoln. In this stanza Whitman depicts the beauty of Manhattan and then, radiating out from Manhattan, other regions of America – the physical beauty and the beauty of human activity. Nussbaum holds that:

> images of natural beauty are always heart-rendering for their link to mortality and the passage of time. Here, they are more profoundly heart-rendering for their link to Whitman's imagined ritual of morning for Lincoln – and, of course, their implied link to all that Lincoln stood for, a nation of free activity and the equality of all Americans beneath the sun
>
> (2013, p. 12).

Lincoln – the 'large sweet soul who has gone' – symbolizes, in Whitman, the great American ideal of equality and justice, and then he – as a morally praiseworthy symbol – is put in relation with the 'already loved feature of the land and the varied people who inhabit it' (Nussbaum, 2013, p. 13), that is, with America and the Americans. In other words, Whitman reflects on what it means to be an American, what are the core values that define one belonging to the American nation, and Lincoln becomes the symbol that embodies these values.

Whitman's poem reflects on what it means to be member of a political community. And more specifically, it serves a function: through the comparison between the moral values symbolized by Lincoln (equality and justice) and the land and its inhabitants, Whitman reflects on the values shaping the identity of Americans. He teaches patriotism.

Such reflections on collective identities are inherently political, as they aim to highlight the values that shape unity (or disunity). We can take other relevant examples from the Italian artistic production in the period of the

'Resistenza'. 'Resistenza' was the movement of opposition to the Nazi-fascist occupation of Italy. The Italian Constitution is the outcome of that wartime period, and all the movements that were fighting in the anti-fascist front took part in the Constituency assembly. Carl Schmitt considers the constitutional process the true political moment because it is the process through which the friend/enemy distinction is actually limited: Constitutional processes are characteristic of postwar periods, and the constitution embodies the agreement that allows a management and a relativization of social conflict so that it does not reach the utmost disruptive polarity of friend/enemy. The agreement that grounds the constitution is not only a legal bond among political forces, it also expresses the values that are (or should be) at the core of one's feeling of national belonging. In order to limit the disruptive force of the friend/enemy distinction, there is the need for a feeling of solidarity that could bind members of different and competing social groups within the greater framework of a unique, inclusive, collective identity (see also Böckenförde, 2010). According to Jürgen Habermas (2009, 2013), the constitution grants such inclusiveness, thanks to its reference to universal human rights, the endorsement of which should suffice to instill solidarity among citizens. Italian scholars, like Gian Enrico Rusconi (1993) and Gaspare Nevola (2003), have developed Habermas's notion of constitutional patriotism, arguing that the endorsement of universal human rights as expressed in the constitution does not suffice to grant that sense of social cohesion and solidarity necessary to contain social conflict. Nevola (2003), in particular, argues for a developed form of constitutional patriotism, entailing other grounding aspects of the constitution. Indeed, the constitution is not just a public endorsement of universal rights; it also stems from specific, particularistic, circumstances. Nevola advocates for a form of constitutional patriotism that also entails a reference to the historical and political context from which the constitution stemmed.

Hence, the importance of reflecting on the contradictions and values of the 'Resistenza'. Elio Vittorini's novel *Uomini e No* (*Men and not men*, 1980) – and the homonymous film of Valentino Orsini (1980) – is one of the deepest and most touching reflections on Italian's 'Resistenza'. Enne2 is the head of a small group of partisans organizing military actions against the Nazi-fascist army in Milan. Enne2 is not a determined and resolute fighter. On the contrary, he is a multifaceted character whose political views are affected by his private life, in particular by his tormented love for Berta, a married woman who cannot decide to leave her husband. The Nazi-fascist army is described as unscrupulous and ruthless, and the Capitan of the army has the symbolically eloquent name of 'Cane Nero' (Black Dog). From a contraposition between Enne2 and Cane Nero we can get a first interpretation of the title, as confronting 'men' (Enne2) to 'not-men' (Cane Nero as a beast-like figure). Yet the book is not a shallow celebration of the Resistenza; rather it is a reflection upon it. Indeed, after Enne2 scarifies his life in order to kill Cane Nero, the book focuses on a worker who tried to help

Enne2 and who joined the partisan force. This worker, who remains anonymous, takes part in military actions against the German army; yet, he will prove himself incapable of killing a German officer, as he can see 'humanity' in the eyes of the enemy. In this last part of the book, Vittorini reassesses the ignobility of killing, and he also wants to leave a spark of hope and a sign of solidarity, as recognizing the humanity in each other is a necessary condition for future coexistence. Works on the 'Resistenza' are political works in this sense.[5] They serve the same function as Whitman's poem: to reflect on collective political identity and the values that ground it.

5 'Being' political

So far we have clarified what the 'political' refers to. We know what a political issue is – namely, an issue that shapes social conflict and grouping along the distinction of friend/enemy. So, at least one part of the tautology 'political films are about political issues' is explained. But this is not enough. We need to clarify when a is film political. I hold that a film is political when it is *intended* to be about a political issue.[6] It means that in tracing the intentions of the author we should be able to see how the 'political issue' was intended to be the subject of the film. With the term 'subject' I refer to what David Bordwell (1989) calls the implied meaning of a work. For instance, *Gravity* is (explicitly) about a space-catastrophe, but it is ('implicitly') *about* mourning. I call the implied meaning 'semantic', because I take it to be linked to the authorial semantic intentions: the intentions to *mean* something through a text T (Levinson, 1996a, 1996b, 2006).

Jerrold Levinson makes a distinction between semantic and categorical intentions. Categorical intentions refer to the

> author's intentions that T be *classified* or *taken* in some specific or general way. . . . Categorical intentions involve the maker's framing and positioning of his product vis-à-vis his projected audience; they involve the maker's conception of what he has produced and what it is for, on a rather basic level they govern not what a work is to mean but how it is to be fundamentally conceived or approached
>
> (1996a, p. 206).

Levinson takes categorical intentions to be imperative with regard to classification, and this can be understood in light of the importance classification acquires in evaluating an artwork: a director may intend to shoot a comedy and yet produce a movie that is anything but funny, hence attracting negative judgments. Something similar, I take it, can happen with political films, although some clarifications need to be introduced. Contrary to Levinson, I do not take categorical intentions to be imperative. An author may intend to make a political film and yet be mistaken about what counts as a political issue, so he would not be making a political film. Also the contrary can happen: an author may state that he did not intend to make a political film, and yet his film may be political.

Understanding when an artwork is about political issues requires an exegetical effort. I take it that the semantic meaning should be the focus of our interpretative effort and the central element for the classification and appraisal of political films. It means that in our interpretation we should not consider what Bordwell calls 'symptomatic meaning' (1989). This meaning emerges from the analysis of those cultural and social forces or unconscious psychological forces in the artist or viewer that have an impact on the creation of the artwork or on the standard ways of watching and responding to it. This type of meaning was central in some interpretative efforts in the seventies and eighties. Laura Mulvey's essay 'Visual Pleasure and Narrative Cinema' (1989) is an example of this approach to interpretation; she argues that 'fundamental features of narrative and its presentation in classic Hollywood films are muted manifestations of unconscious and pathological male fascination and anxiety engendered in contemplating the erotically charged female body' (p. 18).

This approach takes artworks to be the manifestation of cultural, political and social forces that are typical of the society of which artworks are expressions. That is to say, this interpretative practice takes artworks to be the place of cultural, political and sociological critique due to the fact that artworks are, inherently, cultural products. I do not hold that this practice is not legitimate; artworks are indeed cultural products, and we may get to know a great deal about different societies at different times through their analysis. However, I do hold that this approach is limited from the perspective of who is interested in the analysis of the aesthetic value of artworks. The main limit is that it makes every single artwork apt for political, cultural and sociological criticism. Evidently, if this were plausible, then we would not need a category of political films, simply because all films would be political – in this 'symptomatic' sense. This is counterintuitive, since we actually appreciate films as belonging to other, different categories that have nothing to do with the political. Most importantly, this interpretative practice has the drawback of extending the category of political artworks to the point of uselessness. If any film belongs to the category of political cinema, then such a category has no specific tools that may enable a pertinent assessment and evaluation. Moreover, though this is not a problem for my argument, this practice may also raise methodological issues for the cultural theorist: can the analysis of artistic products be the best method to conduct sociological and political analysis? It would seem that cultural studies and sociology need a better grasp of the real world and probably a more intensive use of empirical research.

Hence, the semantic intentions of the author are the focus of our attention, as they allow for a more accurate classification of artworks. Symptomatic interpretation does not help to circumscribe the category of political films, whereas authorial semantic intentions can also help discriminate among different cases. For instance, if a film is set within a political institution, this does not suffice to make it political. There may be artworks using political institutions just as a set to tell a story that has nothing to do with political problems; even referencing real-life political roles or personalities does not necessarily make an artwork political. After all, Hugh Grant in *Love Actually* (Richard Curtis, 2003) plays the British prime minister, and yet we would hardly say that the film is political. At the same time, though, there is the possibility that a film may be political even if it does not seem to overtly address a political issue. It can take the form of an allegory, and interpretation will be required to understand what it is implied by the story told.[7]

Before I say something more on the kinds of intentions that are relevant for political films, I just want to emphasize that films, and artworks in general, may aim to convey a number of messages, not just one. The idea that artworks can convey several messages is coherent with the idea that genres can overlap and intersect. For instance, we can have films belonging to two (or more) different categories at the same time, as in the case of sci-fi-thrillers. However, genres do not simply overlap; they can also have a hierarchical order. For instance, a film may primarily be a comedy while also having elements of another genre, say, 'road movies' or melodrama. It means that political films can belong to other categories (e.g. political thrillers belong both to the political and the thriller genres), but they may also have secondary elements that would count toward their belonging to another category (for instance, a political film may have elements of film noir or action movies), and vice versa, film belonging (primarily) to different categories may also have a political point. For instance, Van Groeningen's film *The Broken Circle Breakdown* (2012) is a drama on the breakdown and tragic end of a family. Subsequently, the film also mentions the ethical debate on the sacredness of life and the limits of scientific research. Despite this being a possible political theme, the film is not political. Even if we were to grant substantial importance to this theme in the process of interpreting the film (and I believe such importance would not be warranted by the work), this would be, at most, a secondary message.

The focus on authorial semantic intentions allows for an accurate classification and understanding of films. We have seen how political films can be so diverse. Adding to this diversity the possibility of symptomatic interpretation would make the category itself pointless, as it would lose any specificity that could serve as index in our assessment.

Notes

1 As we have seen previously, closed categories cannot be 'genres'.
2 I understand that any time I name a genre I may run into objections: what is a psychological drama? And is it a genre? I will not try to define other genres I refer to, and I take everyday usage of that genre as a substantial hint for its actual

existence – specifically, major movie databases use 'psychological drama' to classify films. This may not suffice to prove that 'psychological drama' is a genre but that goes beyond the remit of this work.

3 Perhaps a Brechtian may hold that films with a political commitment need to be characterized by a particular use of the medium that aims to avoid transparency and prevent identification with the characters of the work. However, this route would be strictly prescriptive: it sets certain formal criteria and artworks should adhere to them in order to be political. This is a limiting approach, as it does not deal with divergences from the established norm (see the plague of *normativism* discussed previously).

4 These two problems clearly mirror my intended aims: that of clarifying the concept of the 'political' and that of clarifying how films can articulate such a concept.

5 Among the films on the 'Resistenza', a few are: Carlo Lizzani, *Achtung! Banditi* (1951); Roberto Rossellini, *Il Generale Dalla Rovere* (1959); Gillo Pontecorvo, *Kapò* (1959); Luigi Comencini, *Tutti A Casa* (1960) and Ettore Scola, *Una Giornata Particolare* (1976). Among the novels on the 'Resistenza', a few are: Cesare Pavese, *La Casa in Collina* (1948); Giuseppe Fenoglio, *I Ventitrè Giorni della Città di Alba* (1952), *Una Questione Privata* (1990) and *Il Partigiano Johnny* (1992).

6 This is a rough formulation of a definition on which I will elaborate in the course of the chapter. Moreover, I will also explain how intentions can fail in different ways: for example, an author may fail to make a work political, or he or she may fail to make a successful political work. I will illuminate this difference later and expand on the second kind of failure in the third chapter of the book.

7 This seems to be the case with Henry Koster's *The Robe* (1953) or other films in the blacklist era (see Jeff Smith, 2014).

2 The purpose of political cinema

Now we have defined the concept of the political, and we have clarified the kind of interpretation we need to favor in order to classify and assess political films. Authorial intentions are crucial for the classification, and now I turn to the analysis of such intentions in order to clarify when a film is political.

I propose to follow Catharine Abell's account of genre membership. Abell (2015) claims that what is distinctive about genres is their purpose. That is to say, different genres have different purposes, and if we are to make a theory of a specific genre, then we need to identify the purpose of that genre. For instance, comedy has the purpose to amuse, a thriller to thrill and horror to frighten an audience.[1] Abell defines genre and genre membership as follows:

> GENRE: A genre is a category of works determined by the purpose for which they are produced and appreciated, where the means by which they pursue that purpose rely at least partly on producers' and audiences' common knowledge that the works are produced and to be appreciated for that purpose.
>
> GENRE MEMBERSHIP: A work belongs to a given genre iff it was produced with the intention that it performs the purpose characteristic of that genre by certain means; and these means are such that, if they were to enable the work to perform the purpose at issue, they would do so partly in virtue its producer's and audience's common knowledge that it is produced and to be appreciated for that purpose (Abell, 2015, p. 32).

We can see how it is 'purpose', broadly construed, what defines the category, and if we are to define a specific genre, we need to look for the specific purpose characteristic of that category. This chapter is devoted to this task. I focus my analysis on the functions of political cinema, and I analyze these functions in depth, providing a theoretical framework that

DOI: 10.4324/9780367816872-3

can facilitate the classification and assessment of political films. First, I develop an historical account of political cinema, focusing on Bertolt Brecht's theory of political art (Section 1), and then I spell out the two functions of political films drawing from Brecht's theory as well as from the Schmittian theory that grounds my definition of the concept of the political (Section 2). We will then have a definition of political cinema: a film is political when its intended aim is to (1) persuade the audience about the validity of a political standpoint or (2) elicit reflection around a political issue. A political issue is an issue that shapes social conflict and grouping along the friend/enemy distinction, and a political standpoint is a specific position within the debate shaping social conflict. The first function is a 'rhetorical' function and the second is an 'explorational' function.

In the remaining sections of the chapter I analyze these functions introducing a theoretical framework that can facilitate the classification and assessment of political films. I suggest that to classify and assess political films we ought to analyze three epistemic dimensions: (1) epistemic voice, (2) epistemic merit and (3) pedagogical method. In order to develop and explain this theoretical framework, I introduce Carl Plantinga's typology of nonfiction films (Section 3), which is the source of inspiration for my framework. I then highlight what I take to be the main weaknesses of Plantinga's typology (Section 4), and move to articulate my own theoretical framework, explaining the interrelation between a film's epistemic dimensions and their interaction with the aesthetic value (Section 5).

1 Political functions at a glance

After World War II, political cinema or social cinema were labels used in everyday practice of film criticism. European national cinemas, particularly in France and Italy, were concerned with the opportunities of social and political criticism brought by the cinematic medium. The label political cinema was then quite common although it was used to identify, almost exclusively, arthouse or avant-garde cinematic production (Thompson & Bordwell, 2010). The themes of this political cinema are easily listed, as they included class struggle or a general contraposition between the proletariat and the bourgeoisie, power conflict within political institutions and colonialism or, more broadly, problems of international relations among nation-states. It is evident how political cinema was, at least implicitly, related to Marxist or broadly left wing ideologies. Surely, Marxism had a more prominent role in political life after World War II than it has nowadays, and left wing parties, which overtly called themselves communists, welcomed and promoted artistic production dealing with political problems.

The passing of time and international political events have fostered what seems to be an obsolescence of the classic political jargon linked to Marxists and left wing ideologies. Such political changes have also affected the understanding of political cinema. If political cinema was defined as such by virtue of a close relation to Marxist ideologies, it seems only reasonable that with a decline of Marxism, cultural production as well as artistic criticism may have adapted and shifted their references. However, I hold that the relation between the label 'political cinema' and Marxism is only contingent, and that we are not to understand such a relation as a normative specification of what political cinema needs to be if it aims to be political. Nonetheless, we cannot deny the widespread influence that Marxism had on the cultural production of the postwar period and its influence in shaping public debate as well as art theory. With the decline of Marxism, if not among intellectual debate then at least in the public sphere, even art criticism seems to have dismissed the clothes of political commitment.

Indeed, with the obsolescence of the classical Marxist jargon there has also been less attention to what had been the central issues of the then called political cinema. Class struggle, colonialism and the contraposition between proletariat and bourgeoisie became the syntax of an old conception of the political. Subsequently, as it had been related to this lexicon, political cinema acquired a much less clear identity (see also O'Shaughnessy, 2007). The previous correlation between political cinema and Marxist ideology was certainly limiting and, I hold, inaccurate, but it had the overt advantage of clearly identifying the issues that would make films political.

Defining a political film right now is a much more complex matter. Is there political cinema at all? And can political cinema exist when decoupled from Marxism? My reply to both questions is positive. The relation between Marxism and political cinema was only historically contingent. I have defined the 'political' as that category characterized by the alignments of social groups along the continuum defined by the disruptive dichotomy of friend and enemy. Any issue that shapes the public debate in this fashion is a political issue. Hence, political films need not be related to Marxist ideology, as they just need to problematize issues that shape conflict within public debate. We can say that this kind of cinema has never disappeared. Rather, issues shaping social conflict have changed, and artistic production has mirrored such changes.

Despite my rejection of an ideological approach to the definition of political cinema, it is instructive to see what was previously meant by the label 'political' when originally applied to artistic production. In this sense the work of Bertolt Brecht is central to our analysis, not just because he was an active playwright but also because of his contribution to art theory and his influence on the political cinema of the sixties. To understand Brecht's theater, we are to put it in relation to the Marxist ideology he endorsed. In Marxist theory, human history is a history of struggles that have led to the crystallization of a modern, capitalistic social structure. However, as history is characterized by struggles and changes in the social structure, in the same fashion we are to consider contemporary social organization as transient. Historical materialism permeates Brechtian theater: Brecht wanted to highlight the attitude and behavior that people adopted in specific historical situations (see *Mahagonny* and the *Threepenny Opera*) in order to emphasize the very fact that insofar as they are historically determined, social institutions and practices are transitory and therefore subject to change. Historical specificity and particularization trumps the romantic ideal of art mirroring the essence of humanity and manifesting universal traits and feelings connected to the 'human condition'. Quite the contrary, Brecht is concerned with representing the particular and historically determined social practices, since these practices can be subject to change. Such possibility of change is central to Brecht's view of political art. We can say that Brecht was concerned with manifesting the possibility of change. That is, to be political, art needed to have such a tension toward change. In this sense Brechtian theater aimed at being revolutionary, that is, capable of inspiring and promoting changes in unjust and historically determined social practices.

How to instigate change? In order to make the audience aware of the possibility of change, the play was meant to draw the attention of the audience to avoid passive spectatorship. The plays were to be designed in order to raise critical reflection on social institutions, arrangements and practices that were to be subverted. Hence, the play had to be intended to estrange and distance the spectator, through the use of the Verfremdungseffekt or V-effect. The play needed to defamiliarize a theme or situation in order to draw attention to it and elicit a reflection. Empathy and identification were the main mechanisms to be avoided if the play wanted to have an impact on its audience.[2] The spectator was to be estranged and distanced rather than immersed in the play.

The central point, here, is that immersion inhibits reflection, hence it inhibits political and revolutionary art. This is why Brecht's theater is usually juxtaposed with the so-called culinary theater (Kellner, 1980), which was meant to provide the spectator with a pleasant experience or moral for easy digestion. Brecht rejected that kind of theater on the grounds that it was not capable of serving revolutionary purposes. To put it roughly, revolutionary, or epic, theater was meant to elicit reflection about those practices and social structures that were the product of history and that, as they were historically determined, could have been changed or subverted. Walter Benjamin said that the reaction to epic theater should be that of shock and surprise: 'Is this the way things are? What produced this? It's terrible! How can we change things?' (Benjamin, 2003, p. 8).

In order to reach the audience's attention and critical reflection of the social practices presented in the play, the formal organization of the play itself was meant to be the driving force of the process of defamiliarization of the subject. Where traditional or, say, culinary theater aimed at being transparent in order to favor the audience's immersion in the story and identification with the characters, epic theater wanted to be self-reflexive and used formal techniques to overtly draw the attention of the audience, so that the audience could be reawakened from the passivity that was, instead, promoted by a transparent medium (as an example, see Saltan Dudow's *Kuhle Wampe* (1932)).

However, it is with his later works that Brecht developed an even more pedagogical approach to theater. In his last works, he was much more concerned with the idea of theater as a means for learning. The 'learning plays' (Lehrstuecke) were meant as a moment of reflection that could foster individuals' political education. The learning plays did not advocate for specific standpoints, doctrines or courses of action, but rather they were conceived to engage the public in a process of learning. The play *The Measures Taken*, for instance, confronts the audience with various issues related to revolution – violence, discipline, the structure of the party, the relation with the masses, revolutionary justice and so on – but it does not set forth any specific view: the actors are to present a scene and then discuss it with the audience.

This shows that political or, as Brecht called it, revolutionary theater was meant especially as a moment of reflection and education. It required the active engagement of the audience, which was meant to engage in critical reflections on the unjust social practices.

2 Functions of political cinema

We need not subscribe to the claim that political films aim at changing social practices. Whether art could actually have an impact on our everyday life is a fascinating problem that requires much more empirical research – and this is beyond the remit of this work. Nonetheless, Brecht's theory of art is helpful as it stresses the importance of what I take to be the main characteristic we are to assess when we assess political works: their epistemic value. Brecht actually believed that art could play a role not just in the life of the individual but as a social tool that could serve to instigate action to improve social practices and political institutions. If we leave aside such an empirical claim, we see how Brecht's focus is on the idea of critical reflection. Theater, and artworks in general, should find ways to engage the audience in order to elicit reflection on critical issues. 'Critical reflection' implies a mobilization of our system of beliefs and works that can bring any kind of contribution to our system of beliefs have epistemic value.[3]

It is such epistemic value that is unique to political artworks and to political cinema. It is the main dimension we are to assess when we assess works belonging to this category. However, the epistemic value per se does not denote any specific function that would identify a political film, although it is surely related to any such function.

To spell out the purpose of political cinema we need to think of the main criterion that identifies the category of the political: the contraposition between friend and enemy. An important political aim will be that of convincing the opposition of the validity of our standpoints in order to expand our allegiances. Artworks and films in particular, as means of communication, can perform this very function: that of persuading the audience of the validity of a standpoint.[4] I call this function 'rhetorical'. However, not all political films need aim at persuading their audience. Brecht's late works were not intended to advance a specific point of view or to persuade the viewers. On the contrary, the 'Lehrstücke' were exclusively meant to elicit the reflection of the audience on important political themes. No solution was proposed, but the aim was that of having the audience think about the problem. I call this the 'explorational' or 'observational' function of art.

Now we have all the elements to draw a definition of the category of political cinema. We have a definition of the concept of the 'political', an understanding of the functions of political cinema and an emphasis on the authorial semantic intentions to stress how the author needs to problematize the political issue in order to make it relevant for the classification and assessment of the film. Political cinema may aim to persuade its audience, but it may also limit its intentions to elicit critical reflection about a specific political issue. We can then say that a film is political when its intended aim is to i) persuade the audience about the validity of a political standpoint (the film has a rhetorical function) or ii) elicit reflection around a political issue (the film has an 'explorational' function). A political issue is an issue that shapes social conflict and grouping along the friend/enemy distinction, and a political standpoint is a specific position within the debate shaping the social conflict.

In both cases, we see that the epistemic value of the films is going to be central for the assessment, as in order to persuade or elicit reflection a film needs to make a contribution to our system of beliefs.[5] There may be different strategies to reach such aim but all of them are to be appraised in relation to the actual capacity of the work to bring forward an epistemically meritorious argument – that is, a sound and consistent reasoning. It also means that we need not endorse the standpoint advanced by the film in order to assess its epistemic qualities; artworks are like good arguments: we do not need to share their conclusions in order to appreciate their quality. Even the explorational function is strictly dependent on the epistemic value of films, as reflection is an epistemic activity. With reflection I imply a conscious process of weighing up different considerations; a process that aims at reaching a conclusion, although such a conclusion need not be reached. What is crucial in the process of reflecting on something is the active engagement with different considerations, that is, the activation and mobilization of our system of beliefs.

We can see that if we want to analyze political cinema then we are to look at its epistemic value and I propose a model for the analysis of film's epistemic value that could consider all different dimensions of this value. Indeed, the analysis of a film's epistemic merits does not exhaust per se all the possible ways we can look at a film's epistemic value. I hold we should assess: (1) the degree of authority the work has toward its subject (what I call the epistemic voice); (2) the actual proofs provided to support a standpoint or used to elicit reflection (epistemic merit) and (3) whether and how the film engages the audience in relation to the communication of the political message (pedagogical method).

Before I get into the details of this analytical schema, let me remark on how the pieces of the puzzle are coming together. We said that the genre membership is related to a work performing the function that is typical of that genre. Here I argue that political cinema can have two functions that are strictly related: (1) a rhetorical function and (2) an explorational function. So far, I have also analyzed what constitutes the 'political' and when it is accurate to label a film as such. I have showed that the main criterion that defines the political is contraposition between social groups, and for a work to be political we need to retrieve authorial intentions: if the author intends to persuade the audience of a particular standpoint, or at least elicit reflection on an issue shaping the public debate, then we can say the film is political.

There is more to be said about the process of classification: how do we differentiate between the rhetorical and the explorational function? And there is more to be said about the interrelation of such classification – a work belonging to the category of political cinema – and a film's assessment and aesthetic appraisal: is it possible that the functional properties could affect the epistemic and aesthetic value of the work? The explanation of the criteria that make up the analytical schema I propose here for the assessment and interpretation of political cinema will frame the last two questions and unravel the initial interaction between epistemic and aesthetic value; interaction that will be analyzed at length in the following chapters.

3 A typology of nonfiction films

I hold that political film can serve one of two different functions. How do we differentiate between the two? In order to differentiate between works with a rhetorical and explorational function we need to look at the degree of epistemic authority implied by the work. The epistemic authority of a work depends on its narrative voice, that is, on the degree of assertiveness in the elaboration and articulation of the work's meaning. Indeed, a film that tries to advocate for a particular cause or persuade its audience about the goodness of a particular standpoint on a given issue will adopt an *authoritative voice*, which is characterized by a high degree of epistemic authority; contrarily, a film that only wants to elicit reflection or raise awareness of a political problem will use a *hesitant voice*, which is characterized by a low degree of epistemic authority.

In order to explain the difference between *authoritative* and *hesitant* narrative voices, I introduce Carl Plantinga's typology of nonfiction films (1997b, 2005). Plantinga uses a different terminology that I will avoid since

I do not entirely endorse his typology. Nonetheless, a discussion of Plantinga's typology will help me justify the reason why I hold that epistemic authority is the main criterion that can be linked to a work's function. So, now I turn to Plantinga's classification of nonfiction film, whereas in the next section, I highlight what I take to be its main weakness by discussing the case of the *California Reich* and show that even if we cannot transpose Plantinga's model to categorize fiction films, we can still export what I take to be the most important contribution of his typology: the idea that we should classify films according to their epistemic voice. The discussion of Plantinga's classification will then lead to an outline of my proposed analytical schema, comprising three criteria: (1) epistemic voice; (2) epistemic merit and (3) pedagogical dimension.

Plantinga proposes a typology of nonfiction films based on their narrative voice. The narrative voice of a work is not to be understood as a verbocentric concept. Films presents their projected world from a given perspective (or perspectives) and they assume a specific tone and attitude toward the subject matter (Plantinga, 1997a, 1997b, p. 99). Such perspective, with its tone and attitude, makes up the concept of discursive voice. I take it that this concept substantially overlaps with the idea that a work manifests a specific attitude toward the subject presented and, following Berys Gaut

> the notion of an attitude should be understood broadly . . . to cover not just characteristically affective states, such as showing disgust towards or approval of the characters, but also to cover more purely cognitive states, such as presenting characters in such a way as to imply judgements about their being evil, good, inspiring and so on
>
> (2007, p. 9).

Hence, a work's voice can be considered as the author's attitude toward the work's subject matter.

According to Plantinga, nonfiction films can use a formal or open voice,[6] and there are three major points that can help us distinguish between the two: (1) the degree of their epistemic authority, (2) their formal characteristics and (3) a relation to fiction cinema. Plantinga remarks that such typology is just a heuristic device, so we are to consider the models of works with a formal and open voice as Platonic ideal types. I discuss these three points in turn.

1) The formal voice aims to explain portions of the world to the viewer (1997a, 1997b, p. 107). Surely this is a typical enterprise for a nonfiction film, but more specifically, films with the formal voice adopt what we may call a pedagogical approach: they stand out to teach their audience about a specific subject. Due to such assertiveness, works with a formal voice reserve for themselves a high degree of epistemic authority.

However, let me note that such an authoritative epistemic stance is not to be related to the actual epistemic merits of the work. Rather, it only relates to the discursive voice: the work claims epistemic authority on the subject matter – it conveys a specific viewpoint, and it does so overtly, stating it to the audience. Whether such authority is mirrored by actual epistemic merit has to be appraised separately.

Where the formal voice is epistemically authoritative, the open voice is epistemically hesitant. Works with an open voice acknowledge the epistemic difficulties in gathering knowledge. Instead of claiming authority on the subject matter, the open voice takes an unclear, open stand. As Plantinga puts it, the open voice, instead of explaining, observes or explores (p. 108), and it is reticent to impart presumed knowledge.

2) Works with a formal voice are also associated with a particular kind of form, that is, they are classical in form. They tend to have the 'classical aesthetic characteristics of harmony, unity, and restraint' (p. 107). Such classical aesthetic characteristics are evident not just in the structure of the films – symmetrical, unified and closed – but also in the techniques used, which are going to be instrumental for the communication of the intended message. The correlation between classical form and formal voice is then justified by the intent of the work. The classical form is well suited to explain and convey messages with a high degree of narrative authority. The classical form is instrumental as it allows for a clear question, or questions, to be asked and answered, always providing knowledge to fill in the gaps opened up by its questions.

As opposed to the formal voice, which uses classical structure, films with an open voice use open structure, a form that developed in opposition to the classical form. The open structure is, ideally, characterized by a complete lack of structure. The ideal type of this structure would consist of uncut footage, randomly shot. Hence the association with direct cinema and cinéma vérité. This type of approach to filming, as direct and as unmediated as possible, seems to fit works with an open voice because it aims at distancing the director from the facts depicted.

3) Works with a formal voice are compared to classical fiction film due to their capacity to expose the narrative with clarity, asking and answering questions. The classical fiction film develops what Carroll calls an erotetic narrative, that is, a mechanism similar to practical reasoning that unfolds the plot, posing questions and providing the answers. In particular, we are able to find a macro-question that guides the entire narrative and a number of micro-questions that are dealt with scene by scene.

On the other hand, works with an open voice are compared to arthouse films, as they are developed in contrast to a classical form of fiction making and propose an opposite approach to narration. Instead of having an omniscient voice guiding spectators, arthouse films accept that reality may be unknowable, characters are not one dimensional and the narration may unfold erratically. Classic fiction films are mainly plot driven, with characters that are goal oriented; therefore, the organization of the narrative tends toward the resolution of the events in order to provide conclusive knowledge about the story. Arthouse films are character centered, but the character may lack clear goals and may be caught up in events beyond his or her control.[7] Similarly, works with an open voice abdicate their epistemic authority to explain the world.

Summing up, Plantinga's typology is defined by three dimensions: (1) epistemic authority, (2) form and (3) relation to fiction film. Works with a formal voice are characterized by (1) a high degree of epistemic authority, (2) classical form and (3) significant similarities to classical fiction film. Works with an open voice are characterized by (1) epistemic hesitance, (2) open structure and (3) significant similarities to arthouse cinema.

4 Independence between form and authority

Plantinga argues that this typology needs to be understood as an ideal type, and we should accept some variations from the model, but the relation between the dimensions used to trace the model remains unclear. Are all dimensions equally important? Or should they be ordered hierarchically? The problem is pressing, as we can imagine the case of a film that fits in one dimension and not in the others. How are we to classify the voice of this film? Let me try to elucidate this problem through the case, also analyzed by Plantinga, of the *California Reich* (Parkes & Critchlow, 1975).

California Reich is a documentary shot in 1975 that uses little intervention in the filming and in the exposition of the events. The film begins with some explanatory titles that serve to establish a background to the documentary. These titles show the numbers of the American Nazi Party, which counts more than 2,000 members and is divided into different units across the country. Four of these units are in California. The final part of the titles also contains a specification of the modus operandi of the film: 'There is no narration in this film. It is the filmmaker's belief that the characters' own words are the most eloquent indictment of their racial philosophy'. The film then develops as studies of personalities, where members of the Nazi Party explain their viewpoints, interspersed with various events – including the celebration of Hitler's birthday – and social gatherings. As Plantinga notes: 'after becoming acquainted with the neo-Nazis, the spectator suspects that some suffer from serious mental problems, including paranoid feelings of isolation from society' (1997b, p. 142). This is, indeed, the impression the viewer has when watching the film, corroborated by the opening titles, where there is a clear moral judgment of the neo-Nazis' racial philosophy. Does *California Reich* have an open voice? It seems that Plantinga would defend the idea that the film has an open voice by virtue of the fact that it uses an open structure. He argues

> where the formal voice might analyze the psyches of the neo-Nazis and identify their possible mental disorder(s), *California Reich* refrains from such identification. Where the formal voice might define the word 'Nazi', or the California brand of Nazism, *California Reich* simply presents us with their words and actions, without such a conceptual framework. *California Reich* does not give the information necessary to constitute an analysis, but merely presents images and sounds
> (pp. 143–144).

It is true that *California Reich* refrains from commenting on the images it shows, but this is not sufficient to claim that the work has an open voice. The only thing the work is omitting is second-level propositions about the images that are actually doing all the talking. The work omits second-level propositions in the sense that it does not go on to explain the significance of the images. According to Plantinga, second-level explanations are typical of the formal voice. For instance, in *The Times of Harvey Milk* (Rob Epstein, 1984), the voiceover comments on the relevance of Milk's political activity overtly extending such relevance to the entire gay rights movement in America, making patently clear what is implied by the events narrated. *California Reich* lacks such a pedantic attitude. Nonetheless, the opening titles openly state the authorial stance on the moral issue at stake, and the images show such obviously disturbed individuals that second-order explanations would have only been redundant.

Moreover, the film deals with moral issues that are not perceived as controversial: condemnation of Nazism and of racial philosophy is considered obvious by a vast majority of the audience. When producing films, authors are aware of the perception their audience has of the issues they deal with; hence, this creates a sort of paradox for the open structure: if the work takes a distanced perspective form a moral issue which is generally accepted as flawed, such distance may be legitimately and intuitively perceived as a manifestation of the blame toward the immoral standpoint. In the case of *California Reich* this is particularly evident; as Plantinga notes, the spectator comes to feel that some neo-Nazis may suffer from some serious mental problems. That implicitly creates a link between mental disorder and immoral standpoint, once more reiterating an implied attitude of contempt – which is indeed overtly claimed in the opening titles. Perhaps, with different contextual information we may have a different reaction to the film. For instance, if the directors of *California Reich* had openly stated the intentions to celebrate the Neo-Nazi groups in California, we may have been appalled and outraged by the film.

So, what kind of voice does the film have? Despite the fact that this was meant as a clear example of the open voice, this does not seem to be a clear-cut case. *California Reich* has an open structure, but we cannot clearly say that it is epistemically hesitant, as right from the opening titles it expresses condemnation for the Nazi racial philosophy, so we cannot say that the film refrains from judging the persons endorsing Nazism.

The point I want to make is that the film form and narrative voice need not be linked. It is not necessarily the case that works with an open structure have a hesitant epistemic voice and, similarly, it can be the case that works with a clearly dramatic structure may adopt a more hesitant stand on a viewpoint, since, through the dramatization of their content, they may aim to convey the epistemic complexities that are typical of real-life scenarios.

Errol Morris's *Mr. Death: The Rise and Fall of Fred A. Leuchter, Jr.* (1999) can be a relevant example, especially because it is related to Neo-Nazism, so it makes for an interesting pairing with *California Reich*. Fred Leuchter carried out a series of tests on Auschwitz's ruins that allegedly supported 'negationism' of the Holocaust. Morris's documentary is, from a formal point of view, the complete opposite to *California Reich*. Where *California Reich* is inspired by direct cinema, and there is little intervention in the narration, *Mr. Death* has a much more organized and dramatized structure, which is guided by interviews with Leuchter and members of the scientific community.

I contend that despite such a different formal organization *Mr Death* shows a more hesitant epistemic voice. In *California Reich* the authors clearly condemn the Nazis, and our own feelings cannot be other than contempt and indignation. Even the psychological insights we gather are just superficial impressions of disturbed individuals. Something more complex happens in *Mr. Death* as we have a completely different, and much more multifaceted and nuanced, reaction to Fred Leuchter. In the first part of the documentary, through direct interviews with Leuchter, Morris focuses on his life and personality, so that we slowly get to know the man. The use of interviews permits a deep understanding of Leuchter's character traits. Plantinga himself, discussing the philosophy of Errol Morris, noted how Morris preferred the use of interviews as he found this method particularly well suited to exploring the invisible mental landscapes that he found fascinating. In the case of *Mr. Death*, this method clearly manages to create a complex and multifaceted portrait of Leuchter.

Shelly Shapiro, who is among Leuchter's detractors, hastily identifies him as pure evil and claims that 'there is no slippery slope for Mr. Fred Leuchter. The man is an anti-Semite. There are hate-mongers in this country, and he's one of them'. However, this is not the impression we get from our engagement with *Mr. Death*. Morris sees Leuchter as 'a completely benighted human being who still deserves our sympathy' (Singer, 1999, p. 39), and he manages to convey his sympathy and pity for the man. Plantinga agrees and argues that 'after having learned something of Leuchter's biography and the complexities of his personality, such pronouncements [Shapiro's] seem not only simplistic but void of the sympathy Morris clearly takes toward Leuchter' (Plantinga, 2009a, p. 58).

Hence, the judgment we elaborate about Leuchter is not as clear-cut as the one we have about the Nazis portrayed in *California Reich*. Yet the situation is quite similar. Leuchter supports theories that negate the Holocaust, and yet our judgment about him is hesitant. Such hesitance mirrors Morris's epistemic hesitance in the film. The director refrains from claiming authority on the judgments we are to elaborate about Leuchter, and he does so through an attentive investigation of Leuchter's personality. With *Mr. Death* we have an example of a work that expresses epistemic hesitancy, and yet it does not make use of an open structure.

5 A Theoretical framework for the analysis of political cinema

Plantinga's typology is meant for the classification of nonfiction films, but we can export a minimal characterization of such typology in order to build up a schema that may serve for the classification and analysis of fiction as well as nonfiction films with a political purpose.[8]

I showed previously that the multidimensionality of Plantinga's typology may create inconsistency in the classification – *California Reich* is classified as a work with an open voice because of its open structure, even though its voice is not hesitant. However, this typology does not actually need all three dimensions. What is really crucial for the classification process is the degree of narrative authority asserted by the work – the first dimension. To properly understand why we need not include the last two dimensions in our model, we need to return to the main reason behind Plantinga's typology. Plantinga's aim was to classify nonfiction films according to the broad purposes or functions that films may serve (1997a, 1997b, p. 106). However, we have seen previously that we do not need to establish a connection between function and form. *California Reich*, despite its open form, cannot be said to have a hesitant voice and, indeed, it seems to 'indict' the moral claims held by the Nazi groups portrayed in the film. On the other hand, despite its dramatic structure, *Mr. Death* has a hesitant epistemic voice, and it aims to explore the personality of Leuchter, showing that our judgments are to be weighed in light of all relevant information. Moreover, as I want to export this classification model to fiction films, we do not need the third dimension of Plantinga's proposed typology. After all, arthouse film can assert a high degree of epistemic authority and try to persuade or convince the audience of their viewpoint (see my discussion of *Two Days, One Night* in Chapter 7), and we can think of classical films that only explore an issue without advancing a specific standpoint.

The difference in the degree of narrational authority is the only criteria that is needed in order to discriminate between the various political functions of film. Yet a further clarification is in order. For Plantinga, epistemic authority comes together with a tendency to *explain* the viewpoint of the work. Plantinga holds that works with a formal voice make use of second-level propositions that are apt to explain the viewpoint of the film. For instance, *The Times of Harvey Milk* 'not only recounts the story of Harvey Milk's life and brief political career, but invests them with significance for the gay rights movement in America' (1997a, 1997b, p. 111). It would seem that *epistemic authority* requires *explanation*. This is not necessarily the case. A work that has epistemic authority may use second-level propositions to explain its standpoint, but the two, *epistemic authority* and *explanation*, are not mutually dependent. Let me consider again the case of *California Reich* to show how such separation can redesign our understanding and classification of films. Due to its opening titles and the fact that it deals with a vastly condemned moral standpoint, we can hold that *California Reich* has (contrary to what Plantinga holds) an authoritative voice, yet it refrains from overtly asserting second-level propositions that would (redundantly) explain its standpoint. To claim epistemic authority, a work need not explain or overtly assert its standpoint – although this may be a standard correlation.

Epistemic authority and *explanation* can be conceived as two separate criteria for the analysis of films with political functions. Here I propose a schema which groups these criteria together with the analysis of films' epistemic merits and which, I hold, allows for an accurate analysis of a film's overall epistemic value. The analytical schema I propose then has three criteria: (1) epistemic voice, (2) epistemic merit and (3) pedagogical method.

We have said that political film may aim either to persuade or to elicit reflection about political issues. The epistemic voice of a work is the criterion that helps with the classification of political cinema. We are to conceive of epistemic authority and hesitance as two extremes of a continuum, as films can have a lower or higher degree of narrative authority. Films with a high degree of epistemic authority aim to persuade the viewer of the validity of their standpoint, and I call them rhetorical, whereas works with a low degree of epistemic authority, that is, those that are epistemically hesitant, only aim to explore the issue at stake; their function is observational or explorational.

Films that aim to persuade need to provide the equivalent of proper arguments. Just as I aim to persuade you of the validity of the schema I propose, so too such films have to provide arguments supporting their claims. When we assess a film's capacity to contribute to our system of knowledge, we assess its epistemic merits. A work is epistemically meritorious if it brings a positive contribution to our system of belief, that is, it may yield true beliefs, or clarify some of our previously held beliefs, or it may foster our understanding of a complex issue. On the other end, a film is epistemically defective when the beliefs it yields are either false or connected to other beliefs in a way that is misleading or unwarranted. A claim like the 'unemployed are just lazy' is a perfect example of an unwarranted generalization (Carroll, 1996a, p. 279).

The epistemic merit of a film is conceptually independent from the other dimensions. For instance, even if a film's voice assumes a high degree of epistemic authority, that does not grant any actual epistemic merit to the work. A work may claim epistemic authority on a subject matter, but whether such authority is mirrored by actual epistemic merit has to be appraised separately (e.g. David Guggenheim's *An Inconvenient Truth*, 2006 or also Michael Moore's *Roger and Me*, 1998).

Also, the epistemic value of a work comes in degree: a work can be more or less epistemically meritorious or defective, or it can be meritorious and defective in some aspects rather than others.

I hold that the criterion of epistemic merit is linked to the aesthetic value of films and it plays a role in the persuasive process. The interrelation between the epistemic and aesthetic value will be analyzed at length in the following chapters, so here I only want to stress the role that epistemic merit plays in the persuasive process. And to do so, I take as my starting point Aristotle's conception of rhetoric. In his eponymous book, Aristotle (2015) holds that persuasion depends on *dispositio*, the structure of the discourse, *elocutio*, the style, and *inventio*, the argument or proof provided. The proofs are related to (1) ethos, (2) pathos and (3) logos: (1) the ethical proof is related to the supposed credibility of the persuader; (2) with pathos Aristotle refers to the capacity of emotions to move the audience, that is to say, the persuader can stir the audience's emotions in order to prove his point and (3) the third mode of persuasion refers to the capacity to provide evidence for the argument through examples and data.

It is in this third mode of persuasion that we can measure a work's epistemic merit. Indeed, considering this third mode of persuasion, we can see why Aristotle believed that rhetoric was closely related to dialectic. It is true that the rhetor can make use of emotions and appeal to his own credibility in order to persuade the audience, but Aristotle's *Rhetoric* differed from previous manuals on the subject because he wanted to highlight how the best way to persuade the audience was to present an argument that could demonstrate that something is the case (Rapp, 2009). This kind of demonstration works, just as in the dialectic, with inductive and deductive processes. However, rhetoric is intended for a more general public, less versed in logic inferences, and this is why, following Aristotle, rhetoric does not use full-fledged syllogisms. Nonetheless, dialectics and rhetoric, for Aristotle, use the same logical mechanisms. Inductive reasoning is supported by paradigms and examples, and deductive reasoning uses what Aristotle calls enthymemes.

This means that epistemic accuracy is also crucial for rhetorical purposes, beyond its possible interrelation with aesthetic value. And we can also appreciate how the use of examples, which can take the form of thought experiments (analyzed in Chapter 6), and of enthymemes make art apt to exercise persuasion, as these rhetorical modes of persuasion can be well adapted to what we can call literary or filmic persuasion.

The enthymeme is the rhetorical counterpart of the dialectic deductive syllogism. The deductive reasoning that links premises to conclusions is the same, but the enthymeme is meant to be easier to understand by the untrained public, so it is characterized by brevity (Rapp, 2009). The enthymeme takes the shape of a syllogism with some of its premises or conclusions omitted. The reason for such omission is that it makes the argument more effective from a rhetorical perspective: when the premises or the conclusions of an argument are familiar facts, or become obvious, then the hearer will be able to fill them in without further indications from the persuader.

The enthymematical reasoning calls for an active engagement of the public, which is part of the reason why its rhetorical force is augmented, as it invites participation in the construction of the argument. This kind of rhetorical articulation makes use of the maieutic method, in that it invites the audience to actively participate in the act of truth-seeking (see also Danto, 1983, and Carroll, 1993). This brings us to the third criterion of the schema I propose, what I call the pedagogical method, which measures the capacity of films to call for the active participation of the audience in the articulation of the work's meaning. A work can call for a more or less active engagement of the audience. If the work makes use of second-level propositions to explain its meaning and standpoint, we say that the work is pedantic; on the contrary, if it engages the audience with the use of enthymemetical reasoning then it adopts the maieutic method.

In order to engage actively with the audience, films with rhetorical purposes are better off if they avoid asserting second-level propositions, that is, propositions that are meant to overtly explain the work's meaning. These kinds of statements make the works exceedingly pedantic in their overt formulation of the lesson they want to impart. Enthymematical reasoning is well suited to engage the audience, as it implies an active participation in the articulation of the film's message. Clearly, artistic texts that articulate their points with enthymemes can invite different levels of engagement, and participation, and to different levels of complexity. Also, an enthymeme is a neutral form with regard to epistemic accuracy: the epistemic merits of the argument are to be assessed with regard to the truth of its premises and the soundness and consistency of its conclusions.

So, films can call for a more or less active engagement of their audience, but we can say that from a rhetorical perspective a work is better off if it uses enthymematical reasoning and avoids asserting second-level propositions about its meaning. However, the pedagogical criterion, as the epistemic merit, is not just related to the rhetorical purposes but also to the aesthetic value of artworks. More specifically, works that are epistemically meritorious and use engaging rhetorical strategies are also aesthetically meritorious; first, because they are intellectually engaging and second, because they avoid pedantry, which is often considered an aesthetic defect.

Second-level propositions are usually considered an aesthetic defect because they tend to make the work pedantic and overtly concerned with its attempt to impart a lesson. This is a standard line of assessment in literary criticism that I believe we can import into film criticism. Peter Lamarque holds that 'a novel like Dickens's *Hard Times*, for example, is frequently criticized for its overbearing moral message and its extremes in characterization aimed at drumming home the point' (2009, p. 253). In general, Lamarque argues, overtly didactic works that are obviously trying to teach a lesson are seldom valued highly (p. 253). Conolly and Haydar (2008), in their analysis of three political literary works – Shakespeare's *The Tempest*, Ibsen's *The Pillars of the Community* and again, Dickens's *Hard Times* – hold the same point. According to the authors, the works fail as political artworks not because they fail to be political but rather because they have little aesthetic value, which they had sacrificed in order to promote a political lesson. Conolly and Haydar argue that it is the excessive attention these works devote to their political message that leads them to oversimplify characters' psychology and flatten the works, which use dialogues between the characters to express those second-level propositions that pedantically restate the point they want to bring home (Conolly & Haydar, 2008).

The three criteria I have analyzed are useful on their own and they also interact with one another and with the aesthetic value of films. More specifically, these dimensions are independent from one another, but when we start to link them together, we can draw some inferences on their bearings on aesthetic value.

Works that call for an active engagement of the audience, I hold, are maieutic works. It is possible to say that the relation between maieutic films and epistemic merit is indeterminate. Maieutic works can be epistemically meritorious or defective: that a work calls for the audience's active engagement in the elaboration of its meaning is not tantamount to saying that it is epistemically meritorious; quite importantly, narratives with an assertive or a hesitant voice can both fall within the category of maieutic works. Indeed, works with a hesitant voice seem to be maieutic in nature, as they highlight epistemic difficulties, and since their voice is hesitant they naturally call for the audience's engagement. But we have also seen that narratives with an assertive voice not only can be epistemically meritorious but can also use rhetorical methods (enthymematical reasoning) that are apt to engage the audience (as in the case of *Two Days, One Night* – discussed in Chapter 6 – or, again, *California Reich*).

The enthymeme is the rhetorical form that works in place of the dialectic syllogism and that invites an active participation of the audience. Such rhetorical device can make a work with the assertive voice a maieutic work, avoiding the use of second-level propositions that explain the meaning of the work. Yet, saying that a work makes use of the maieutic does not imply that it allows for any kind of interpretation. Quite the contrary, it just invites the audience to actively look for the interpretation intended by the author.

In the case of an enthymematical reasoning, premises and conclusions are implied by the author, who just leaves an open space for the audience to exercise intellectual engagement with the work. Moreover, in the case of open works with a hesitant voice, the epistemic hesitance does not translate into an indeterminacy of meaning, but rather an epistemically hesitant discursive voice that wants to remark that the author himself believed the topic worthy of accurate reflection and the subject of the work to be epistemically complex.

These dimensions have some bearing on the aesthetic value of films, but I have not provided here an argument for a direct correlation between epistemic and aesthetic value. Nonetheless, from the analysis that I have carried out in this chapter, we can hold that works that are epistemically meritorious and that make use of a hesitant voice are always aesthetically meritorious to the extent that they call for an active engagement of the public. Whereas if they use an assertive voice, their aesthetic merits are to be evaluated also in light of their capacity to engage the audience and to call for their active participation in the elaboration of the work's meaning.

Notes

1 In the examples provided, the purpose of the genres is always related to the elicitation of some effects on the audience, but this need not be always the case, as some genres can be characterized by appealing to aspects of the content. For instance, Abell holds, 'the purpose of science fiction is arguably to describe logically coherent alternative worlds' (2015, p. 36).

2 I consider this issue at length in Chapter 6.

3 I say 'any kind of contribution' in order to define epistemic value quite broadly, so as to entail not just contributions that are related to the acquisition of new true beliefs but also contributions to our understanding of an issue and clarification of extant beliefs.

4 Here I use the term 'opposition' instead of enemy, as political confrontation requires that we do not reach the extreme contraposition of friend and enemy (when this happens, according to Schmitt, there is war and not political confrontation).

5 This is not necessarily true. A film, or even a speech, may persuade its audience while being epistemically defective. I will spell out all possible scenarios later, or for a more accurate treatment of the possibility of persuasion by an epistemically defective work, see Chapters 3 and 7.

6 Actually, Plantinga distinguishes between three different voices: formal, open and poetic. I do not discuss poetic voice here as the concern of works with a poetic voice is mainly aesthetic, and not epistemic, and I take it that works that aim to persuade, explain or even just observe and explore need to have epistemic concerns.

7 See also Bordwell (1985).

8 With 'political purpose' I imply that a work aims to persuade, or at least elicit reflection, on a political issue.

3 Political cinema and propaganda[1]

In the previous chapters I defined the category of political cinema. I argued that a political film is one that (1) aims to persuade its audience of the validity of a particular standpoint around an issue that shapes public conflict along the friend/enemy dichotomy ('rhetorical function') or (2) aims to elicit refection about an issue that shapes public conflict along the friend/enemy dichotomy ('explorational function'). Political cinema aims to contribute to our system of beliefs, so we need to assess its epistemic dimensions if we are to appraise its capacity to succeed, as well as its aesthetic value. Political films can be more or less epistemically meritorious: a film can provide an attentive and thorough characterization of a political issue, or a shallow and defective one. In this chapter, I will focus my analysis on this difference. Here I argue that in both cases the film is a political one; to fail to be political, films need to be about nonpolitical issues. However, films about political issues that are epistemically defective belong to a subcategory of political films, that of propaganda films.

To develop my argument, I first introduce and define the category of propaganda (Section 1); I want to show that propaganda films are a particular kind of political film, those with epistemic defects. I then clarify the relation between political and propaganda films (Section 2) and, as an example, I analyze the epistemic merits of *Dead Man Walking* (1995), showing how this is a case of a successful political film (Section 3).

1 What is propaganda?

The word 'propaganda' was used for the first time by Pope Gregory XV when he created the 'Congregatio de Propaganda Fide', an organization tasked with the job of spreading Catholicism in response to the Protestant Reformation. Here, propaganda meant something similar to education and preaching. However, despite having its origins in the seventeenth century, the term has only achieved widespread usage in the twentieth century, and despite such widespread usage its definition remains contested. What seems to be something like a necessary condition for propaganda is the intention to persuade. This is probably the only uncontroversial feature of

DOI: 10.4324/9780367816872-4

propaganda, and some general definitions use this feature as both sufficient and necessary, as they tend to equate propaganda with *mere persuasion*. Hummel and Huntress (1959) simply define propaganda as 'any attempt to persuade anyone of any belief' (p. 14); David Welch provides a similar definition: 'put simply, propaganda is the dissemination of ideas intended to convince people to think and act in a particular way and for a particular persuasive purpose' (Welch, 2013, p. 2); and the Institute for Propaganda Analysis, that was formed in United States in the thirties, goes in the same direction: 'propaganda is an expression of opinion or action by individuals or groups deliberately designed to influence the opinions and actions of other individuals or groups with reference to a predetermined end' (Lee & Lee, 1939, p. 4). These definitions use a different phrasing to say that propaganda is mere persuasion; the first definition is the most straightforward, whereas the others paraphrase the idea using synonyms like 'convince people to think and act' or 'influence the opinions and actions of other individuals'.

These definitions are flawed because while 'persuasion' is a necessary condition, it is not a sufficient one. If this were the case, any quarrel or debate would become a battlefield of propaganda. Even in philosophical debates, arguments aim to persuade opponents, but that does not suffice to make them propaganda. Furthermore, political films with rhetorical functions would all be propaganda, and rhetoric itself, which is the art of persuasion, would be the form of propaganda. Clearly these definitions are not capable of identifying what is specific to and characteristic of propaganda and what could differentiate it from any other attempt at mere persuasion.

Jowett and O'Donnell provide a definition of propaganda that goes in a better direction: 'propaganda is the deliberate and systematic attempt to shape perceptions, manipulate cognitions and direct behaviour to achieve a response that furthers the desired intent of the propagandist' (1992, p. 4). This definition has the advantage of underlining how there may be something wrong with propaganda, something deceptive. Indeed, while the term had been introduced in the seventeenth century, propaganda received far greater attention during the twentieth century, when it was associated with totalitarian regimes. The fact that propaganda was used as a tool by these regimes to move the masses indicates that one ought to make a distinction between mere persuasion and propaganda.

However, Jowett and O'Donnell's definition is not accurate enough, as it is not clear what it means to 'shape perception and manipulate cognition'. Even film directors deliberately and systematically shape perceptions and manipulate cognitions but that does not make film narration a form of propaganda. Clearly, films can be used for propaganda purposes, but we need to clarify what is actually typical of the methods of propaganda and, to be accurate, our definition also needs to account for the pejorative connotation propaganda has come to receive.

Some other definitions of propaganda have focused on its capacity to elicit emotions. For instance, Lippmann suggests that propaganda 'consists essentially in the use of symbols which assemble emotions after they have been detached from their ideas' (1927, p. 37) and Harold Lasswell argued that 'propaganda is the management of collective attitude through the manipulation of significant symbols' (1927, p. 627). In his definition Lasswell emphasizes how the communication of the message is mediated through the manipulation of symbols, hence implying that the type of engagement the propagandist aims to elicit is based on affective responses to the symbols employed. These definitions imply that propaganda has an impact on the audience's beliefs through the mobilization of an emotional response that is detached from rational deliberation. So, they hint at the fact that in propaganda there may be something to be wary of, but they do not clarify whether and how emotional responses actually bypass rationality (I inquire into this possibility in Chapter 7), and their definitions do not account for propaganda that relies not on emotions but simply on bad arguments, like syllogisms based on false premises.

Sheryl Tuttle Ross (2002) develops what I take to be the most accurate analysis of propaganda. She provides a definition that works for all instances of propaganda, and that is extremely relevant in the case of propaganda films.[2] Following Tuttle Ross, propaganda is a communicative process that involves a 'sender' (the agent or group who aims to persuade), a 'receiver' (the targeted group that is to be persuaded) and a 'message' (the means used for persuasion). According to Tuttle Ross, for something to be propaganda the sender needs to be a political institution, organization or cause (2002, p. 19). This is because, the author argues, propaganda is necessarily a political phenomenon, and this condition serves to capture this intuition. I share Tuttle Ross's view here, even though we must acknowledge that there can be communicative processes that work just as propaganda. Advertisement is an example that is often compared to propaganda (see Stanley, 2015), as it has senders and receivers and its message can be epistemically flawed. The working mechanisms may be the same, but there is a substantial sociological difference – the message is not about political issues – and Tuttle Ross's definition manages to capture it, reinstating also an historical coherence of the concept, which has always been linked with political problems – first within the church and then in relation to totalitarian regimes aiming at manipulating the masses.[3]

As for the message of propaganda, Tuttle Ross holds that what differentiates propaganda from other persuasive processes is the epistemic character of the propagandistic message. More specifically, she says that

> we should characterize propaganda as being epistemically defective or lacking epistemic merit, where this criterion not only applies to propositions and arguments but also to conceptual schemas (ways of carving up

> the world) as well as moral precepts. We can say that a message, M, is epistemically defective if either it is false, inappropriate or connected to other beliefs in ways that are inapt, misleading, or unwarranted
> (2002, p. 23).[4]

So, Tuttle Ross's definition highlights how the epistemic dimension of propaganda and its relation to political causes are what differentiates propaganda from any other persuasive attempt. When a message, sent on behalf of a political institution or cause, aims to persuade its intended receivers and is epistemically defective, then it is propaganda. We can see that there are four conditions for a message to be propaganda, which I take to be conjointly necessary and sufficient. A message M is propaganda when: (1) it is intended to persuade its receivers about the validity of a given viewpoint; (2) it is sent on behalf of a political institution, organization or cause; (3) the recipient of propaganda must be a socially significant group of people and (4) M is epistemically defective – that is, M is either false, or inappropriate, or connected to other beliefs in ways that are inapt, misleading or unwarranted.

Tuttle Ross's definition has several advantages. It manages to highlight what is actually distinctive about propaganda and what differentiates it from cases of mere persuasion. The propagandistic message is always political, as it is sent on behalf of a political institution, organization or cause, and what is peculiar to this message, what makes it propaganda, is that it is epistemically defective. These two elements distinguish propaganda from mere persuasion. Not all persuasive attempts are about political issues and not all of them are epistemically flawed. Moreover, Tuttle Ross's definition also manages to pinpoint and clarify what is so negative about propaganda. As the term has been so deeply associated with totalitarianisms and mass manipulation, it has come to receive a pejorative connotation, and Tuttle Ross identifies this negative side of propaganda: its epistemic defectiveness. This allows Tuttle Ross to avoid some oversimplifications in the definition of propaganda. For instance, it is not the case that propaganda can be used only for morally despicable causes, like the Nazi regime's degrading campaign against the Jews. There can be messages for good causes, like gender equality, that are epistemically defective and that are to be classified as propaganda. Moreover, it is not the case that propaganda, necessarily, involves deception. There are three possibilities to be distinguished here: (1) the persuader believes in the ideas they want to communicate but are aware that the message through which they communicate these ideas is epistemically flawed or (2) the persuader does not endorse the ideas they want to communicate but pretends to believe in them anyway (say, for personal interests). Both conditions can be realized in the case of propaganda, but they are not necessary, as there can be (3) the case of a persuader who believes in the ideas they want to communicate and also believes that the message through which they communicate these ideas is not epistemically flawed (while it actually is). For instance, it may have been the case that Leni

Riefenstahl really believed that Hitler was a great leader capable of elevating Germany, and she may have also believed that her message in *Triumph of the Will* was not epistemically flawed. Yet the film would still count as propaganda.

Jason Stanley, in his recent book *How Propaganda Works* (2015), holds that we should not include, what he calls, the *insincerity condition* in our definition of propaganda. This condition implies that the author of propaganda is insincere: he is aware of the epistemic flaw of the message he wants to communicate but he pretends to endorse it anyway. Stanley argues that such condition does not hold because 'propaganda relies upon the existence of *flawed ideologies* present in a given society' (2015, p. 4, italics mine). It means that the persuader may actually endorse a 'flawed ideology'; the expression 'flawed ideology' itself highlights the presence of an epistemic defect within the ideological system, which is then transported from the ideology itself to the message that aims to persuade the audience. A 'flawed ideology' is a set of ideals and beliefs that is incoherent or that is characterized by some sort of epistemic defect; it means that some of the ideals or beliefs that make up that ideology can be false, inaccurate or their connection may be misleading or unwarranted. The propagandistic message of 'true believers' is epistemically flawed because it reflects the epistemic flaws of the ideology behind it.

2 The relation between propaganda and political films

So far, we have defined propaganda, and now I turn to analyze how it relates to political films. Sheryl Tuttle Ross defines propaganda as an epistemically defective message, sent on behalf of a political institution, organization or cause, with the aim of persuading its audience. Political speeches can be propaganda, but epistemically defective messages can also be conveyed through artworks. When we apply Tuttle Ross's definition to films, we can see that there is a clear relation between my definition of political cinema and her definition of propaganda films. I define political films as films with rhetorical or explorational functions that are about political issues (issues shaping the public conflict along the lines of the friend and enemy dichotomy). Films with rhetorical functions aim to persuade the audience of the validity of a standpoint, whereas films with explorational functions only aim to elicit a reflection around a political problem. Moreover, as political films aim to have an impact on the audience's system of beliefs, to assess their value we should analyze their epistemic qualities. We can see that there are relevant similarities between the definitions of political and propaganda films, in particular between propaganda and political films with a rhetorical purpose, as they both aim to persuade their audience of the validity of a particular standpoint on a political issue. Political films with explorational functions are not directly related to propaganda films as they do not try to persuade their audience, so, in the remainder of the chapter, when I say that there is a relation between propaganda and political films, I always imply political films with a rhetorical function.[5]

In order to analyze the relation between political films and propaganda I suggest we focus on (1) the rhetorical function and (2) the epistemic value of films. I defined political films with rhetorical function as films that aim to persuade the audience about the validity of a given standpoint within a political debate – a debate that shapes social conflict along the line of the friend/enemy distinction. This means that propaganda films *are* political films, as they aim to persuade their audience about the validity of a given standpoint within a political debate (so they share the same rhetorical function). However, not all political films are propaganda. I contend that propaganda films are political films of a particular kind – epistemically defective. Within the broad category of political films (with rhetorical functions) we are going to have films that have great epistemic merits while some others are going to be epistemically defective. Epistemically meritorious political films are those that bring relevant and valuable insights regarding the standpoint they are advocating and that acknowledge the epistemic complexity of the debate to which they aim to contribute. Epistemically defective political films are those aiming to persuade their audience of beliefs that are either false, or inappropriate, or connected to other beliefs in ways that are inapt, misleading or unwarranted. Both kinds of films, epistemically meritorious political films and epistemically defective political films, intend to persuade the audience about the validity of a particular standpoint within a political debate, but they can be differentiated by their epistemic value. Hence, I propose to imagine these two categories of political films as two ends of a continuum, where the feature that determines the position along such continuum is the epistemic value of artworks.[6] The relation between these two categories is aptly described by the idea of a continuum because the epistemic value is not an either/or property.[7] A film can be more or less epistemically valuable, or valuable in some respects but not in others. Indeed, in any analysis of a film's epistemic value, it is going to be hard to give a clear-cut judgment. However, such differentiation based on the work's epistemic value allows a more accurate classification of political films with rhetorical function. In particular, those political films with a rhetorical function that are epistemically defective are going to be instances of propaganda. Epistemically defective political films with rhetorical functions are propaganda, and we find instances of these kinds of film on one end of the continuum defined by differences in the epistemic value of political films with a rhetorical function. Hence, at the other end of the continuum we find instances of epistemically meritorious political films. For the sake of brevity, when, in the chapter and in the rest of the book, I refer to political films with a rhetorical function, I always imply that these are 'epistemically meritorious' political films, to stress their divergence from propaganda films, which always imply epistemically defective political films.

In light of these specifications, are we justified to say that political films (epistemically meritorious political films with a rhetorical function) are always successful exemplars of the category (of political films with a rhetorical function), whereas propaganda films (epistemically defective political films with a rhetorical function) are failed attempts? To reply to this question, we need to consider different aspects of artistic production. I will first introduce some considerations on authorial intentions before analyzing the possible success of the film in light of its intended aim.

We have seen in the previous chapters how, in the classification and assessment of a film, we should consider both categorical and semantic intentions, but I also hold that none of these intentions are authoritative: i.e. capable of establishing membership to a category or a specific meaning of a film even against contradictory evidence.[8] A deluded author may intend to make a political film and yet have no clear understanding of what constitutes a political problem, so that his film will have nothing related to the political. Similarly, the same deluded author may assert that he has no intention to make a political film and yet shoot a film on a political problem. For instance, he may hold that his intention was not to make a political film but simply to persuade its audience of the immorality of euthanasia. As moral problems around euthanasia are political issues and he intends to persuade his audience, he is actually shooting a political film. In the first case, when the author declares his intention to make a political film but his film has nothing to do with the political, we say that the film fails to be political.

Moreover, an author may intend to make a political film and yet produce propaganda. That is to say, the author intended to produce an epistemically meritorious film on a political issue (aiming to persuade its audience), but his work is epistemically defective. We will not say that his work fails to be political, but it simply provides a shallow treatment of the political problem. I hinted at this possibility before, and now that we have introduced the category of propaganda we are better equipped to analyze these cases. These kinds of works, political films with little epistemic value, can be seen as belonging or at least leaning toward the category of propaganda. So, shall we conclude that propaganda films are unsuccessful political films?

Propaganda films are surely defective (at least from an epistemic point of view), but to claim that they are also unsuccessful, we must introduce some proviso that could consider all possible authorial intentions. Before I introduce such a proviso, let me also clarify what I mean when I say that a film is successful or unsuccessful as a political film. We could define a work's success in a broad fashion, referring to its popularity or to the fact the work has great artistic merits. However, I actually use a narrower definition, and I use the term 'successful' in relation to the actual realization of the author's intention. So, a film is successful when it reaches its intended aim. And this is why we cannot so easily say that propaganda works fail as political films.

There may be authors whose intentions are to produce propaganda. This may seem peculiar; propaganda has been recognized by authoritative regimes as a tool to spread the ideologies that served for their legitimization, and its pejorative connotation does not make this category particularly appealing. Moreover, as the definition of the term implies the presence of a defect (specifically, an epistemic defect), to have the intention to produce propaganda requires the will to make a work defective – from the epistemic point of view. But while it may appear counterintuitive, I cannot intend to make propaganda if I actually hold that my ideas and the message through which I aim to convey them are not epistemically flawed. Indeed, 'true believers' are not aware of the fact that they are making propaganda, they just aim at persuading the audience of what they take to be a laudable idea. At best, they can conceive of their work as 'educational'.

This is a peculiarity of what we may call 'propagandistic intentions': they require a will to deceive or to make something epistemically defective. We have seen previously that we do not need the *insincerity condition* to define propaganda but that does not mean that there may be cases where the propagandist is actually insincere. The aim of propaganda is that of persuading the audience, so the epistemic defectiveness may be part of a rhetorical strategy. We have seen how, among the Aristotelian modes of persuasion, rational proof is not the only way to persuade the audience. The persuader may exploit some unwarranted generalization or false belief in order to stir the audience's emotions. I hold that there is the possibility of there being authors willing to produce propaganda, and this does imply that they have conscious beliefs about making a work epistemically defective. It also means that a work's epistemic defect does not, per se, make a work (wholly) unsuccessful, in the sense of not achieving its intended aim. Indeed, if I have propagandistic intentions, then my work is meant to be epistemically defective.

A great many cases of propaganda may be non-intended cases. The majority of authors probably do not recognize their work as epistemically flawed. Nonetheless, their works are to be classified as propaganda, for the very reason that we did not list the *insincerity condition* in the definition of propaganda. That is to say, an author may sincerely endorse a standpoint or ideology that is itself epistemically flawed – and not recognize the flaw. Such a flaw will necessarily be present in the artistic production of the author. For this reason, even if a work is not intended to be propaganda, it may actually be so.

Now we can imagine the case of a film that is epistemically defective and yet not intended to be propaganda (not intended to be epistemically flawed). Can we then say that this is an unsuccessful political film? Again, not so hastily. In the opening of this section, I said that to analyze the relation between political and propaganda films we must pay attention to (1) the rhetorical function and (2) the epistemic value of films. The two dimensions are also able to identify where the intentions of an author can fail. To say that a film fails as a political film with a rhetorical function, the film has to be defective in these two dimensions. It needs to fail to be epistemically meritorious when it was intended as such, and it needs to fail to persuade its audience, when it was intended to have a rhetorical function.[9] Indeed, despite its epistemic defect, the film may actually reach one of its intended aims: that of persuading its audience. We say that the aim of political films with rhetorical functions is that of persuading the audience of the validity of a specific standpoint around a political issue. I also hold, drawing from Aristotle's view of rhetoric, that the epistemic value of a work is the most important tool to persuade the audience, but this does not rule out the possibility that even epistemically defective works may persuade the audience. We would need to be able to measure the actual impact of films on the audience's system of beliefs, but this is a matter of empirical research, which is beyond the remit of this work.

Probably the major problem for this kind of empirical research is related to the composition of the audience. When philosophers of art talk about problems of interpretation, they always postulate the existence of, what is usually called, an 'intended' or 'ideal' audience.[10] This is an interested and well-prepared audience that is capable of understanding complex semantic relations, has a general knowledge of topics and issues at stake in artworks and knows the author's public persona as well as his or her *oeuvre*. Such an audience exists in reality, but clearly it does not represent the totality of the audience, and perhaps not even the majority or the average of the audience that is engaged with artworks in general, and with rhetorical films in our case. The concept of an intended audience is useful for philosophers as they can avoid the uncertainties that an uncharacterized audience may leave open in their theories. Philosophical theories deal with so many different variables that it makes sense to fix some of them axiomatically. Nonetheless, in reality, the intended audience is not the only audience engaged with films and it may not be unrealistic to think of part of the audience being persuaded by a bad argument. This would be a situation in which our appraisal of the epistemic merits of the work does not suffice to establish its actual success, in terms of its impact on the audience's system of beliefs.

Despite these difficulties we should not underestimate the relevance of our assessment of the epistemic value of a work. We can say that our assessment of the epistemic value is generally a good indicator of the work's capacity to persuade its audience. I have argued earlier that the epistemic value is the distinguishing factor between political films and propaganda, and we can imagine political films and propaganda as two extremes on a continuum.[11] For example, at the left end there are instances of propaganda works, and at the right end of the continuum there are instances of epistemically meritorious political works.[12] If we were to also assess the success of these works we would need to add an axis to the analysis and imagine a Cartesian plane. On the x-axis there is the epistemic value and on the y-axis what we may call a rhetoric value, intended as the capacity to persuade the audience. Ideally, the higher the epistemic value, the higher should be the rhetoric value. So, we should find at the right end of the quadrant the highest scores for rhetoric value. Similarly, as we go toward the left end of the quadrant the rhetoric value should diminish. This is not always the case, and we are aware of the fact that some propaganda films have, or at least had, a great impact on the masses (as it has been the case for Nazi propaganda), so we could also expect a different scenario, where works that are epistemically defective manage to succeed in persuading the audience (the work could be positioned on the left top corner of our imagined quadrant), and perhaps we can also imagine the case of an epistemically meritorious work which is unsuccessful in persuading its audience (bottom right of the quadrant).[13]

Unfortunately, we will not be able to predict when an epistemically meritorious work fails to persuade its audience, and vice versa when propaganda succeeds in its intent. But what we can do is to appraise films in light of their epistemic value and take such value as a measure of their success. In reality, works may be more or less successful than what their epistemic merit may suggest, but this need not affect our theory. For our purpose we can postulate that the intended audience responds predictably to changes of the epistemic value, following the positive correlation between epistemic and rhetoric value.

3 Analyzing the epistemic value

In this last section, I want to introduce an example that could illuminate the distinction between political and propaganda films. The distinguishing factor between the two categories is the epistemic value of the film. I posit that these two categories are to be imagined as the extremes of a continuum. A political film with a rhetorical function that is epistemically defective will be classified as propaganda; otherwise, it belongs to the category of an epistemically meritorious political film with a rhetorical function. Hence, our appraisal of the epistemic value of a film determines both its classification and its capacity to succeed in persuading its audience.

I will now question Tuttle Ross's analyses of Tim Robbins's film *Dead Man Walking* (1995) to prove that we can actually analyze and even quarrel about the epistemic value of a work in order to classify and assess the film.

Tuttle Ross, discussing Robbins's film, argues that the film is an example of propaganda as the film is about a political issue – the abolition of death penalty – and it is epistemically defective. It is true that the film advocates against death penalty and the director also publicly stated it, but I question the fact that the film is epistemically defective. On the contrary, I want to prove that the film provides an attentive exploration of moral and psychological problems related to the death penalty. It is an epistemically meritorious film, I hold, and it cannot be classified as propaganda. So, I want to show that her interpretation is unwarranted and that, actually, Robbins's film is an example of a successful political film.

Matthew Poncelet (Sean Penn) is convicted and sentenced to death through lethal injection for having killed a young couple after having raped the girl. Sister Helen Prejean (Susan Sarandon) helps Matthew to promote a final appeal and will then become his spiritual advisor before the execution. This is why Tuttle Ross takes the work to be epistemically defective:

> The message that the death penalty is unjust is, in part, conveyed through a powerful visual metaphor at the end of the movie. . . . The character [Matthew Poncelet] is shown from a variety of camera angles strapped to a medical table which is visually similar to being tied to a cross. The final allusion of the film is that the person being executed is Christ-like. This strikes me as an inapt metaphor, for even if the death penalty is immoral, the comparison of a convicted killer to Christ seems unfair. For they are in essence comparing a person who might be regarded as evil to someone who represents the divine
>
> (2002, p. 28).

I hold that this interpretation is misguided. First, even if this had been the actual metaphorical meaning of the last scene, the film would not have been epistemically defective. Or better, we would have needed to acknowledge that this metaphor may not have been warranted, but we could not judge the entire film as epistemically defective on the basis of a single unwarranted metaphor. As I have argued previously, the epistemic value comes in degree, and a single scene does not suffice to categorize the entire film. Indeed, the film is far from being a unilateral accusation against death penalty. After a first appeal to the court, Sister Helen decides to meet the family of the victims, and they speak as the voice in favor of death penalty. Robbins captures the pain caused by the loss they suffered, and he even prompts empathic engagement with the victims' family. One scene is particularly relevant: Sister Helen visits the parents of the girl who has been raped and killed by Matthew, and in her visits the couple gives an extremely detailed and touching reconstruction of their daughter's last day of life, adding disturbing details from the medical report. This scene brings the audience the perspective of parents who have lost their daughter. In the scene, while she recounts her daughter's last day of life, Mrs. Percy cries for her loss, and her pain is emphasized by close-ups of her face transfigured by the tears.[14] Here we feel the same sadness and rage Mrs. Percy is feeling, and Robbins provides a powerful representation of the perspective in support of the death penalty, fostering the understanding of the victim's family standpoint.

Also, throughout the film, Matthew Poncelet is not depicted as a saint. Quite the contrary. After Sister Helen has accepted to help him with the appeal, he releases interviews where he praises Hitler and proudly shows his Nazi tattoos. We never properly sympathize with him because the main character of the film, who guides us in unfolding the story behind Poncelet, is Sister Helen. And to erase any doubts over his possible innocence, he even confesses the murder and the rape before the execution, so that it is really impossible to see Poncelet as a martyr.

Second, Tuttle Ross is surely right in pointing to the final scene as a possible reference to Catholicism, yet this does not grant the accuracy of her interpretation. The cross is a leitmotif of the film. We first see it in one of the initial scenes, and our attention is accurately drawn to it. Sister Helen goes for the first time to visit Matthew in prison, and she activates a metal detector; the camera then zooms in on the metal cross hanging from her neck, lingering for a few seconds on the image. This is the first of many times we see the cross. Yet, the reason why our attention is drawn to the cross is that the film aims to question the role of religion in shaping the debate around the death penalty. Throughout the film, the director seems to ask 'Where should religion stand in this debate?' 'Which side is it on?' Indeed, the families of the victims do not just claim to be fervent Catholics; they are also appalled by Sister Helen's efforts to help and comfort Poncelet as they are convinced the nun should be 'on their side'.

Third, if the last scene has a metaphorical meaning, this might not be as defective as Tuttle Ross claims. This last scene could be interpreted as a sort of provocation toward Catholicism. That is, Poncelet is not compared to Jesus; rather the aim of the scene is to question once more the role of religion in the debate. This scene may be intended as a provocative statement: 'this is what they did to Jesus – does religion now justify the same treatment?'

Tuttle Ross's interpretation is not just weakened by these considerations; there is also some textual evidence that goes against it. Talking with Poncelet a few days before his execution, Sister Helen describes to him the life of Jesus. Particularly, she refers to Jesus's help and love for the poor and how this love

> changed things. All people nobody cared about – prostitute, beggars, the poor – they finally had somebody who respected them, loved them. Made them realize their own worth. And they were becoming so powerful that the guys on top got really nervous, and so they had to kill Jesus.

Here Matthew asks 'kinda like me, uh?' The camera alternates between close-ups of their faces so we can see that Sister Helen's expression changes drastically, becoming serious and worried, and she replies, putting an end to our quarrel, 'No Matt . . . not at all like you!'

Dead Man Walking is not epistemically defective; the final scene's metaphor does not seem unwarranted as Tuttle Ross argues, and the film provides an accurate reflection of the problems around the debate on the death penalty, questioning the role of religion in the debate and also providing insights on the opposing standpoint, enquiring into the psychological reaction of the victims' families.

Notes

1 A previous version of this chapter appeared in the *International Lexicon of Aesthetics* (Cioffi, 2020)
2 Tuttle Ross analyzes propaganda as a communicative phenomenon, but her definition is meant to cover all instances of propaganda, be they art or not, and indeed, the main examples she refers to come from art and film in particular.
3 It means that we can coherently conceive of Church propaganda as political propaganda. Pope Gregory XV created the 'Congregatio de Propaganda Fide' as an instrument to convert the masses and as a response to the Protestant Reformation. Religion was, and still is, an issue that divides the public along the friend/enemy distinction.
4 Note that this definition of epistemic defectiveness is Carroll's definition (1996b), which is the same one I used in the first chapter.
5 However, it is still possible that a work intends to be epistemically hesitant but mistakenly portrays a problem one sidedly and misrepresents a party in the quarrel. In this case the work can be labeled propaganda. However, successful attempts of epistemically hesitant films are not related to propaganda, as they do not even share the intention of persuading the audience.
6 These two categories – epistemically meritorious political films and epistemically defective political films – are subcategories of the general category of political films with a rhetorical function, which is itself a subcategory of the wider category of political films entailing films with rhetorical and exploration functions.
7 This also implies that we do not have clear boundaries between these two categories.
8 I hold that this position is compatible with any Intentionalist theory of interpretation (Livingston, 2005), except from a strong version of Actual Intentionalism, which sees intentions as authoritative. However, this position would also be incompatible with a caveat of Levinson's Hypothetical Intentionalism, as he takes categorical (and not semantical) intentions to be authoritative (Levinson, 2006).
9 Note how the two dimensions are also the first two dimensions of the theoretical framework proposed in the first chapter. I hold that to classify and assess political films we are to analyze their 1) epistemic voice, 2) epistemic merit and 3) pedagogical method. When a work has an authoritative epistemic voice it has a rhetorical function, and when it is also epistemically defective, the work is propaganda. Classification of propaganda or political films is neutral with regard to the pedagogical method. Both political and propaganda films can make use of maieutic or be pedantic. The third criterion may play a role in the assessment of the work's capacity to succeed. For instance, Aristotle emphasizes how the rhetor should make use of enthymematical reasoning as it would make the argument more effective: that is, capable of persuading the audience. However, such normative correlation is not entirely apt to explain the actual capacity of a work to persuade its audience, and the capacity of persuasion also depends on the other epistemic dimensions of the work (a work which is epistemically meritorious, yet pedantic, should have better chances to succeed in persuading its audience than a maieutic work that is epistemically defective). Later, I linger on some empirical problems related to the composition of the audience, even though it falls outside of the remit of this dissertation to inquire into the audience's actual response to the work.
10 See for instance Levinson (2006) and Gaut (2007).
11 Even if I do not spell it out overtly, I always imply that propaganda works are still political works. More specifically, there is just a difference between

'epistemically meritorious political works' and 'epistemically defective political works' (which are instances of propaganda).

12 As I stated earlier, works with explorational functions do not fall on this continuum.

13 Note that works that can be posited around the left top area of a quadrant can be seen as examples of successful propaganda, when they are intended to be epistemically defective.

14 In Chapter 7, I provide a full account of empathic engagement, which is also based on affective mimicry and emotional contagion – two reactions that are triggered by close-ups.

4 Epistemic values in art

The definitions of political cinema and propaganda cinema developed in the previous chapters are linked to the idea that cinema can afford epistemic values. This is an issue that I have taken for granted so far, and I now address: can art yield knowledge? And more specifically, can political cinema afford epistemic values? Finally, are these values in any way related to the value of a work *qua* art? These are going to be central questions for this chapter and the following ones.

My main focus is cinema, and my main examples come from political cinema. Nonetheless, in philosophy of art, the debate around the epistemic value of art is shaped, generically, on art's capacity to yield knowledge, with no distinctions made between art forms. I will frame the debate in the same fashion, and I talk generically of art's epistemic value – even though I will use cinema as my primary source of examples.

I hold that cinema can be epistemically valuable, and I argue that cinema can have an impact on the audience's system of belief. The expression 'have an *impact* on the audience's system of beliefs' is intentionally vague, and this is intended to cover all the possible ways that artworks can affect a system of beliefs: they can clarify already-held beliefs, make them more vivid, they can also bring new knowledge that can be articulated in propositional terms, they can foster understanding of specific issues, characters or situations, and they can foster empathic and sympathetic imaginings that are relevant skills for moral reasoning.[1] In this chapter and the next, I argue that artworks can affect our system of beliefs in all these ways.

However, suppose we can prove that art has epistemic value, how does this affect our assessment of artworks? Surely being epistemically valuable is a merit of a work, but a lecture also aims to teach us something, and yet its epistemic merit does not make it an artwork. We need to link the epistemic merit of a work with its value *qua* art. Is epistemic value relevant for the value of the work *qua* art? We may find that art can be epistemically valuable, but we would still need to prove that such value has bearings on the value of a work *qua* art. Artworks can have a wide array of different values, but I want to demonstrate that the epistemic value can be among those that contribute to the value of a work *qua* art.

DOI: 10.4324/9780367816872-5

To do so, I open this chapter (Section 1) with an overview of the debate around the distinction between artistic and aesthetic value. The aim of the first section is to map the debate and establish my position on this issue. I begin with an overview of this debate as it outlines the possible interactions between values, in general, and the value of a work *qua* art. Surely this reconstruction alone will not suffice to provide a fully-fledged reply to the question related to the capacity of epistemic value to contribute to the value of a work *qua* art, but it is a necessary starting point that frames my enquiry. In the second section of the chapter, I tackle the question of the possibility of epistemic value: can art yield knowledge? I provide a reply focusing on the possibility of justifying acquired beliefs through testimony (Section 2). However, I also emphasize the limits of testimonial justification: as testimony depends on the trustworthiness of the testifier, it bypasses the artwork. That is to say, testimony cannot establish a connection between the epistemic and aesthetic value of an artwork. By way of example, I analyze the film *Leviathan* to prove this point (Section 3).

1 Epistemic value between the aesthetic and artistic

We could hold that art should not be assessed for its nonartistic aims. Social, moral and political aims of artworks should not be taken into account when assessing art's value. This claim has been held by artists and philosophers alike (Wilcox makes a helpful introduction in his history of *l'art pour l'art*, 1953) and it revolves around the alleged distinction between art's intrinsic and instrumental values. Instrumental values are those that use art as a means to an end, where the end can be moral, political, pedagogical and so on. Art's intrinsic value is its value as such, for its own sake. But as it stands this formulation of art's intrinsic value does not make clear what it means to appreciate an artwork for its own value. Some say that the traditional understanding of the term 'aesthetic' has to do with matters of form and appearance (Carroll, 2001, p. 399, §11; Zangwill, 1998, p. 75). Perhaps, such understanding of the 'aesthetic' is the 'proper' value of art. Yet, even if we were to endorse such a formalist approach to art, that would not, per se, eschew consequentialist explanations of art's value: perhaps, form and style are of value because they please us. Then pleasure would still be the end of such a formalist approach.

However, we need not deny the possibility of art's intrinsic value to admit that art can have other instrumental values. A simple way out of the problem is to say that art can have other instrumental values, but they do not affect art's 'proper' value.[2] Whatever other values art may have, epistemic, historic, moral and so on, this will not affect its value *qua* art. For instance, an artwork may aim to criticize a political regime or endorse a particular moral standpoint, but these issues would not affect our assessment of the work *qua* art. Hence, the values, here, are not related anyhow. The artwork's intrinsic value is its value *qua* art, or, let us call it, aesthetic value.

Here aesthetic value and intrinsic value are coextensive. And this value is neatly separate from other instrumental values that art may have. It is a bit like saying that a frying pan is perfect for frying and it is also great for personal defense. One value does not add or detract to the other.

If this were actually the case, what would we make of the category of political cinema? Such a category would serve, at best, to identify those artworks dealing with political issues, but any kind of criticism about the political or epistemic element of the work would not affect these artworks' value *qua* art. Perhaps an artwork develops a particularly shallow critique of a political regime, and yet such consideration would not affect our appreciation of the work *qua* art.

It is worth noticing that the relation between instrumental values and intrinsic value can be bidirectional. So, instrumental values may or may not affect intrinsic value, and art's intrinsic value may or may not affect any other instrumental value artworks may have. It means that if a moral standpoint may not affect the value of the work *qua* art, such intrinsic value may still have a bearing on the moral value. For instance, the artistic value can actually enhance the instrumental moral value. As the work is artistically valuable, it can also be considered capable of imparting a moral lesson more effectively.[3]

Another possibility is to admit that art's value is, at least partially, instrumental. Art's value would then be dependent on a combination of instrumental value and intrinsic value. This is, for instance, the suggestion made by Paisley Livingston. He rejects the view that art's proper value is exclusively intrinsic, as

> some, if not all, of art's properly artistic value is instrumental, since it is a matter of serving as a means to a valued end, such as the occasioning of valuable emotional experiences, or, again, of influencing other artists to make valuable works. Given that at least some 'properly artistic' value is instrumental, why not further allow that one of art's legitimate artistic pay-offs is the advancement of cognitive or epistemic goals?
>
> (2009, p. 24).

Hence, Livingston suggests that art's value is affected by the work's capacity to reach other ends while, at the same time, he admits the possibility that art may have a specific intrinsic value. Livingston is actually not interested in delving deeper into a definition of such intrinsic value, and perhaps we need not be interested in that either if we just want to prove a relation between epistemic and art's value *qua* art. However, some clarifications are in order. First, is it the case that the intrinsic value is actually the aesthetic value? If so, then we also need to acknowledge that this is not 'unique' to artworks; indeed, it seems that more generally we talk of aesthetic experiences as something that do not relate exclusively to art, there are other types of aesthetic appreciations that are not artistic, like the appreciation of nature.[4] Second, Livingston introduces the concept of 'artistic' value, as the value of art *qua* art, and as something that we can distinguish from the aesthetic value. But then one would still need to qualify such value: Livingston seems to imply that the artistic value is a compound of other values, but what are the values that constitute the artistic value? How do we trace a line between those values that are part of the artistic value of a work and those values that are not?

We have seen two main positions so far. In the first case, art's 'proper' value is its aesthetic value defined in a very narrow sense, related to matters of form and appearance. In this case we do not need to use the concept of artistic value, since art's value *qua* art is its aesthetic value; we can imagine the two values – aesthetic and artistic – overlap. We have also seen that artworks may have other values, but when the aesthetic and artistic values overlap in such a narrow definition, any other value does not affect them. A second position is proposed by Livingston. He claims that we can conceive of the artistic value as broader than the aesthetic. The two values no longer overlap, and the aesthetic is a component, among others, of the artistic value. This second formulation seems to revitalize what has been called 'the pluralist debate' – the debate around the possible interactions of values in art – as other values, like the epistemic, moral, pedagogical and so on, can affect the value of a work *qua* art.

Dominic Lopes (2011) shows that the concept of artistic value, however, remains quite obscure. If there have been several attempts to characterize the idea of aesthetic value, it is even less clear what is meant by artistic value. The appeal to the idea of artistic value comes from the argument regarding indiscernible counterparts. Two objects having the same perceptual features may have different artistic values, as, for instance, Duchamp's work 'Fountain' and any urinal. Why is that? It means there must be something more than mere perceptual features to an artwork. Lopes spells out the argument for artistic value as follows:

(i) If the value of a work of art is wholly aesthetic, then its value supervenes on its perceptible features
(ii) If the value of a work supervenes on its perceptible features, then no work differs in value from an indiscernible twin
(iii) Some works differ in value from indiscernible twins
(iv) So the value of a work of art is not wholly aesthetic
(v) So works of art bear artistic value distinct from aesthetic value (Lopes, 2011, p. 519).

From this characterization, the aesthetic value, then, is a subspecies of the artistic value, and it is defined as the value supervening the perceptible features of a work. The artistic value on the other end is not clearly defined, if not as a value that seems to be a compound of other values. A list of the values that can be part of the artistic value may include:

> aesthetic value, cognitive value, moral value, therapeutic value, political value, propaganda value, economic value, decorative value, entertainment value, hedonic value, distraction value, prurient value, theological value, communicative value, bragging value, collector value, . . . The inventory is lengthy indeed
>
> (Lopes, 2011, p. 520).

What this list shows is that advocates of an artistic value entailing 'something more' than the value supervening perceptible features need to spell out what that 'more' is. An artwork can be valuable because it covers a hole in the wall, or because it is made with precious materials, or because it provides factual knowledge. An artwork can have, potentially, any kind of value. What is it that makes it valuable *qua* art? The challenge, here, is to separate mere values from values of a work *qua* art (Lopes argues that such a challenge cannot be met, 2011, pp. 521–535). If such a differentiation cannot be made, then claims about a given value affecting such artistic value are only trivially true, as any value can be taken to be part of the artistic value. In this case the pluralist debate becomes trivial, because there are no clear boundaries as to what can be defined as 'artistic value'. If anything can be part of this value, then it is only trivially true that the artistic value can be affected by other values.

We have seen previously that artistic value and aesthetic value can also be coextensive. Let us call the view that aesthetic value and artistic value are coextensive 'Aestheticism' (Hanson, 2013). Aestheticism comes in different versions. We have seen previously that aesthetic value and artistic value can overlap and be defined in a very narrow sense. That is the narrow version of Aestheticism, one that would make the pluralist debate pointless. But there is also a broader version of Aestheticism, where the aesthetic value is defined in a much broader fashion to entail more than just formal qualities. In this second version, the aesthetic value is 'expanded', so we can still say that it overlaps with the artistic value, but in this second version the pluralist debate acquires relevance again as the aesthetic value is defined in a broader fashion including the possibility of a work having complex meaning, being intellectually engaging or expressive of emotions. We can imagine, though, how such a broader version of Aestheticism may encounter the same troubles faced by any theory advancing the idea of a non-aesthetic artistic value: how do we establish the boundaries of the aesthetic?

Dominic Lopes's conception of an artwork's value *qua* art, indeed, seems to face this very problem, even though his strategy is slightly more complex, as he advocates a hybrid theory. On the one hand, he uses an aesthetic theory of artistic value, that is, he claims that we should return to the view that the characteristically artistic value is aesthetic value independently conceived (Lopes, 2011). On the other hand, he also advocates for a 'deflationary' account of the artistic value, so that the value of a work as art is its value as a song, painting, film, etc. So, following Lopes, 'V is an *artistic* value *if it is the aesthetic value* of an artwork *as a K*, where K is an art form, genre, or other art kind' (Lopes, 2011, p. 533, italics mine). Here, the artistic value is 'deflated' to include *only* what is aesthetically valuable *for a particular genre or art kind*. It means that Lopes deflates the concept of artistic value (relating it to art forms, genres and art kinds), but at the same time he inflates the concept of aesthetic value. His view of the aesthetic value is related to the specific art kind to which the work belongs – to make it coherent with his buck-passing theory of art (see Lopes, 2014) – but, as Louise Hanson shows, his understanding of aesthetic value is quite broad, as he lists among the features we may count as aesthetic things like 'being expressive of emotion, being intellectually challenging, having complex meanings, being formally complex and coherent, being original, and being the product of a high degree of skill' (Lopes, 2011, p. 525). So, Lopes's account actually confronts the same troubles faced by theories of non-aesthetic artistic value. As Hanson notes,

> if aesthetic value is to include all these things, it becomes less clear that aesthetic value is a single kind of value at all, and crucially it becomes less clear that the advantage Lopes claimed to set his theory apart from its rivals really obtains
>
> (Hanson, 2013, p. 506).

Berys Gaut (2007) also endorses a broad conception of the aesthetic value, but the justification of his theory has its roots in art-critical practices.[5] The starting point of Gaut's theory is the analysis of what we take to be part of what we call 'aesthetic'.[6] This is the list of what Sibley considered aesthetic properties: being beautiful, elegant, graceful and dainty; being tightly knit, unified, integrated and lacking in balance; being serene, somber, lifeless, dynamic, tragic, sentimental; being deeply moving, exciting, full of tension; being trite and vivid (Sibley, 1959). Sibley was not in the business of defining the 'aesthetic', but Gaut suggests that we may understand what pertains to it, and what is of aesthetic value, if we identify what all these properties have in common.

Sibley's list primarily shows the complexity and diversity of aesthetic properties. Such properties are not just formal, although some of them are (like balance and unity); they are also expressive properties (like being somber) and affective (like being deeply moving or sentimental). What these properties have in common is that they are evaluative, yet of a specific kind: they are terms used in art-critical practice.[7] A list so conceived accounts for a broader conception of our experience of artworks, one that is not merely, or not exclusively, perceptual, and such experience is what makes a work valuable *qua* art.[8] Hence, following Gaut, 'the aesthetic value of an artwork is . . . its value qua work of art; and its aesthetic properties are those of its evaluative properties that have aesthetic value, as so defined' (2007, p. 35). That is to say, the aesthetic properties of an artwork are those that make it a work of art (I say more on the possible threat of circularity later). Therefore, the work's value as art is its aesthetic value (the value of the properties that make it art).[9]

There are two major considerations I want to make about this account, which is going to be the one I use throughout this work. The first is that it establishes a priority of our art appreciation over the concept of the aesthetic. It may seem that this makes the aesthetic appreciation of nature implausibly dependent on the aesthetic appreciation of art. As if we would need to know about art in order to have an aesthetic appreciation of nature. This is not just implausible, as we may think that human beings appreciated nature aesthetically even before they invented art, but also inaccurate as it is possible to appreciate nature even without being aware of the existence of art. The aesthetic experience is phenomenologically akin in both cases, and we can aesthetically appreciate nature even when we do not know art, because we are capable of appreciating specific and individual aesthetic properties. But this is not to say that we can bring these properties under the notion of the aesthetic. This is what art theory does: it unifies the items that we categorize as 'aesthetic' (Gaut, 2007, p. 37).

Therefore, we have experienced individual aesthetic properties when appreciating nature aesthetically, but art theory allows us to unify all the terms under the umbrella of the notion of 'aesthetic'. So, art-critical practices simply provided the tools for the unified explanation of the phenomenon – the experience of the aesthetic qualities – and, as a matter of fact, they provided the name for the phenomenon as well. As Gaut highlights, in *Aesthetica* Baumgarten explicitly connects beauty to values such as truth and certainty; these are qualities that only works of art can possess, so the history of key concepts in aesthetics also seems to repeat the claim that aesthetic appreciation of art is prior to that of nature, when we understand aesthetic as a unified notion. Hence, it is worth noting that the class of aesthetic properties is divided into two: those that can be attributed to natural objects and those that cannot as their application presupposes that their bearers are the products of agency.

The second consideration is about a possible objection that such an account of the aesthetic value may raise. It may seem that the artistic theory of the aesthetic value simply shifts the problem: from the definition of the aesthetic value to the definition of art. Indeed, it tries to define what the aesthetic value is, and to do so it appeals to the values of the work *qua* work of art. Do we need a definition of art to make this theory work? If so, we could not appeal to the notion of aesthetic value to ground such a definition, as it would be circular – the aesthetic value is the value of a work *qua* art, and art is any work that possesses aesthetic value. However, we need not look for a definition of art, as we are after something else: its evaluation. To say that something is good art we need not appeal to the criteria that make it art.[10] Moreover, Gaut's artistic theory of the aesthetic value presupposes a plurality of aesthetic values, which makes it perfectly integrated with his cluster account of art. Gaut eschews a definition of art based on necessary and sufficient conditions; rather he holds that art is a cluster concept. That means that we can identify a number of criteria that *count toward* an object falling under the concept (Gaut, 2005). The criteria proposed by Gaut include: being beautiful (or possessing other narrow aesthetic properties), being expressive of emotion, having the capacity to convey complex meaning, exhibiting an individual point of view, being an exercise of creative imagination, being the product of a high degree of skill, belonging to an established artistic form and being the product of an art-making intention (Gaut, 2005). None of these criteria alone counts as sufficient for something to fall under the concept of art. If all the properties that are criteria are instantiated then the object falls under the concept of art, but a combination of fewer properties also counts toward an object falling under the concept, which means that there are jointly sufficient conditions for the application of the concept. Also, none of the criteria alone is a necessary condition, but some of the properties must be instantiated for something to fall under the concept of art, so there are disjunctively necessary conditions for the application of the concept. Finally, as the meaning of the concept is given by a cluster account, it is not even possible to apply the concept fixing individually necessary and jointly sufficient conditions.

Gaut's art theory of the aesthetic value allows for moral and epistemic values to contribute to the value of a work *qua* art. However, the fact that art may have epistemic value does not, per se, make such value contribute to the artistic qualities of the work. A work may have epistemic and moral values, but that does not mean that they are necessarily aesthetically relevant. To be aesthetically relevant these values need to contribute to the value of a work *qua* art. Gaut himself admits this possibility, as he claims that 'the cognitivist must hold that sometimes cognitive values are aesthetically relevant and sometimes not. . . . We need to prove that the relation between values is not adventitious, and that cognitive values can contribute to artistic ones' (Gaut, 2007, p. 170). So Gaut proposes a general criterion that can link cognitive and moral values to the artistic: 'moral and cognitive claims tend to be aesthetically relevant *when expressed by artistic means*: it is the *way* or *mode* in which ethical and other insights are conveyed that makes them of relevance' (ibid., italics mine). So, a work can be epistemically valuable and yet this value may not contribute to its value *qua* art. Consider the recording with a single long take and a static shot of a philosophical lecture; even if the lecture is intellectually engaging, this does not contribute to make the recording valuable as art. The importance of the mode of presentation explains why even if profound truths were inserted into a text, they would not necessarily transform the text into a profound work of art.[11]

In particular, Gaut holds that it is

> factors such as the development of a *persona*, the way that insights are integrated into the particulars dealt with by the works, and the way that we are affectively moved to feel the force of these insights, that are germane to securing the aesthetic relevance of the insights
> (Gaut, 2007, p. 171).

This last criterion, that of 'bringing home' insights by presenting them with affective force, has, according to Gaut, a peculiarly pervasive role in securing aesthetic relevance. Indeed, while we should allow at least for the *possibility* of aesthetic relevance being secured without this factor – due to the presence of the other factors in the artistic mode of expression – Gaut holds that there are in fact few and perhaps no plausible examples of works that manage to secure the aesthetic relevance of completely 'cool' (lacking in affect) cognitive judgments. So much so that, given the importance of the affective criterion, 'we should think of the value of art as partly deriving from a kind of cognitive-affective perspective onto the world: its ability to bring home an understanding of the world through affective means' (Gaut, 2007, p. 171).[12]

Gaut also suggests a second way to prove that the connection between cognitive and aesthetic value holds, and this method is related to the art-critical practice that frames its theory of the aesthetic value. Indeed, Gaut argues that our use of cognitivist evaluative terms shows not only that works have epistemic virtues but also that such epistemic merits are relevant to their artistic merit. As Gaut puts it:

> consider someone who said 'this novel is a profound and insightful exploration of death without a trace of sentimentality, but this of course has nothing to do with its artistic merit'. This is as bizarre as someone who said 'this novel is well written, elegant and witty, but this of course has nothing to do with its artistic merit'.

The point that Gaut wants to stress is that it is, at least partly, in virtue of their epistemic merits that some works are valuable *qua* art.

Now let me wrap up this section by refocusing the discussion on political cinema. The previous discussion is relevant to our purposes as it provides an overview of different characterizations of the relation between values in art. First, we need a theory of the aesthetic and artistic value that could be used as a framework to make sense of the debate around value interrelation in art. Second, we need to prove that a given value can actually be aesthetically relevant. I use Berys Gaut's art theory of the aesthetic value as a framework for the discussion that follows. Such theory makes the aesthetic value permeable to other values that are used in our art-critical practice for the assessment and evaluation of artworks.

Political cinema aims at persuading its audience of the validity of a political standpoint or at eliciting reflection on a political issue. These are epistemic aims: political cinema aims to have an impact on our system of beliefs. So, we are to tackle two questions: can films afford epistemic gains? And when are such gains aesthetically relevant? Indeed, the fact that a film has epistemic merits does not make them, per se, aesthetically relevant. In the remainder of the chapter, my task is twofold. First, I argue that film can afford epistemic values. Second, I consider the possibility that such epistemic values may not be aesthetically relevant. In this chapter, I will provide a possible example of when an epistemic value is not aesthetically relevant, whereas in following chapters I will focus on epistemic values that are conveyed via artistic means and are, therefore, aesthetically relevant.

2 Art's epistemic value[13]

My position is that artworks *can* be epistemically valuable, by which I mean that they can contribute to our system of beliefs, even though such contribution varies case by case; artworks can make already-held beliefs more vivid, bring new propositional knowledge or foster understanding of characters, situations and events. I want to stress that art can yield knowledge, but knowledge is not the only epistemic value. So, more generally, we can say that art can bring what Berys Gaut calls 'cognitive gains', as this entails knowledge and other epistemic values, like understanding, clarification of already-held beliefs or even training of cognitive skills like empathy and sympathy.

Too often the debate on cognitive value has been focused exclusively on art's capacity to yield knowledge. Knowledge is surely an important epistemic value and I do take into account the possibility of acquiring knowledge through art and the limits of such process. But we would probably miss out on art's main potentiality if we were to limit the discussion to knowledge itself. Especially if we consider that other epistemic values, like understanding, are not to be seen as subordinated to knowledge.

Following Gaut, let us use the term 'Cognitivism' to refer to the view that art can afford cognitive gains. The main problem with such a view is that art is considered unreliable and unfit to convey knowledge (and epistemic values in general). I take it that cognitivists have two main strategies to reply to objections about the unreliability of art as a source of knowledge. On the one hand, they can point to the fact that art can convey knowledge through testimony, and testimony is accepted as a reliable source of knowledge. On the other hand, they can point to the fact that some epistemic values are afforded through imagination, and imagination should be considered just as reliable as other sources of knowledge, like testimony, or memory and perception. I hold that both strategies are successful to prove that art can convey knowledge and that more generally it affords cognitive gains. However, the first strategy severs the connection between the cognitive value and the aesthetic: justification through testimony bypasses the artwork *tout court*, as it depends on the trustworthiness of the author. It means that while we can say that an artwork has epistemic value, this does not affect its aesthetic value. The second strategy can secure a connection between the epistemic and aesthetic value, and I analyze this in depth in Chapter 6. Here I want to expand on the first strategy, showing its epistemic reliability while also underlying how it cannot contribute to the aesthetic value (Section 3). I support my argument with an analysis of the film *Leviathan* (Zvyagintsev, 2014).

The strand of Cognitivism I defend is the one that sees artworks as being able to teach us something. Another form of Cognitivism could be described in terms of the possibility of *learning* from art. This form of Cognitivism mistakenly shifts the focus of attention from the artwork's communicative intentions to the audience's capacity to learn from it. As Gaut puts it, 'the fact that one can learn from something does not entail that it has taught one that thing, or even that it understands that thing' (2007, p. 139). Gaut gives the example of the incompetent plumber: someone who does not know what he is doing and yet he tries to fix a house's plumbing and ends up flooding the house. We may well learn from him – for instance, we may learn not to use the specific tools or techniques he used. But while we may say that we have learnt something from him, we cannot say that he has taught us anything, since he did not understand what he was doing and could not communicate knowledge to us. The same can happen with art. We can watch a film that completely trivializes a serious political problem, depicting flat characters and overlooking important aspects defining the complexity of the issue. Watching such a film, we feel contempt for the treatment of such an important issue, and we can then reflect upon the issue itself. We can realize that we have been neglecting arguments in favor or against a particular standpoint, and we can even come to form new beliefs about the problem. Reflection has been triggered by a bad film, but this does not amount to the film teaching us something. On the contrary, the film was shallow and should not be praised for any cognitive gain afforded, which in this case is merely circumstantial.

There are two main objections advanced by non-cognitivists. The first is that art cannot teach us anything because it does not reference the real world. To quote Diffey: 'how can a work of art be faithful to the facts it would teach if art is not by its nature fact-stating?' (1995, p. 208). A second objection is advanced by Stolnitz (1992) who argues that, at best, art can convey knowledge that is trivial, as it cannot provide confirmation of the knowledge conveyed.

A first move to reply to both objections is to point out that non-cognitivism usually conflates artworks with works of fiction. There are nonfiction works that are artworks and these objections seem at least weaker when directed at these works. Nonfiction artworks clearly reference the real world, and they are capable of providing the same confirmation offered by nonfiction (non-art) works: a confirmation based on the reliability of testimony. A high-school history book, for instance, teaches knowledge about real-world individuals and events. How do we know that the beliefs acquired from the text are non-coincidentally true? There needs to be something about that particular text, or document, that grants it reliability. Usually, we can infer the reliability of such a text from our considerations about its author. We trust that the historical research has been thorough, and we can take propositions expressed in the text as reliably true. The same sort of epistemic check needs to be done for nonfictional artworks. Nonfictional artworks reference the real world just as general nonfiction works do. Their reliability is also granted by the trustworthiness of the author. Surely, there are nonfiction artworks that are unreliable, and even mistaken or deceptive, and we discriminate among these artworks checking the reliability of the author.

It is usually held that nonfiction communicates empirical knowledge via testimony,[14] and since we usually consider testimony a reliable source of knowledge, we tend to consider nonfiction capable of conveying knowledge and information about the actual world. So, nonfiction artworks are in the same position: they can convey knowledge and information about the actual world via testimony. Clearly testimony is not always reliable, as we would need to establish whether the source is trustworthy, but this seems to be the only 'epistemic' caveat afflicting nonfiction works.

Fictional works seems to be in a much more difficult position than works of nonfiction. Such a disadvantageous position is due to the fact that, in fiction, 'making things up' is perfectly legitimate. However, Stacie Friend (2012) has convincingly argued that the difference between fiction and non-fiction in terms of their capacity to convey empirical knowledge is one of degree rather than of kind. She holds that

> If we define testimony as 'the assertion of a declarative sentence by a speaker to a hearer or to an audience' (Adler, 2006), then (i) at least some sentences of works of non-fiction do not count as testimony, and (ii) at least some sentences of works of fiction do count as testimony
> (Friend, 2014, p. 231).

So, on the one hand, works of nonfiction contain questions, hypotheses, counterfactuals, arguments, illustrations and so on, which does not count as plausibly testimonial. And on the other, fictional works frequently contain straightforward assertions. Why should we accept that propositions asserted in the world of fiction can never count as testimony? The answer to the question seems to be somehow related to the fact that in fiction authors can purposely include falsehood in their works. But this is also the case for works of nonfiction; authors of nonfiction may be unreliable because of ignorance, incompetence or a will to deceive, but it is surely the case that works of nonfiction can contain falsehood. So, as Friend would have it, there are no reasons to hold that there is a difference in kind between fiction and nonfiction. Rather, there is a difference in their degree of reliability. That is to say, if both of them can contain assertions and both of them can contain falsehood, then the difference is only about the degree of reliability: we take nonfiction to be, generally, more reliable than fiction when it comes to transmitting beliefs about the actual world.

Yet we must face the problem of the different degrees of reliability. To follow Friend, the beliefs we can acquire from fiction are unsafe. They are unsafe because in fiction we can find more statements that are not intended to hold in the actual world, hence, the higher epistemic unreliability of fiction. As an example to illustrate the problem, Friend uses Goldman's paradigmatic case of the fake barns.

> Unbeknownst to you, the county through which you are driving is full of fake barns: barn façades that from your car look like real barns. Suppose that you happen to stop in front of one of the very few real barns in the county and form the true belief that there is a barn in front of you. Since you would have formed exactly the same belief in front of a barn façade, the standard intuition is that the truth of your belief is too much a matter of luck for it to be knowledge. But this judgment hinges on matters of degree: in particular, the proximity and number of fake versus real barns
>
> (Friend, 2014, p. 232).

As we have seen, the difference between nonfiction and fiction's reliability is a matter of degree. So, how do we solve the problem? Shall we just give up on any epistemic-based evaluation of fiction? Friend argues we should not, and she does so by appealing to Ernest Sosa's approach to epistemology (2007, 2009), which gives a new focus on the agent's role in the epistemic process. Friend takes Sosa's virtue epistemology to help clarify how and why we can get empirical knowledge from fiction, and I find her argument convincing. Specifically, Friend wants to give more responsibilities to the audience.

As Friend argues, fiction is not a safe environment: we cannot safely export beliefs from the world of fiction to the actual world. However, a competent reader can still distinguish between beliefs that are meant to hold only within the story and beliefs that are meant to hold in the actual world. Indeed, we have seen that the difference between fiction and nonfiction in terms of their capacity to provide empirical knowledge is not a difference in kind but just in degree of reliability. Nonfiction is still able to deceive and to provide false beliefs; the audience needs to vet and assess the claims made. With fiction, the level of attention required is higher, and the audience needs to master specific skills in order to detect the veracity of the beliefs communicated. Sosa (2007) gives the example of an archer who may be *adroit*, skilled, in the discipline and yet misses the target. Her performance can be evaluated along three dimensions: accuracy (how close she gets to the target), adroitness (the level of her skills) and aptness (her capacity to be accurate because adroit). The point is that the archer can hit the center of the target out of sheer luck, because of the wind, or because someone bumps into her right at the moment of shooting. Or, contrarily, she can miss her target even when being perfectly adroit, skilled, in the discipline. We should consider not just the outcome of the shooting but rather the aptness of her performance.

In our appraisal of fiction's capacity to yield knowledge, we ought to adopt the same kind of assessment. It is difficult for an archer to hit the center of the target, yet with training she can acquire skills that will increase her chances of doing so correctly and her performance will become apt to get it right. Fiction, as we have seen, is less reliable than nonfiction, which makes it more difficult to detect beliefs holding in the actual world. Yet, an adroit audience can more easily get it right. Audiences grow used to stylistic conventions, understand and distinguish different genres, can be more or less acquainted with an author's *oeuvre* and with her public persona. The point is that even if it is difficult to detect the veracity of beliefs in fiction, we need not discard fiction's capacity to yield knowledge; we just need a more adroit audience that can detect beliefs about the actual world (Friend, 2014).

In the literature on meaning and interpretation there is always an initial reminder of the kind of audience to which philosophers refer. Indeed, it is possible for a work to be misunderstood by an audience that is not used to specific stylistic patterns or genre conventions. I have highlighted this issue in the previous chapter, and this is why philosophers refer to an appropriate audience that can correctly understand and interpret the artwork. Jerrold Levinson refers to this audience as the targeted or appropriate audience while Gaut calls it a 'normatively specified audience' (2007, p. 139). The concept is the same: an audience that can grasp the communicative aims of the work. More specifically we can say that this is an audience whose adroitness makes its interpretation accurate.

An adroit audience has a critical approach to artworks, as it has a general knowledge of the author's *oeuvre*, public persona and general trustworthiness, and it masters genre and stylistic conventions. Such an audience is in a better position to interpret artworks and to differentiate among beliefs that are meant to hold in the actual world and those that are not. As an example of the difficult, yet not impossible, task of the audience, let us consider Jean-Marc Valèe's film *Young Victoria* (2009). This is a romanticized history of Queen Victoria's early reign. Toward the end of the film, Victoria and Albert have a heated fight that seems to undermine their relationship. Immediately after the fight, the couple is portrayed riding in a carriage together when someone attempts to take Victoria's life by shooting a gun. Albert shields Victoria and gets injured. This act of bravery seems to reconcile the couple. But are we justified in exporting the belief that Albert has been injured trying to save Victoria? In this case, the event seems suspiciously convenient for the dramatic development of the plot. Indeed, while it is true that there have been several attempts on Victoria's life, Albert was not injured as a result of any of them. However, this possible inaccurate account is not just anticipated by a suspicious dramatic development but also by public declarations of the film's scriptwriter Julian Fellowes. In an interview to an online magazine, he said

> There are two different accounts [of the attempt], one says the gun went off but the bullet missed him, and another says the gun jammed and we don't know which is true. Albert saw the gunman, she didn't, and he flung her into the well of the carriage and then pushed himself across her and put his back to the gunman. Of course, this was fantastically brave. His instinct was to cover her with his body. What I felt was, if the gun jammed in the film, there was a danger it would become comic and it would deflate the bravery of the moment. It's hard to make people appreciate that he was prepared to take a bullet for his wife, if he doesn't take the bullet for her. So that's why I changed that
>
> (2009).

It may not be possible to ascertain the truth of an event based on its dramatic role in the fictional world, but Fellowes's words are public, so the appropriate audience is able to differentiate between those beliefs that hold exclusively in the world of the story and those that can be exported into the actual world.

3 Testimony and aesthetic value

Following Friend, we can say that when we analyze the epistemic reliability of artworks, the difference between nonfiction artworks and fiction artworks is not a difference in kind but in degrees. Exporting a belief about the actual word from nonfictional artworks is safer than exporting it from a fictional one. This does not mean that there are no epistemic risks when engaging with nonfictional artworks, and it does not even mean that we cannot export beliefs from fictional artworks. The burden is on the audience, which needs to check the reliability of the author and the veracity of the beliefs that may also hold in the real world. So, fictional artworks can convey empirical knowledge, and the beliefs we acquire from fictional artworks are justified by the fact that we trust the author who is holding such beliefs – as we take them to have the relevant expertise. Testimony serves to justify the beliefs we export from the fictional to the actual world. This kind of justification grounds fictional works' epistemic value. They can teach us something about the actual world. But this does not suffice to hold that since these works teach us about the actual world, they are also aesthetically valuable – in virtue of the knowledge they convey. More precisely, testimony is a reliable source of knowledge that leads us to conclude that artworks can be epistemically valuable, but it does not explain whether such epistemic value contributes to the aesthetic value of a work.

The peculiarity of testimony is that it depends on the trustworthiness of the testifier. Whether a testimony is reliable, ultimately, does not depend on any artistic means that may be used to convey the testimony itself but exclusively on the quality (and specifically the reliability or trustworthiness) of the testifier. Hence, testimony, as a justificatory source, completely bypasses the artwork. This short circuits the connection between the aesthetic and the epistemic value; the latter is not expressed through artistic means – as it depends on extra-artistic qualities that are not instantiated in the work – so it cannot contribute to the former.

I use as an example to prove this argument, Zvyagintsev's *Leviathan*. I take it that the film is a political film, yet it fails to be a successful political film. The film does not fail to *be* political, but it fails *as* a *political artwork*. In Chapter 3, analyzing the differences between political and propaganda films, we made a distinction between successful and unsuccessful films that was limited to the epistemic merits of a work. That is to say, we have been describing a work as successful when it could actually afford epistemic values and unsuccessful when it failed to do so. Now we can enrich our characterization of the distinction between successful and unsuccessful films. If, previously, we were simply focused on the epistemic dimension, now we can see how to be (also) 'artistically' successful, a political film needs to provide a connection between its epistemic value and aesthetic value. In other words, a (non-art) *work* may be successful insofar as it affords epistemic values, as in the case of a lecture that aims to teach us something, but a political *film* (you can read it as 'political *artwork*', as I want to stress here that we are analyzing a token with an art-status) aims to afford epistemic values which are aesthetically relevant, that is, according to Gaut's principle, epistemic values afforded through artistic means. This means that a political film needs to succeed on two fronts: it needs to be epistemically valuable and aesthetically valuable *in virtue* of its epistemic value. Testimony does not require any artistic means, hence, works that exclusively rely on testimony to convey their message may not be epistemically defective, but any aesthetic merit they have cannot be traced back to their epistemic values justified by testimony.[15]

Leviathan is a political film that fails to be successful as a political artwork, as the main political message it intended to convey can be justified only through testimony. But this implies that any of its aesthetic merits cannot be brought back to its epistemic contribution. We can imagine the case of political films that are not epistemically valuable and yet remain aesthetically meritorious (perhaps because of the skillful use of some cinematographic techniques). And it can be the case that films are both epistemically and aesthetically valuable, and yet the latter value does not depend on the former. When this happens to a political film, we may say that it is unsuccessful. This may seem counterintuitive. After all, the artwork seems to have everything it needs to be deemed successful; it has epistemic as well as aesthetic value. However, its aesthetic merits do not depend on the (politically relevant) epistemic value.[16] Note that the film can be a successful artwork (while its aesthetic value is not linked to the epistemic one, there can be other qualities that make the work aesthetically successful) and epistemically successful, but it is not a successful political artwork (where this last combination implies, roughly, that a token is art (also) in virtue of its political content). This is, admittedly, a peculiar combination, that I claim can actually be realized only in a specific circumstance, that is, when we resort exclusively to testimony to justify the epistemic merits of a work. This is the case in *Leviathan*.[17]

Leviathan is a political film because it is about the political conflict between the state and the individual. There is little doubt that the film is about this contraposition. The first hint lies in the title: Leviathan is a biblical sea animal imbued with great power and strength, and with this reference in mind Hobbes gave the title to his seminal work on the social contract and the absolute state. The Leviathan, in Hobbes's title, is a symbolic representation of the absolute state, with a huge body whose limbs are made of each individual.

More specifically, the film is about the Russian state, although this is not overtly stated. I take it that only this association brings one to the right interpretation of the film. The film is about the contraposition of the monster-like bureaucratic and corrupt state versus the inert powerless citizen. Precisely, Leviathan tells the story of Kolya, a handyman living in Pribrezhny, a small coastal town in northern Russia. And this is a story of a fall. Kolya has a house, a friend and a family, but the corrupt mayor of the town wants Kolya's land in order to build a shopping center.

Surely this is a story about injustice. Everything that happens to Kolya is unjust. Him losing his house due to the economic interests of a corrupt politician, the prosecutor conspiring with the mayor, the police unjustly placing Kolya into custody and then charging him for murder without evidence. His friends, like Pasha and Stepanych, also seem to care more for his skills as a mechanic than anything else, and his best friend Dima, a Moscow lawyer who came to help Kolya with his trial against the mayor, has an affair with his wife.

The intended message of the film is to show contemporary Russia's corruption and the helpless situation of the individual, who cannot confront such a monster-like state exercising uncontrolled power over the individual.

But let me consider two alternative interpretations, which I consider at the most complementary, but which do not replace the above as the main intended meaning.

(i) Perhaps the film is just about Kolya's personal ordeal. So, the film has little to do with politics, as it is primarily a drama about the tragedy of life. Such an interpretation may not be compatible with the one

I suggest, as it shifts the focus from the political meaning to the characters' story. I discard this interpretation though because the political and religious symbolism is just too prominent in the film. Moreover, to make a psychological drama, the author should have provided a better, or indeed any, psychological analysis of the inner state of the characters. *Leviathan*'s characters indeed are shallow and mono-dimensional. Kolya is just a drunk, hot-headed handyman, and even Lilia's suicide is not explained from a psychological point of view, and it actually seems a contrived plot device.

(ii) It may be possible to hold that the film's focus is religion. I do believe that the religious symbolism is central to the analysis of the film, but overall, the film is not religious in its scope.[18] There are clear references to the book of Job and not solely because the film's title references the Leviathan. In the book of Job, Satan challenges God to prove Job's faith, so God has Job lose all his possessions, hurts his beloved and plagues him with a deadly disease. I claim that Kolya's suffering is meant to be compared to that of Job – Kolya's suffering has to do with his incapacity to deal with the monstrous creature that is the Russian state. However, the religious theme is only used instrumentally to emphasize the political aim of the film. Indeed, Job's book analyzes problems of extreme salience for Christianity that are not relevant to the film analysis, as it questions the redistribution doctrine found in the Deuteronomy. Job's book is about suffering and its meaning. Job asks God the reasons for his suffering. All of Job's friends try to explain his suffering in light of the retribution doctrine: if you are good, God will reward you, so if God brings suffering, and God cannot be unjust, then it must be Job who is unjust, or, alternatively, if God is bringing suffering then this is just to prove Job's actual faith. The doctrine of the proof does not stand in Job's case because it is Satan who challenges God, and the doctrine of retribution does not apply either, because Job is a righteous person. Job, deaf to his friend's explanation, questions his own life and curses the day he was born and the night he was conceived. However, Job, despite the suffering imposed upon him, does not renounce God. Instead, Job invokes God in searching for an explanation, believing that only in God can there be answers. This aspect of the book of Job is overlooked in the film *Leviathan*. Zvyagintsev focuses the attention exclusively on the monstrosity of the Leviathan.

Moreover, toward the end of the film, after Kolya sees Lilia's dead body, he meets Father Vasiliy and their dialogue again references Job's book. Kolya asks Vasiliy where is 'his merciful God almighty', and Vasiliy replies quoting Job:

KOLYA: Where is your merciful God Almighty?

VASILIY: Mine is with me. As for yours I wouldn't know. Who do you pray to? I haven't seen you in Church. You do not fast, take communion or go to confession.

KOLYA: If I lit candles and all, would things be different? Maybe it's not too late to start? Would I get my wife back from the dead? And my house? Or is it too late?

VASILIY: I don't know. Our Lord moves in mysterious ways.

KOLYA: You don't know. Then why do you call me to confession? What do you know then?

VASILIY: Can you pull in Leviathan with a fishhook, or tie down its tongue with a rope? Will it keep begging you for mercy? Will it speak to you with gentle words? Nothing on earth is its equal, it is king over all that are proud.

KOLYA: Father Vasiliy, I am talking to you as a regular person, why the fucking riddles? What for?

VASILIY: Have you ever heard of a man called Job? Like you, he was preoccupied with the meaning of life. Why, he asked, why me of all people? He worried so much he became covered with scabs. His wife tried to talk some sense into him; his friends told him to not evoke God's anger. But he kept kicking up dust and sprinkling ash on his head, then the Lord relented, and appeared to him, in the form of a hurricane, and explained everything to him in pictures.

KOLYA: And?

VASILIY: Job resigned himself to his fate, and lived to be 140. Got to see four generations of his family. And died old, and content.

This dialogue shows how the director aims to compare the lives of Job and Kolya (despite the fact that Zvyagintsev himself admitted that the idea of the story was inspired by what happened to an American citizen: Marvin Heemeyer). However, and most importantly, Father Vasiliy misinterprets Job's book. Indeed, it is not resignation that Job feels but rather the understanding of the necessity of God despite the suffering.[19] But such misinterpretation leads us to the actual main theme of the film: Vasiliy and, by extension, the entire church collude with the political power and can only suggest the individual to 'resign' to his destiny, accept whatever comes, because he cannot compete with the power of the Leviathan-State. So, the religious theme is arbitrarily manipulated to serve only as a prop for the political message of the film.[20]

There is more religious symbolism in the film, but rather than being linked to Job's book, it focuses on the general suffering of Kolya. In one scene, the director lingers on a statue of a suffering Christ, with the inscription 'Ecce homo'. We see the statue in Father Vasiliy's office, after he had a meeting with the mayor. The scene comes right after Kolya discovers Dima and Lilia's affair. After the meeting between the priest and the mayor, which shows the collusion between the religious and secular power, the mayor bends to take Vasiliy's blessing and to kiss his hand. We see a medium shot of the profile of the two, who then part ways. The camera changes the range of focus, switching from the foreground to the background, and then it tracks in to show the statue of Christ. The words 'Ecce homo' were used by Pontius Pilate when showing the suffering Jesus to the Jews after he had been flagellated. Pilate was not convinced of Jesus's guilt, so he thought that flagellation was a sufficient punishment. Pilate ended up being wrong, as the Jews wanted Jesus crucified. The words 'Ecce homo', literally 'Behold the man', became a synonym for human suffering in general and the iconography of the scene also reiterates how the central aim of the words was to highlight the suffering, which, from the suffering of Jesus, became the suffering of men. Zvyagintsev probably draws attention to highlight the suffering of Kolya. However, this further religious symbolism does not add to the story. Indeed, the story told in the Leviathan does not aim to explain the suffering condition of human being, as it is not sufficiently abstract and does not even provide hints of such abstract ambitions. Also, the story does not aim to bring any sort of insights into the suffering condition of Kolya, as we are never led to empathize with him, and we barely feel a superficial sympathy for him simply because he is afflicted by such a paroxysmal concatenation of tragic events.

The Leviathan is then a metaphor for the Russian state, but instead of being a unifying entity capable of granting order, the state is an untamable monster. More specifically, we need not think of a general, abstract, contraposition between the state and the individual; rather, the film is specifically about the contraposition between an individual (Kolya) and the *Russian* state. This is not simply due to the fact that the film is set in Russia, but there are clear indications that the state being described is the contemporary Russian state. Indeed, there are obvious references to Russian institutions and, most importantly, to Russia's leaders.

A symbolic shooting happening during a picnic with family and friends reveals quite clearly the author's intention to refer explicitly to Russia's government.

Kolya and his friends' families are off for a picnic, and they carry their shotguns as they enjoy some shooting while drinking vodka. At first, they use empty bottles as targets, but after destroying all the targets with his automatic machine gun, Stepanych takes out the new targets: a number of portraits of former Soviet leaders, from Lenin to Yeltsin.

Kolya asks Stepanych if he has a more current portrait, and Stepanych answers that he has all kinds of stuff, but it is too early for the current ones: 'Not enough of a historical perspective; Let them ripen up on the wall a bit'.

This sentence alludes to Putin's portrait that we have just seen hanging on the mayor's office wall. We were in Vadim's office when Dima threatens him with some apparently dangerous information he collected in Moscow. But more significant is the scene in which Vadim has a meeting with his 'men': the court judge and two high-ranking police officers. In this scene, we see all the main branches of the political system plotting against one citizen. Where the main idea of a democratic regime is that of having 'checks and balances', this scene shows the complete collusion of all powers, and Putin's portrait overlooks the events with a satisfied expression. The mayor, Vadim, symbolizes political institutions in general, and I take it that his behavior is to be seen as a parody of Russian political power. Vadim is a drunk with no scruples about solving problems with force, and when he hears of Kolya's fifteen-year sentence for murder, he is shown stuffing his face with food in a gaudy restaurant, evidently pleased with Kolya's conviction.

Religion serves as a further justification of the system of corruption. Father Vasiliy's misinterpretation of the book of Job, together with his overt support of Vadim, gives a sense of inevitability, with religion serving as ideological justification for the corrupt state of affairs.

Zvyagintsev wants to show Russia's political corruption and how individuals are powerless against this Leviathan-State.

Does it succeed? Can we say that after watching *Leviathan* we learn that Russia is a corrupted state? The first thing to notice is the peculiarity of the kind of knowledge the film aims to convey. Propositions like 'Russia is a corrupt state' or 'Russia's state is a monster-like apparatus' or 'Russia's political power is ruthless and exclusively driven by particularistic interests' are empirical propositions that are meant to hold in the actual world. However, in the film *Leviathan* there is nothing that could justify the exportation of these beliefs to the actual world. The film does not aim to foster our understanding of what it means to live in a corrupt country or of what it means to suffer from injustice. Rather it simply uses Kolya's tragic fall to exemplify Russia's corruption. We have seen that empirical knowledge from fiction can be justified through testimony: we take the author to have the relevant expertise, and when we consider him trustworthy, we are justified in adopting the beliefs he intends to communicate. As we are justified in adopting these beliefs only to the extent that we find the author trustworthy, there is nothing in the work itself that justifies these beliefs.

We can hold that the film is not epistemically defective because we can still adopt these beliefs through testimony.[21] However, its aesthetic value is by no means affected by its political content.[22] This is a case where aesthetic and epistemic values are merely adventitious.

Notes

1 It can be the case that films, and artworks in general, may have a negative impact on the audience's system of beliefs: we can imagine an audience that gathers false or unwarranted beliefs from its engagement with artworks. I will not consider this possibility in this book. I have argued in the previous chapter that the intended audience can identify epistemic merits and flaws of artworks, so, here and in the remainder of the book, when I say that films can have an impact on the audience's system of beliefs, I always imply a beneficial or positive impact, one that can enhance the audience's system of beliefs. Implicitly, I always assume that epistemic defects can be detected, even though I acknowledge the difficulties we face when engaged with artworks; I will say something more on these difficulties later.

2 The debate on the relation between art's 'proper' value and other instrumental values is often framed in light of the possible relation between moral value

and aesthetic value (see, for instance, Carroll, 2002; Harold, 2008). Within this debate, the position that art's instrumental values do not affect its proper value *qua* art is called 'Autonomism' (for a recent defense of this position, see Harold, 2011).

3 I take it that for an Autonomist, it would still be possible to hold that an artwork's intrinsic value affects its moral or political insights, despite the fact that the contrary does not hold.

4 For this reason, it seems implausible to hold that the aesthetic value is the intrinsic value of art. There seems to be another viable option: to hold that the aesthetic value is not art's intrinsic value, yet it is in itself an intrinsic value. Or perhaps it is an instrumental value, and yet it is not affected by any other instrumental value an artwork may have. In these cases, the pluralist debate – the debate around the possible interactions of values in art – would be limited. It would be possible for epistemic value to affect the artistic value but not the contrary, because we have defined the artistic value as a compound of other values. Moreover, if we held that aesthetic value was not affected by any other value, we could still accept that it may affect other values that are part of the artistic value.

5 I do not take Lopes's and Gaut's theories of aesthetic value to be compatible. I just want to highlight how these are two interesting attempts to 'inflate' the concept of aesthetic value, albeit to different extents. In particular, Lopes inflates the concept of aesthetic value to what is valuable for an artwork *qua* artwork belonging to a particular category K, where K is an art form, genre or other art kind, whereas Gaut inflates the aesthetic value to what is valuable for a work *qua* art – I expand on this later.

6 Gaut's theory is the one I favor and endorse throughout this dissertation. However, what I will say on the aesthetic relevance of the epistemic value will also make sense for proponents of different conceptions of the relation between artistic and aesthetic value, as long as such conceptions do not trivialize the pluralist debate.

7 It means that not all evaluative terms can be part of such a list but only those that are used in art-critical practice.

8 Indeed, an artistic theory of the aesthetic value is also underpinned by the idea that aesthetic experience constitutes the value of the aesthetic (Goldman, 2006).

9 For an extensive defense of the artistic theory of aesthetic value, see Gaut (2007, pp. 35–40).

10 Gaut argues that not all the criteria we use to evaluate something need be constitutive of its definition. With an analogy: 'We can evaluate an individual qua business man, and what is to be a businessman can presumably be defined. But what makes someone a good businessman is partly determined by factors [being disciplined in one's work habits, being a good communicator, etc.] that are not part of the definition of the concept' (2007, p. 40).

11 Nozick (1973), criticizing Goodman (1968), provides a wonderful example of this scenario.

12 Art's capacity to provide understanding through affective means will be particularly relevant in our later discussion of the artistic relevance of political cinema's epistemic values (in the remaining chapters of this book).

13 I use the terms 'epistemic' and 'cognitive' as synonyms, as I understand the notion of epistemic value in a very broad sense, to also entail those skills that are mainly cognitive, like the capacity to empathize or sympathize with a character; this is because they play an important role in the acquisition of knowledge and in fostering understanding.

14 Stacie Friend uses the term 'empirical knowledge' and she argues that fiction and nonfiction can convey this kind of knowledge via testimony. However, testimony

could be considered a reliable source also for moral knowledge. I do not analyze the possibility of acquiring moral knowledge via testimony, as such epistemological problems fall outside the scope of this chapter. Yet, I want to stress that if the argument for empirical knowledge holds, then it could possibly be expanded to justify also the acquisition of moral knowledge from fiction via testimony. However, I take it that this argument would suffer from the same weaknesses suffered by the argument for empirical knowledge; indeed, the problem concerns the (in)capacity of testimony to link epistemic and aesthetic value.

15 An artwork may afford many epistemic values. Empirical knowledge may be justified by testimony, but other values need not depend on the same justificatory source. Hence, these other values may still be presented through artistic means – and, therefore, be aesthetically relevant.

16 I add the specification 'politically relevant' epistemic value to concede the possibility that artworks may have different kinds of epistemic values which may also have nothing to do with the political dimension of the film. Yet, when the main intended aim of the film is political, even when there may be other non-political epistemic values interacting with the aesthetic dimension, we are justified in saying that film is unsuccessful as a '*political* film'.

17 I do not need to assess the potential aesthetic merits of the film; here I just aim to prove that the film is not aesthetically better off in virtue of its (politically relevant) epistemic value; and the intended aim of the film is political. Hence, the failure.

18 Had it been the case that the film had a primarily religious aim (say, to reflect on the doctrine of retribution), then we would need to stress the mistaken interpretation of the book of Job provided by Vasiliy, the local priest.

19 Resignation implies a passive attitude of acceptance, not understanding. But Job did not resign to God's might or will. He understood the need of God in times of despair as a shelter where comfort and hope could be found.

20 Also, the comparison between Kolya and Job is stretched, given that Job was to find shelter in God, whereas Kolya is doomed, crushed by a Leviathan-state.

21 However, let me highlight that the knowledge that Russia is a corrupt country seems quite trivial. It does not come as a surprise that Russia is corrupt; we already possess this knowledge. If the difference between epistemically meritorious works and epistemically flawed ones is a difference in degree, then perhaps we can say that the Leviathan is not defective, but it surely is not that epistemically meritorious either.

22 I did not analyze the possible aesthetic merits of the film, since this is not relevant to my argument. I just needed to prove that its aesthetic merit is not enhanced by the empirical knowledge conveyed through testimony.

5 Epistemic values afforded by political films

The aim of this chapter is to show that political cinema can have an impact on the audience's system of beliefs. In the previous chapter we have seen how fictional artworks can convey empirical knowledge justified via testimony. In this chapter, I consider alternative replies to the alleged inability of art to convey nontrivial knowledge. I analyze Propositionalism, as proposed by Conolly and Haydar (2001), and Clarificationism, as advanced by Noël Carroll (1998). Clarificationism can be seen as a moderate version of aesthetic cognitivism; it holds that art can have an educational function, but it cannot convey new propositional knowledge; at best, art can clarify beliefs that we already hold and make them more vivid. Propositionalism, instead, holds that art can also convey new propositional knowledge. I reconstruct Conolly and Haydar's argument against Clarificationism in detail. I want to dwell on the authors' argument for two reasons: the first is to provide a further argument supporting a stronger version of Cognitivism that could also entail the acquisition of new propositional knowledge. The second reason is that the authors are the only ones, in the analytic tradition of philosophy of art, to sketch an account of the possible cognitive values of political artworks. Specifically, they argue that while Propositionalism holds for artworks that aim to convey propositional knowledge about personal morality, the cognitive value of political artworks is best explained in Clarificationist terms. I show that their conclusions about political artworks are mistaken as they are grounded on an arbitrary distinction between personal and political morality.

As in the previous chapter, I frame the debate on art's cognitive values in general terms, speaking of 'art' with no overt reference to films. However, I use films as examples, and later in the chapter I focus more closely on the capacity of film to be epistemically valuable analyzing Emanuele Crialese's film *The Golden Door* (2006).

In the first section of this chapter, I reconstruct the debate between Conolly and Haydar and Noël Carroll. Conolly and Haydar hold that political artworks cannot convey new propositional knowledge because they are about problems that are not sufficiently complex to challenge, or to elicit connection between, our already-held beliefs. In the second section, I delve deeper

DOI: 10.4324/9780367816872-6

into this argument, as I deem it flawed and in the third section, I analyze how art can actually have an impact on the audience's system of beliefs. First, I argue against Conolly and Haydar's distinction between political and personal morality: political artworks can be about 'personal stories', so they can convey propositional knowledge, and their epistemic relevance can be explained through the belief-application and the connection-making models. This discussion will remark the usefulness of the theoretical model introduced in the first chapters. In the fourth section, I argue that political films can afford different kinds of epistemic values. The analysis of *The Golden Door* serves as an example to prove that works that foster understanding of what it is like to be in a given situation can also be conducive to new propositional knowledge.

1 Can art convey new propositional knowledge?

Clarificationism can be seen as a moderate view between anti-cognitivists and cognitivists who believe that art can convey propositional knowledge. It implies that art has educational value, particularly in the moral realm, yet such value does not entail the capacity to convey new propositional knowledge. Clarificationism, as advanced by Noël Carroll (1998), holds that art may provide moral education by: 'a) prompting us to apply already-held moral concepts to new (imaginary) situations;[1] b) . . . prompting us to make connections between already-held moral beliefs; and c) . . . making already-known moral propositions more vivid than previously' (Carroll, 1998; Conolly & Haydar, 2001, p. 114). We can conceive of these three 'modes' of clarification of our already-held beliefs as separate, granted that they can work together as a process: new imaginary situations prompt us to (1) apply already-held moral concepts, (2) make connection between our already-held beliefs and/or (3) make such already-held beliefs more vivid than they were previously. However, as noted by Conolly and Haydar, (1) is a necessary condition for both (2) and (3). Let us call (1) the concept-application model, (2) the connection-making model and (3) the vivid-making model.

According to Conolly and Haydar, (3) is compatible with Clarificationism. Point (3) implies that art can trigger a more vivid understanding of some already-held beliefs. Indeed, in our reading of *Crime and Punishment*, engaging with the strong emotional consequences felt by Raskolnikov may reinforce our belief that killing is wrong. This is something that we already knew, yet engaging with Raskolnikov's reaction to murder reinforces the wrongness of the action. A quote from Shelly Kagan backs up this possibility, marking a distinction between the mind's representations of pale and vivid beliefs:

> we must distinguish between two ways that beliefs can be represented in the mind: a belief can be *vivid* or *pale*. Pale beliefs are genuine

> beliefs – but they are displayed to the mind in such a way that the individual does not fully appreciate their import
>
> (1989, p. 283).

So, our engagement with an artwork can reinforce a belief, making us 'fully appreciate its import'. We do not form a new belief, so this kind of educational capacity is well explained in Clarificationist terms: our engagement with art makes some of our already-held beliefs more vivid.

Clarificationism has problems at points (1) and (2). Consider (1): we do apply our already-held concepts to imaginary situations, but this is not always unproblematic.[2] Carroll holds that narratives can provide us with new (imaginary) situations that require the application of moral concepts, but is it also the case that these narratives, with such new scenarios, never pose a challenge to our moral knowledge? Some cases seem to be obviously challenging. Berys Gaut analyzes Styron's novel *Sophie's Choice* that can be interpreted as a fictional rendering of a typical philosophical dilemma: would you kill someone to save someone else's life? The debate between consequentialist and deontological ethical theories is often enriched by thought experiments and examples; *Sophie's Choice* can be seen as a more vivid and detailed characterization of a thought experiment, where the application of our beliefs is not so unproblematic. Now, if a fictional work challenges our beliefs, then the cognitive activity it elicits is not so shallow as Clarificationism seems to imply. Challenging fictional works surely elicit reflection which is, per se, cognitively valuable. Indeed, in order to apply a belief to a newly imagined situation – a situation we may have not considered yet – we need to reflect upon our already-held beliefs. After careful consideration of the moral dilemma, as in *Sophie's Choice*, we may still not change our already-held beliefs, and the artwork may have still achieved the valuable aim of triggering careful consideration. However, reflection on such challenging new scenarios may also show the inappropriateness of our beliefs, as vividly imagining a certain situation can change our perspective on it; hence, such challenging fictional works can (1) elicit reflection and (2) (potentially) change our perspective on the issue at stake. As such, we cannot exclude the possibility that challenging scenarios may be conducive to new propositional knowledge.[3]

As for (1), Conolly and Haydar rightly note that it is hard to explain how connecting already-held beliefs could be cashed out if not in propositional terms. Indeed, newly imagined situations can elicit connections between beliefs that had never been thought in conjunction before. But connecting two beliefs is like creating a new proposition altogether. Following Conolly and Haydar, we can interpret the notion of 'making connection between beliefs' only in two ways:

> it can mean either the making of logical connections that entail new beliefs, or simply the juxtaposition of previously held beliefs with no

> change in their content or one's belief-set generally. If the former is meant, then propositional knowledge clearly follows. If the latter is meant, it is hard to see the point of bringing together in one's mind two beliefs, unless logical connections are made between them
> (2001, p. 116).

So, if it is true that newly imagined situations can foster connections between already-held beliefs, then we can say that the result of such connections is new propositional knowledge. It is important to note that while Propositionalism need not reject art's capacity to reinforce, or clarify, some already-held beliefs, Clarificationism does deny art's capacity to yield new propositional knowledge.[4]

Carroll's basic assumption to support Clarificationism is that in order to understand fiction, we must mobilize and access our 'moral repertoire'. So, fictional artworks do not teach us anything because they actually depend, 'as a condition of their very intelligibility, upon our possession of the relevant knowledge of various moral precepts and of concepts of vice and virtue and so on' (Carroll, 1998, p. 142). Carroll says that from Dostoyevsky's novel, *Crime and Punishment*, we understand that killing is wrong, and the novel serves as a reinforcement of an already-held belief. This cannot be otherwise because we need to already hold a belief about the evilness of murder if we are to properly understand the novel itself. However, this argument, without further specifications, can bring unwelcomed consequences. Conolly and Haydar spell out Carroll's argument in the following terms:

(i) Understanding narratives depends on the possession of moral concepts
(ii) In any form of communication depending on X-type concepts, no interesting propositional X-type knowledge can be gained
(iii) From i) and ii) no interesting propositional knowledge may be gained from narratives (2001, p. 111).

We can grant the first premise, but the second seems a great deal more problematic. Moral discussion, for instance, surely requires that the participants have at least some moral knowledge, just as if I were to attend an advanced lecture of extragalactic astronomy, I would need to have some basic notions of astronomy in order to understand what is being said. However, it does not follow that if I have moral knowledge, I cannot gain new propositional knowledge from a discussion on a moral problem.

Carroll's examples of the kind of propositions we need to hold in order to appreciate fictional works – say, 'murder is wrong' or 'justice is good' – are very general and seem to be true by definition. Our belief system surely entails very general propositions, but they clearly are not the only ones. These propositions are linked, as in an epistemic chain, to other propositions expressing attitudes toward more specific and detailed situations. We can think of our belief system as proceeding from a central, general, core of generic propositions to peripheral and progressively more detailed propositions expressing attitudes toward specific issues. Conolly and Haydar refer to Quine's description of our stock of judgments, which is pictured as an interrelated web of propositions, with analytic judgments at the center and synthetic ones at the periphery. 'This picture has the purely "moral judgements" at the centre, and shades off into more specific judgements that respond to changes in "purely factual" propositions' (Conolly & Haydar, 2001, p. 112). To highlight the hierarchical structure of moral propositions, Conolly and Haydar suggest calling propositions expressing analytic judgments as 'LEVEL 1' moral propositions.[5] The more these propositions come to be specified, the further we proceed down the levels. For instance, a general proposition about the desirability of justice can be specified at lower levels: what is the conception of justice we endorse? Be it Platonic, or Rawlsian, or rule-consequentialist, moral propositions at LEVEL 2 specify our attitudes on the matter. And we can think of further levels of specification (e.g. LEVEL 3, LEVEL 4 . . .).

In light of this mapping of our moral beliefs, Conolly and Haydar reformulate Clarificationism. Specifically, Clarificationism can be reformulated in two different ways. In the first case our understanding of narratives depends only on LEVEL 1 moral concepts.

(i)' Understanding narrative depends on the possession of Level 1 moral concepts.
(ii)' In any form of communication depending on possession of LEVEL 1 X-type concepts, no interesting propositional LEVEL 1 X-type knowledge may be gained.
(iii)' No interesting LEVEL 1 propositional knowledge may be gained from narratives (Conolly & Haydar, 2001, p. 113).

In the second case, our understanding of narrative depends on *all* levels of moral concepts. That is:

(i)" Understanding narrative depends on the possession of LEVELS 1, 2 and 3 moral concepts.
(ii)" In any form of communication depending on possession of LEVELS 1, 2 and 3 moral knowledge, no interesting propositional knowledge may be gained.
(iii)" No interesting new LEVEL 1, 2 or 3 propositional knowledge may be gained from narratives (Conolly & Haydar, 2001, p. 114).

The first possibility is far too weak, and it surely does not undermine Propositionalism. Indeed, there is nothing distinctive about the inability of narrative to teach us in this way, and moral propositions can be conveyed at other levels of knowledge. The second reformulation is much stronger than the first, but highly implausible, as the second premise seems to prevent the possibility of knowledge tout court. As the first formulation is the most plausible, we can say that it does not threaten Propositionalism, as artworks can convey propositional knowledge at the lowest levels of specification (LEVEL 2, 3, etc.).

I have reconstructed Conolly and Haydar's argument against Clarificationism to show that art can also convey new propositional knowledge. Now I turn to the second part of their argument, where they hold that Clarificationism is better equipped to explain cases of narratives that revolve around political morality.

2 Can political artworks convey new propositional knowledge?

Conolly and Haydar hold that Clarificationism makes better sense if it is applied to artworks that deal with problems of political morality rather than to artworks concerning issues of personal morality (2001, p. 116). This is because, according to the authors, artworks about political moral issues lend themselves to the vivid-making model (model (3)) of cognitive value, whereas artworks about personal morality lend themselves to the connection-making model (model (2)). This means that political artworks can, at best, make our already-held beliefs more vivid, whereas artworks about personal morality are able to convey new propositional knowledge. Before I explain their argument, I just want to note that their claim here is not sufficiently clear. Is it *always* the case that artworks about political morality can be seen as cognitively valuable because they lend themselves *exclusively* to the vivid-making model? Or is it the case that *sometimes* artworks about political morality are best explained by the vivid-making model? If the latter is the case, then I have no quarrel with the authors. Indeed, artworks can clarify our already-held beliefs or they can bring new propositional knowledge. *Sometimes* they convey new propositional knowledge; *sometimes* they do not. This capacity is not 'typical' of political artworks. So, it seems that the authors must have in mind something closer to the first option: artworks about political morality are *always* best explained by the vivid-making model, so they cannot convey any new propositional knowledge. The reason why I raise the doubt about the actual claim of the authors is that they use a political artwork (*Up the Sandbox*, Roiphe, 1970) to prove how artworks can foster connection between our already-held beliefs. But connecting beliefs, following the authors, is a path to new propositional knowledge. Admittedly, they claim *Up the Sandbox* can be seen as an exception, but nonetheless this seems to weaken their overall claim.

Let me first introduce Conolly and Haydar's argument so we can analyze its incongruences. They hold that narratives are best placed to explore human psychology, as they 'typically focus on individuals and their relationships with one another, rather than on entire societies and social movement' (2001, p. 118). So, narratives can help us investigate issues that pertain to, what they call, 'personal morality'. Among the issues that pertain to this sphere of knowledge there are 'the conditions for personal flourishing and fulfilment, as well as multiple ways in which people may deceive themselves and each other' (p. 118). The authors hold that the personal domain is not reducible to the political, hence, issues of political morality can be distinguished from those pertaining to personal morality. In addition, the authors hold that issues about personal morality are 'less obvious' than those about political morality. To quote the authors: 'apart from the difference in scope between personal and political moral issues, there is a difference in their obviousness' (p. 120). Specifically, narratives about personal moral issues invite the audience to make connections that are 'less obvious' than those prompted by narratives about political morality. This is why narratives about political morality lend themselves to the vivid-making model, as they can only reinforce or clarify beliefs that are already held. Following the authors, narratives about political morality cannot do anything more than reinforce already-held beliefs because political disagreement can be settled with reference to facts only, and narratives cannot 'point to the actual world' as sociological reports can. Let me use the words of the authors to express these points of their argument: 'political disagreement is often settled with reference to facts only, as there is often agreement about moral political concepts such as the nature of justice' (p. 120), and then

> in political argument, changes in one's beliefs often – if not always – depends on changes in our factual beliefs. And since a fictional narrative cannot point to the world in a manner requisite for such changes to takes place, it cannot, it seems, affect such changes in our political beliefs (p. 121).

The authors do not provide any reason to justify the claim that in political disputes changes in one's beliefs depend on changes in factual beliefs. They simply assume that, when it comes to political disputes, there is agreement about more general beliefs about political morality. Let me summarize their argument:

(i) We can distinguish between personal and political morality
(ii) Issues about personal morality are less obvious then issues about political morality
(iii) There is a general agreement about moral political concepts
(iv) Political disagreement can be settled with reference to facts only
(v) Narratives cannot point to the state of the world in a manner that is 'requisite' to change beliefs about facts
(vi) *Therefore*, narratives about political morality can at best clarify already-held beliefs.[6]

Every single premise of this argument seems dubious at best. The authors distinguish between issues about political morality and those about personal morality. There is not a proper argument in the text that could further explain the reasons for such divide. They simply add that 'numerous critics have argued that. . . [the] personal domain is not reducible to the political, and Noël Carroll gives no indication of being in disagreement with them' (2001, p. 118). Then, since the personal domain 'is not reducible' to the political, political morality is distinct from personal morality. This passage needs further clarification. Even if we were to grant such difference, more would need to be said about it: what goes under the umbrella of 'personal morality'? And what goes under that of political morality? Does political morality refer only to issues about justice? It is, indeed, not clear what they imply with the label 'political domain', so it is hard to infer their view of 'political morality'. Commenting on the insights provided by *Middlemarch* they claim that such insights are personal and not political because 'it is hard to see how they could be put to any use in either an abstract theory of justice or a concrete political proposal about how a society ought to be governed' (2001, p. 119). However, to say that some psychological insights cannot be put to use in a political theory is not to say that no insights into human psychology can be used in political theory. Indeed, it is the case that important political theories also imply a theory of human nature; I have in mind theories of thinkers like Machiavelli, Adam Smith, John Locke, and Jean-Jacques Rousseau. In addition, John Rawls has been accused by John Harsanyi (1980) to mistakenly attribute psychological attitudes to people behind the veil of ignorance. According to Harsanyi, Rawls imbues people with an innate aversion to risk – which is a psychological trait. My point, here, is that it does not suffice to presuppose a strict divide between personal and political domains to establish a difference between personal and political morality. So, this first premise is, at least, underdeveloped, and this has important repercussions on the overall argument, which I will explore later.

Premises (ii), (iii) and (iv) seem to discredit centuries of normative political theory. If we were to take the authors' words at face value, we would infer that they take political issues to be more obvious and easily settled – as there is general agreement about moral political concepts. Here, though, their own argument about the epistemic chains that link our beliefs can be used against them. There can be an agreement about general propositions, that is, LEVEL 1 propositions, of the kind: 'justice is good' or 'murder is wrong'.[7] But surely there is no such general agreement at lower levels of analysis. Indeed, a distribution principle like Rawls's maximin principle significantly differs from Nozick's entitlement principle. There is not a general agreement on moral political concepts, so it is strange to hold that moral political issues are more obvious than personal ones. How could this be true? And is it the case that political disagreement can be settled with reference to facts only? Again, returning to the argument advanced by Conolly and Haydar, there are beliefs about political concepts at different levels of abstraction (LEVEL 1, 2, 3 etc.). If the more peripheral beliefs are more directly sensitive to factual judgments, this need not be true for intermediate levels. There are normative issues that are crucial for what Conolly and Haydar call moral political concepts. For instance, disputes about ownership need not necessarily be solved with reference to factual information. The Lockean conception of ownership based on the mixed-labor theory is a normative conception that has factual implications on issues like the ownership of intellectual property or the ownership of the land. This is a normative concept that can change our beliefs in the sphere of political morality, and arguments about this concept need not refer to facts.

Premise (v) is also unclear. What does it mean 'to point to the world in a manner that is requisite for such changes [changes in factual beliefs] to take place'? Conolly and Haydar compare fiction with nonfictional sociological studies, like the Shere Hite reports, which include empirical data related to people's attitudes to sexuality and relationships. The authors argue that the Hite reports have had a stronger impact on the debate on sexual equality. There are no empirical data that could back the claim that nonfictional sociological reports have a stronger impact on a political debate than a fictional artwork – we can actually imagine that the contrary can also hold: that fictional artwork can have an impact on political debates.[8] So, we are to infer that what the authors imply is that nonfictional reports are a reliable source of factual knowledge, whereas fiction is not. But this is a controversial claim. We have already seen in the previous chapter how nonfictional *art*works can be just as reliable as nonfictional works, and I have also noted how the epistemic difference between nonfictional artworks and fictional artworks is a difference in kind rather than degree: it tends to be safer to export beliefs about the actual world from nonfictional artworks, but it is still possible to gather true beliefs about the actual world from fictional artworks. The reliability of testimony justifies the knowledge we gather from artworks; be they fictional or not. It means that fictional artworks can teach us about the actual world just as nonfictional sociological reports can. For instance, I can read a sociological report on the problem of corruption in Russia and learn that Russia's peripheral administrations are extremely corrupted. However, I can also watch Zvyagintsev's *Leviathan* (2014) and trust the author, whom I may consider an expert on Russia's sociological problems, and learn that Russia's peripheral administrations are extremely corrupted. Both the sociological report and the fictional artwork convey the same propositional knowledge about the actual world. It follows that also fictional artworks can 'point to the actual world in the requisite manner', where 'requisite' is the capacity to justify knowledge of factual beliefs that can be exported in the actual world. Even if all the other premises were true, as fictional artworks can convey knowledge of factual beliefs, then we could say that fictional artworks about political morality could have an impact on political disagreement, so they could, potentially, bring new propositional knowledge.[9]

Conolly and Haydar's conclusion – that fictional artworks about political morality can at best clarify already-held beliefs – is not warranted, as premises (ii), (iii), (iv) and (v) are false, and premise (i) is at least unclear. The authors' argument then does not present good reasons to say that narratives about political morality cannot convey new propositional knowledge. The challenge, now, is to provide a positive argument that could show how political artworks can also convey propositional knowledge.

3 Political artworks and epistemic values

Let us return to my initial doubt about the strength of Conolly and Haydar's claim concerning the alleged incapacity of political artworks to convey propositional knowledge. Conolly and Haydar hold that Clarificationism can better explain cases of artworks about political morality, but they still seem to admit the possibility that artworks about political morality can convey propositional knowledge. Indeed, using as an example Anne Richardson Roiphe's novel *Up the Sandbox* (1970) – which has since been made into a film by Irvin Kershner (1972) – they provide an argument that supports the idea that political artworks can convey new propositional knowledge. The novel aims to highlight the inequalities between a housewife, Margaret, and her husband's life, juxtaposing Margaret's adventure fantasies with her daily routine as a housewife. Conolly and Haydar hold that

> one way of characterizing what is going on here [in *Up the Sandbox*] is that the reader may start with the beliefs that (1) men and women are equal; (2) housework is just as fulfilling as other kinds of work; and consequently (3) there is nothing unjust in a division of labour which consigns some to the home. In undermining (2), the novel blocks the inference to (3), and indeed may lead to the adoption of a contrary view (2008, p. 115).

This process shows how, through engagement with the novel, the audience may acquire new propositional knowledge.

However, the authors qualify the propositional knowledge that can be acquired through the engagement with *Up the Sandbox* by adding three provisos. We already encountered one of these provisos: the authors hold that fictional narrative cannot point to the actual world in the way that sociological reports can. We have seen previously that this proviso does not hold if it implies that artworks cannot convey factual knowledge. However, this condition seems to imply that the kind of knowledge we can gather from fictional narratives about political morality is somehow less valuable than the knowledge we can acquire from sociological reports. This impression is reinforced by the second proviso on the knowledge conveyed by *Up the Sandbox*: the moral knowledge to be gained from this novel, the authors hold, if not altogether obvious is at least 'more obvious than the kind of depth-psychological insight offered by George Eliot' (2008, p. 120). Perhaps *Up the Sandbox* is less insightful than *Middlemarch*, but that does not make the knowledge we gather from it obvious. What Conolly and Haydar seem to be doing here is to unduly establish a hierarchy of complexity within moral epistemology – problems of 'personal morality' are more complex than problems of political morality.[10]

The last proviso added by the authors to qualify the 'quality' of the propositional knowledge conveyed by *Up the Sandbox* has to do with what the authors take to be something like a *sui generis* kind of political morality, the one that has to do with gender equality; indeed, they hold that 'feminist themes seem to straddle the divide between the personal and the political, and thus borrow some of the characteristic techniques of both, the making vivid of propositions and the inducement to substantive cogitation' (2008, p. 120). But is it the case that only feminist themes straddle the divide between the personal and the political? Consider, for instance, how some publicly debated ethical problems have important bearings on individuals' lives; consider, for instance, the debates on abortion, euthanasia, the death penalty and civil unions. Also, different conceptions of justice have different bearings on matters of redistribution, so individuals' lives can be affected by a given preference in the allocation of resources. Clearly, immigration and citizenship regulations have an impact on how people can conduct their lives, where they can live and their status in a given society. Do all these cases straddle the divide between the personal and the political? The problem, for Conolly and Haydar, is that they actually do! These cases actually straddle such a divide; and this simply proves that the divide itself is to be reconsidered. As I noted previously, it seems odd to distinguish between personal and political morality, and if such a distinction is to be drawn then we need precise coordinates on how to differentiate one from the other. The authors do not provide any indications; they simply note how a number of critics have argued that the personal domain is not reducible to the political and that Carroll has given no indication of disagreement, so he must hold the same position, hence, narratives can at best clarify already-held beliefs about political morality. I do not intend to suggest that we should reduce the political domain to the personal. Let us admit a distinction, but we cannot be shortsighted. The political domain has clear influences on the personal. Personal experiences are necessarily, if only partially, shaped by the political framework. The feminist example brought by Conolly and Haydar is a case in point: personal life is affected by political conceptions of gender equality. The same happens in all aspects of the political. We have defined the political as the sphere of conflict, and the dimension of the conflict is public, that is, it concerns the entire society. If something is relevant in shaping allegiances along the friend/enemy divide across the entire society, then it surely must have an impact on the life of individuals. This means that narratives focusing on individuals' lives can still tell us something politically relevant. Political artworks and what Conolly and Haydar label artworks about personal morality do not rely on a different set of characteristics. To explore a political problem, we need to look at individuals' lives, analyzing their peculiar circumstances and relations to other individuals. This should have been clear already from the few examples treated so far. *Dead Man Walking* delves into the lives of Matthew Poncelet and his victims in order to advocate against the death penalty, and Errol Morris's *Mr. Death* is even more 'person-centred' as it explores the life of Fred Leuchter since his childhood while in Marco Bellocchio's *The Sleeping Beauty*, personal stories are used to advance different standpoints on euthanasia. That personal stories can be used to make a political work will be even more evident in the examples to come. In this chapter, I examine how the story of the Mancuso family serves to elicit reflection on the problem of immigration, and Sandra's psychology serves to explore the sense of belonging and the need for solidarity within the workforce in the Dardenne brothers' film *Two Days, One Night* (discussed in Chapter 7).

Let me reconsider Conolly and Haydar's argument. They hold that artworks can convey new propositional knowledge because (1) they prompt the application of moral concepts and beliefs to new imaginary scenarios, and such application can be challenging and elicit reconsideration of our standpoint (this is the concept-application model), and (2) they prompt connection between our already-held beliefs, which leads to the formation of new propositions (the connection-making model). However, the authors have it, political artworks can at best make more vivid some of our already-held beliefs, so they lend themselves to c) the vivid-making model. The reason why political artworks lend themselves only to model c) is, according to the authors, an alleged difference between personal and political morality; this is to be paired with the authors' assumption that narrative artworks are best placed to deal with issues about personal morality. However, there is no strict division between personal and political morality, so there is no reason why political artworks should lend themselves exclusively to the vivid-making model. Indeed, the examples of political artworks treated in this book are all examples of scenarios in which the application of our already-held beliefs is challenged (does Poncelet deserve to die? Is Leuchter a hideous hate-monger?) and we are prompted to make connections between our already-held beliefs (like our beliefs about proportional justice and those about the respect for human life).

In the next section, I argue that the vivid-making model can also be conducive to new propositional knowledge, and it should become even clearer how these three models are deeply interrelated. However, I want to stress how proving that political artworks can convey new propositional knowledge is only part of the viewpoint I intend to defend. Indeed, I hold that films, and political films specifically, can afford epistemic *values*. New propositional knowledge is surely an important epistemic value, but it is not the only one nor is necessarily the most important one. I do not intend to hierarchically rank epistemic values that may be afforded by artworks, as I am not interested in proving the superiority of one value over another. I just need to prove that they can actually be afforded. In the next section, I reconsider the vivid-making model, and I argue that, as it entails understanding, it can be conducive to propositional knowledge.

4 The Vivid-making model as conducive to propositional knowledge

Conolly and Haydar's argument for Propositionalism seems to suggest a hierarchical structure of the kinds of epistemic values narratives may afford. Indeed, the authors hold that narratives about political morality can 'at best' make already-held beliefs more vivid, and Clarificationism is fit to explain the kind of epistemic value afforded by narratives about political morality, where political morality, according to the authors, is less controversial than personal morality. The authors stress how the vivid-making model does not add to the audience's knowledge; so it simply 'brings back to mind' existing beliefs, and the narrative does not add anything to such beliefs, they are just made more vivid. Hence, the acquisition of new propositional knowledge is of greater value, as there is an actual epistemic gain. I contend that the authors are unduly restricting the possibilities of epistemic gains. They consider exclusively the possibility of acquiring new knowledge versus the possibility of clarifying already-held beliefs. Furthermore, their understanding of a narrative's capacity to 'clarify' a belief is itself quite restrictive.[11] For instance, they do not consider the possibility that 'to clarify' may imply further specifications of some already-held beliefs, and that such specifications may be cashed out in terms of new propositional knowledge. Consider the previous example about gender equality in *Up the Sandbox*; we could still hold that housework *may be* just as fulfilling as any other kind of work, but the 'may be' implies that we are yet to specify the conditions that make the proposition 'housework is fulfilling' true. Engagement with the narrative can introduce such specifications, which are nothing less than new propositional knowledge. So, the narrative's capacity to clarify a belief implies a gain for the audience.

However, there is another sense in which 'to clarify' actually implies a gain, a sense which is again overlooked by Conolly and Haydar. A narrative can foster understanding of specific situations, scenarios, events and characters' feelings. I may hold the belief that being a housewife may not be just as fulfilling as any other work while lacking an understanding of why this is so. The engagement with a fictional narrative that can show me the boredom of housework through the experience of a character can foster my understanding of the belief that housework is not as fulfilling as any other job. Here there is a gain for the audience that acquires the understanding necessary to hold that belief. The narrative does not just 'bring back to mind' an already-held belief but explains it.

This means that new propositional knowledge is not the only gain to which an audience can aspire when engaging with fictional narratives, and we should not even posit a hierarchy of the possible gains afforded. Knowledge is not just about getting something right. That a belief may be true and that it may be a justified true belief is an important aspect of knowledge. But it is not the whole story. We want more than to just get something right. Ernest Sosa identifies more than one epistemic value:

(i) Truth: we would rather our beliefs were true than not true, other things being equal.
(ii) Safety: we would prefer that not too easily would our beliefs be false.
(iii) Understanding/explanation: often we would like not only to know a given thing but also to understand it, to have an explanation. (And this leads to the next item.)
(iv) Coherence: we would prefer that our minds not house a clutter of mere facts sitting there loose from one another.
(v) Finally, we are often interested not only in *having* the truth but in *discovering* it, which involves not just being visited with the truth by sheer happenstance or through some external agency but to arrive at the truth through our own intelligent doings, by relying on our own reliable abilities, skills and faculties.

(Sosa, 2009, p. 137)

We have seen in the previous chapter that fiction is not a safe environment in which to gather our beliefs about the actual world, even though the 'adroit' audience can distinguish between beliefs that are true only in the world of the story and those that also hold in the actual world.

The last value highlighted by Sosa – the fact we value the enterprise itself of discovering the truth – reinforces the validity of the pedagogical dimension we are to analyze to assess films and narratives that aim to have an impact on our system of beliefs. We have said in the first chapter that some films pedantically state the message they aim to convey and their meaning, and I have argued that this can turn out to be an aesthetic defect. The maieutic method (see Chapter 2), instead, presupposes an active intellectual engagement of the audience. Such intellectual engagement is both epistemically and aesthetically valuable.

Here I want to linger on the values of understanding and coherence, as they are strictly linked and also capable of fostering connection among beliefs – and connecting beliefs, according to Conolly and Haydar, translates into new propositional knowledge. Understanding is a complex value that does not exclusively imply that you believe or know the reason why a proposition 'p' holds, but it implies a set of abilities that makes us treat a reason 'q' as the right reason for 'p'. Following Alison Hills, to understand why p, you need to be able to:

(i) follow an explanation of why p given by someone else
(ii) explain why p in your own words

(iii) draw the conclusion that p (or that probably p) from the information that q
(iv) draw the conclusion that p' (or that probably p') from the information that q' (where p' and q' are similar to but not identical to p and q)
(v) given the information that p, give the right explanation, q;
(vi) given the information that p', give the right explanation, q'

(Hills, 2016, p. 663)

Here I will use this definition of understanding as it has the main merit of highlighting how understanding differs from propositional knowledge.[12] Hills holds that this set of abilities is essential to understanding, for to understand why p, it does not suffice to know that q is the reason why p.[13] To understand why p we need to grasp the relationship between the two propositions p and q. To describe what it means to 'grasp a relationship', Hills uses an example: 'if you grasp a ball, you have it under your control. You can manipulate it, move it, turn it round, and so on, that is you (normally) have a set of practical abilities or practical know how, which you can exercise if you choose' (2016, p. 663).[14] This means that to grasp a relationship we are to be able to control it, manipulate it. She calls this set of abilities 'cognitive control', and we can say we understand why p, and q is why p, when we have cognitive control over p and q, which means that we can (in the right circumstances) manipulate the relationship between the two propositions. Cognitive control comes in degrees, so we should also think of understanding as something that comes in degrees; this is consistent with a range of linguistic evidence, which shows that we can have more or less understanding of why p, and this is also compatible with the idea that artworks can actually *deepen* our understanding.[15] In Hills's definition, to exercise cognitive control on the relationship between q and p we must also be able to draw inferences in similar cases. Suppose you study the life of Napoleon and you come to believe that he was a great general. To understand why Napoleon was great, you need to *grasp* why he was great – for instance, because he was tactically astute, well organized and ruthless. To grasp why Napoleon was great means that you need to have cognitive control over the relationship between these propositions and the conclusion that Napoleon was a great general; therefore you need, among other things, to be able to draw conclusions and give explanations in similar cases. So, if you were to gain true beliefs about Napoleon and then similar beliefs about Wellington, you would be able to draw the right conclusion about their military prowess (Hills, 2016). In this case, you would have cognitive control over the proposition that Napoleon was a great general and the reasons why that is true – so you would understand why Napoleon was a great general. I find these kinds of abilities ((v) and (vi)) particularly interesting as they show how understanding can foster connection among beliefs.

As we can understand and explain our beliefs and make inferences among similar beliefs, we can also judge the coherence of our overall system of beliefs. So, if I hold that p is true, then I cannot hold that z is true, if z implies non-p. The inner coherence of our system of beliefs requires reflective equilibrium: we analyze our beliefs about a specific issue and compare them with beliefs we hold about similar cases, more general principles and other moral and factual issues. We reflect on the relationship among our beliefs and we hope to reach an equilibrium, where we limit inconsistencies. So, in the process of analyzing our beliefs in light of one another we also revise them in order to create coherence. This means that understanding and coherence are epistemic values per se, but they also enable a process of revision that could be characterized as potentially yielding new propositional knowledge.

To make this reasoning less abstract, let me consider an example that can be used to clarify my point. I want to consider Emanuele Crialese's film *Golder Door* (*Nuovomondo*, 2006). This is a political film about immigration, and contextual information can help the analysis of the film. It was released in 2006, when the debate on immigration was particularly lively in Italy. In 2002, the Italian government first took severe measures against illegal immigration, introducing a much-contested law, which established the crime of 'clandestinity' – previously unregulated in the legislation.[16] Moreover, the film is to be viewed in the context of Crialese's *oeuvre*, which is a further clue that testifies to the political commitment of the author: in 2011, Crialese releases another film, *Dry Land* (*Terraferma*), about contemporary immigration problems.

Golden Door is set at the beginning of the twentieth century and is about a Sicilian family, the Mancusos – Salvatore, his old mother Fortunata, and his two children Angelo and Pietro, who is said to have lost the capacity to speak – looking to emigrate to the America. The film follows the journey of the family, from the little village in Sicily to Ellis Island.

The first part of the film serves to present the family. Although a small portion of the narrative, it is quite relevant as it provides background knowledge of the Mancuso family. In the opening of the film, Salvatore and Angelo climb up a hill with a stone in their mouths as a penitence to the Lord, and once they reach the peak, they ask for a Lord's sign: should they leave Sicily or should they stay? Meanwhile, Salvatore's mother practices a sort of exorcism on one of the girls of the village, who is said to be possessed by a snake. The Mancusos come from a rural part of Sicily, and they believe that America is the land of opulence. To symbolize this belief, Crialese uses oneiric scenes of young children carrying huge vegetables, and Salvatore dreams of coins raining down from the sky. Fortunata does not want to leave her native land, as dead souls do not want her to leave. So Salvatore buries himself in a field to convince the dead souls of his family to let them go. The family finally leaves and we follow them on the ship that will bring them to America. This part of the film is particularly interesting: there is no event that guides the narrative, but the time on the ship is used to dwell on the condition of being a migrant. The Mancuso family meets Lucy

(Charlotte Gainsbourg), an aristocratic woman who finds herself traveling with the poorest families; a meeting that, at the arrival at Ellis Island, will highlight the struggle and difficulties of the poorest Italian families.

During the journey on the ocean, a tempest causes deaths among the passengers. A sequence after the event is a central passage in the narrative. An overhead tracking shot shows the survivors carrying the bodies of the dead over the bridge. We are driven to feel sorrow and pity for all the migrants, facing such terrible circumstances just to run after a promise of hope. The message is reinforced by the diegetic soundtrack: Salvatore's mother sings of hope and rebirth after despair. Diegetic music punctuates the narrative throughout the journey on the ship. A couple of passengers play a typical Sicilian song, called 'Amuri Amuri', which is about a man who loses his mind and runs after his beloved. Here, the beloved symbolizes the New World, which drove the men to leave their homeland.

The time in Ellis Island evokes the humiliations and difficulties the migrants are to face in order to pursue their new life. On arrival, migrants are visited and tested for their intelligence; Salvatore and Angelo, when tested for their intelligence, do not know how to solve simple puzzles and Pietro keeps on refusing to speak. The time at Ellis Island also serves to further stress the differences between the Mancuso family and Lucy, who immediately manages to solve the puzzle. She then asks the reason for these intelligence tests, and the US official replies that it has been discovered that lack of intelligence is hereditary, hence contagious, and they do not want below-average people to mix with their citizens. 'What a modern vision' is Lucy's sarcastic reply.

After the tests in Ellis Island, Salvatore's mother is deemed feebleminded and therefore she is not allowed to enter the country. When she is called for the tests, the dialogue she has with the officer can be taken as a relevant hint for the interpretation of the film, probably revealing the attitude of the director. She asks why they ('we all coming from the "Old World"') are to be tested, and the officer replies that they (the US government) are trying to understand whether the immigrants are 'fit enough' to enter the New World. Fortunata bursts out, asking who they think they are: 'Are you God? Is it you who decides whether we are fit or not?'

In the end, Fortunata decides not to enter the New World. In what is a highly evocative and symbolic scene, Pietro speaks up for his grandmother, saying that she has decided to go back to Sicily. In this scene the three male characters need to part from the old matriarch, and they enter the New World accompanied by Lucy, which is translated in Italian as 'Luce' (which also means 'light' in Italian). In this scene, Pietro speaks and announces that grandmother has decided to go back while she wishes that they (Salvatore, Pietro and Angelo) remain in the New World. As Pietro speaks, the camera lingers with close-ups on the face of each member of the family, fostering empathic engagement; we feel the same sadness and fear they feel in having to leave the old woman and the Old World behind them.[17]

The film aims to guide us in the world of migrants, using the Mancuso family as an example. The film aims to tell us what it means to be migrants. It describes the difficulties of the journey, the pain of separation from the homeland and the hope for the future. The Mancusos here are just an example, but the aim of the film is to describe a condition common to all migrants. Let me stress the difference between this film and *Leviathan* (analyzed in the previous chapter). *Leviathan* could also be seen as a film using a family's story as an example. The difference is that the message of *Leviathan* has to do with a factual issue (Russia's corruption), whereas *The Golden Door* wants to describe the condition and feelings of the migrants and to foster our understanding of their situation. *Leviathan* did not attempt to make us understand what it feels like to live in a corrupt country, whereas *The Golden Door* aims to makes us understand what it means to be in a given situation. What does it mean to leave your homeland and face awful difficulties to reach a country that makes you feel unwelcome. The film provides background knowledge of the Mancuso family, which serves to frame their cultural extraction; it provides insights into their beliefs, desires and ambitions. Throughout the film the Mancuso family meets other emigrants; they always introduce themselves in the same fashion, saying their names and the name of the village they come from. None of them comes from a city, and they are not aware of what awaits them. Moreover, Crialese constantly avoids 'particularism'; that is, the Mancuso family is going to America, but the characters always refer to it as the 'New World' ('a Terra Nova'). This way of referring to America points to their hope for the future and a better life, where the 'New World' is just any place where money grows on trees. It is also particularly significant that upon their arrival in the New World, the migrants do not see the Statue of Liberty. They arrive on a foggy day, and they cannot see anything around them. The avoidance of such an obvious symbol of the United States is clearly a deliberate choice that aims to withdraw attention from the country, in order to focus on the conditions of the migrants. It is as if Crialese was reminding us that the migrants' hopes are not bound to a specific place but are directed more generally to a new life – no matter where.

So, we can say that the film actually has two related aims: (1) it aims to foster our understanding of what it means to be a southern Italian immigrant and (2) it also invites us to apply such understanding to similar cases. Even if the film only had the first aim, due to the nature of understanding itself, the film may have been conducive to new propositional knowledge. Indeed, the peculiarity of a value such as understanding is that it actually implies the capacity to be applied to other similar cases. It means that if a work provides understanding of events, situations, scenarios or character traits, this can be applied to similar cases. A work may aim to foster understanding of beliefs at a local level (say, only about what it means to be southern Italian emigrants), but it may have, as a by-product, the capacity to affect other kinds of beliefs that are similar and that can be re-examined in light of the newly acquired understanding. The case of Crialese's film is slightly different since it does not just aim at deepening the understanding of what it means to be southern Italian emigrants, but it also prompts us to apply such understanding to similar cases. The film, indeed, prompts us to universalize the case of the Mancuso family. We are invited to compare the family's situation and feelings with that of all migrants. The film invites such comparison throughout the film, and the final sequence is just another input that aims to trigger a more general analysis of the conditions of migrants. In the last sequence, an overhead shot tracks over the Mancuso family, with Luce, and many other migrants swimming in a sea of milk. The sea of milk is a recurrent symbol that refers to the opulence after which the migrants are running.

Hence, the film aims to have an impact on the audience's system of beliefs that goes beyond specific beliefs concerning Italian emigrants to the United States in the thirties. The understanding of what it is like to be migrants should prompt reflection on the general condition of being a migrant, be they an Italian emigrant of the thirties or a Syrian emigrant of the twenty-first century. *Golden Door*, then, is a peculiar example, as it is not only about Italian emigration to America but also about migration in general.[18]

My discussion of the *Golden Door* served to show how the film aims to have an impact on the audience's system of beliefs. The film aims to foster our understanding of what it means to be a migrant. It does so by taking as an example the Mancuso family; indeed, we are meant to understand what it means to be in their situation. We have little but sufficient background knowledge of the family, and we feel pity and sorrow for them throughout the unraveling of the narrative, as we understand their feelings and struggle. But the film also prompts us to universalize our understanding of the condition of being a migrant. Such an invitation not only pushes further our understanding of what it means to be a migrant, as it overtly invites us to compare the condition and feelings of the Mancusos with those of every other migrant, it also triggers a process of reflection on beliefs that are correlated: how are we to welcome immigrants in our country? Should we forbid them to enter the country and on what grounds? As our understanding of the migrant's standpoint is enhanced, the film triggers the application of reflective equilibrium to check the coherence of our system of beliefs.

As we have seen previously, understanding and coherence are epistemic values, so we can say that political films afford epistemic values even when they do not convey new propositional knowledge. However, an attentive analysis of the implications of these epistemic values (understanding and coherence) shows that these are values that can be conducive to new propositional knowledge. We can then conclude that Conolly and Haydar underestimate the role of understanding (and of other epistemic values), both as a value in itself and as being capable of promoting new propositional knowledge.

Notes

1 Carroll holds that the intelligibility of artworks depends on our application of already-held 'moral beliefs, concepts and feelings' (1998, p. 141), and elsewhere he refers to 'moral precepts, and the concept of vice and virtue and *so on*' (p. 142, emphasis added). And, more generally, he says that 'filling in the narrative is a matter of mobilizing or accessing the cognitive, emotive, and *moral repertoire* that, for the most part, we already have at our disposal' (p. 141, emphasis added). So, when Conolly and Haydar refer to the fact that Carroll holds that we apply already-held concepts, they actually imply that we apply this broadly construed 'moral repertoire', which the authors refer to as a 'stock of moral knowledge' (2001, p. 111).

2 When I say that we apply already-held beliefs, I always imply (following Carroll, and Conolly and Haydar) that we actually mobilize, more generally, our 'moral repertoire'.

3 I will say more on this possibility later, and in Chapter 5, I provide further details on the possibility that fictional narratives may work like thought experiments.

4 However, it is not clear whether Propositionalism, as advanced by Conolly and Haydar, also entails the possibility that art could afford other kinds of cognitive gains, such as understanding. Clarificationism entails understanding, so it seems that this may be accommodated by Propositionalism. However, later I suggest that the authors' stand of Propositionalism downplays art's capacity to afford other cognitive gains.

5 Following Conolly and Haydar, analytic judgments are those that are true by definition.

6 There seems to also be a parallel argument related to narratives about personal moral issues. As these issues do not depend solely on facts, but on moral psychology, narratives are best suited to investigate them – and so narratives can convey new propositional knowledge about these issues. This argument seems underdeveloped in the text, but we do not need to tackle this argument, as it will suffice to demonstrate the problems of the main argument concerning the triviality of moral political issues.

7 I do not delve into the definitional problems around analytic and synthetic judgments, but Conolly and Haydar seem to endorse the view that analytic judgments are true by definition. So, it can only be trivially true that there is agreement on these kinds of judgments.

8 We can pick up beliefs from fiction, even when these are unwarranted (see Chapter 4). Also, there is a general awareness of the capacity of fiction to have an impact on public debates. The release of Kathryn Bigelow's *Zero Dark Thirty* (2012) was delayed until after a presidential election, as the film was charged to support Obama's administration and it may have had an impact on the electoral campaign.

9 Admittedly, this strategy – fictional artworks can convey factual beliefs about the actual world via testimony – can only lead us to a cul-de-sac. As explained in the previous chapter, testimony is a reliable source of knowledge but it bypasses the artwork itself as it depends on the trustworthiness of the author. So, this kind of epistemic value has no bearing on the aesthetic value of the work.

10 Perhaps it is also possible to hold that the authors unduly establish a hierarchy of the kinds of epistemic values an artwork can afford – propositional knowledge seems to be more valuable than understanding (which, at least in Carroll's formulation, is entailed by the vivid-making model). The authors do not overtly express this standpoint, so I cannot say whether they would actually endorse this view. Nonetheless, I hold this can be seen as an unintended consequence of their argument, as the vivid-making model is exclusively associated to what they label

as 'less complex' moral issues; being 'less complex' if not 'altogether obvious', these issues seem to lose their 'epistemic dignity'. Consequently, understanding these issues can be seen as epistemically less valuable.

11 Here I criticize Conolly and Haydar for not seeing the potentialities of the vivid-making model, so my criticism is also directed toward Carroll's original formulation of Clarificationism.

12 For arguments supporting the idea that understanding is not reducible to propositional knowledge, see Knavig (2003), Newman (2014) and Zagzebsky (2001). Some philosophers have argued that understanding is the most significant epistemic gain and should be the focus of our enquiry (Knavig, 2003; Pritchard, 2009), but I can remain neutral toward this debate, as I just want to prove that artworks can afford epistemic values in general.

13 This means, following Hills, that we need to possess *at least* this set of abilities to understand why p. This definition of understanding is quite demanding for two reasons: first because it implies that understanding is something more than just knowing that q is the reason why p holds, but it requires a set of abilities that put in relation the two propositions q and p, and second because among the abilities required there is the capacity to explain why p with our own words. Hills herself acknowledges that this is quite a demanding requirement, as we may actually understand why p and yet not possess the linguistic abilities to explain it; so, she marks a distinction between explicit and implicit, or tacit, understanding (Hills, 2016), where tacit understanding does not require the ability to explain why p with our own words.

14 Grimm (2010, 2012) also conceives of understanding in terms of 'grasping' a relationship between beliefs and provides a similar explanation as to what 'grasping' means.

15 For instance, we say that 'John understands *very well* why he needs to go to the gym', or 'Jane does not understand *completely* why she cannot talk during meetings'. For further analysis of linguistic evidence that points to the idea that understanding comes in degrees, see Hills (2016).

16 The law was named after their political proponents 'Bossi-Fini'.

17 In Chapter 7, I will say more on the different kinds of imaginative engagements we may have with fiction films, and in Chapter 6, I reconsider this final scene.

18 We have seen how there is contextual information (the *oeuvre* of Crialese, and the lively debate on immigration in Italy at the time of release), as well as a number of clues in the film that backs up this reading of the work.

6 Film as thought experiment

In this chapter, I argue that films, like thought experiments, can afford epistemic gains and imagination is the source that justifies these gains. To do so, I divide this chapter into two sections, each one made of four subsections. In the first section, I focus on the epistemological problems surrounding imagination and thought experiments. First, I defend the view that imagination can justify our beliefs in general terms arguing that we can imagine with constraints and that this kind of imagining is a reliable source of knowledge (Section 1.1). I then discuss the epistemic value of thought experiments. I follow Tamar Gendler in characterizing thought experiments as epistemically valuable as they are capable of triggering reflections through processing mechanisms that abstract reasoning is not able to activate (Section 1.2). I introduce some examples of thought experiments to show their epistemic value, arguing that they are capable of playing a role especially in the fields of moral (Section 1.3) and political (Section 1.4) philosophy. The second section of the chapter is devoted to draw the analogy between thought experiments and film. My contention is that thought experiments are epistemically valuable and that films can function as thought experiments. As the first section of this chapter is devoted to defending the epistemic value of thought experiments, in the second section I develop the analogy between films and thought experiments. First, I consider some prominent objections to such analogy (Section 2.1), and then I dwell on the debate on cinema as philosophy. This is where the analogy between films and thought experiments has been developed. I explain the limits of the debate (Section 2.2) and then I analyze in detail Paisley Livingston's position, as it provides a useful starting point to discuss the relation between films' aesthetic properties and epistemic gains (Section 2.3). I argue that aesthetic properties and epistemic gains interplay and, in particular, I hold that, although we can paraphrase and discuss the philosophical import of a film, the epistemic contribution depends on the actual experience of the film, which cannot be paraphrased (Section 2.4).

DOI: 10.4324/9780367816872-7

1 Imagination and thought experiments

1.1 Imagination as a source of knowledge

Can we learn from imagination? It is usually held that perception, memory, consciousness (introspection), reason and testimony are reliable sources of knowledge (Audi, 2003). However, these sources of knowledge that we typically consider as reliable are also defeasible. None of them grants knowledge without risks. For instance, a memory of a past event may not be sufficiently accurate to provide true beliefs about the event; our perception may be altered so to deceive us about reality and, as we have seen in Chapter 4, even testimony depends on the trustworthiness of the testifier, who may make false statements and deceive us.[1] So, a reliable source of knowledge need not be indefeasible; there is always a certain degree of epistemic risk. For this reason, imagination can be seen as a valid candidate to be a source of knowledge: it does not grant, with certainty, true beliefs, but it is sufficiently reliable to justify some of them. Indeed, we do use imagination to deal with everyday situations and to make choices about the future. For instance, if I have to move some furniture with my car I can try to imagine whether they will fit in it. As I have a small car I am sure that my wardrobe does not fit in it, I do not need to try it to prove this belief true. On the contrary, if I dismantle my bookcase, I will be able to fit it in my car. Similarly, we can make decisions that are relevant for our future by imagining possible scenarios. For instance, I may have to decide what to do with my holidays, and I can try to imagine what it would be like to go trekking in the Alps even though I have never been on this kind of vacation. I may have to wake up early every day, and then leave for a walk after breakfast. I will probably be walking many miles per day on footpaths that can be steep, tortuous or even dangerous. I will be tired in the evening, but the tiredness will be paid off by the beauty of the landscapes I will encounter. I can even try harder and imagine what it would be like to trek on a difficult footpath, perhaps recalling a similar adventure or thinking of the kinds of emotions I would feel when facing those situations. Knowing that I am not an adventurous person, that I fear heights and that the last time I was on a hiking trail I felt scared, I may decide to avoid this kind of vacation and prefer a more relaxing holiday at the sea where I can lie on the beach all day.

Surely, when I imagine that something is the case, I can be mistaken. After all, the bookcase may not fit in my car. But the fact that I can err does not make the technique – imagination – inapt to justify beliefs. Imagination can be fallible, just as any other source of knowledge, and this does not make it unreliable.

Let us agree on a 'minimal' definition of imagination as 'the power of entertaining a thought-content – a proposition or a concept – without commitment to the proposition's truth (or falsity), or to the existence (or non-existence) of an object that instantiate the concept' (Gaut, 2007,

p. 151).[2] Imagination enables us to consider different alternatives without necessarily experiencing the imagined scenarios, and it can also provide alternatives that cannot be the case in reality. It is for these reasons, though, that skeptics may argue that imagination is unreliable. Indeed, imagination has, potentially, no constraints and it may misfire. For instance, we can imagine we would behave bravely in a dangerous situation, but when we actually experience that situation we may behave differently. So, the skeptics may have it, imagination cannot teach us about the actual world because I can imagine anything I want. Following Amy Kind (2016), we can put the skeptics' standpoint more systematically. She holds that there are three main reasons why imagination can be taken to be epistemically irrelevant: (1) imagination is typically under our voluntary control; (2) imagination is not world-sensitive, that is, the content of imagining is determined by the imaginer and does not depend on the actual world; and (3) imagination is uninformative, as it does not provide new information. Kind holds that the first two charges are true, but that does not prevent imagination from being epistemically relevant. Indeed, as she has it, truth may not be the constitutive aim of imagination but that does not mean that imagination cannot have truth as its aim (Kind, 2016). Following Kind, what we need, if we want imagination to aim for the truth, is to imagine with constraints: we need to control imagination and pursue the 'aim' of getting things right. Indeed, there are a number of examples whereby we imagine a scenario because we are interested in getting an answer: where will I go on vacation? As imagination is bound to our will, we can also control and guide it, so that it may accurately predict what is true in the actual world. If the first two charges are true, but nonetheless imagination can be epistemically relevant, then the third charge is false, since if imagination can be epistemically relevant, then it is not uninformative; indeed, imagining with constraints, with the aim of getting thigs right can provide new relevant information, for instance, I can decide to avoid that vacation on the Alps as I am not that adventurous, and I hate waking up early.

How do we constrain imagination? Berys Gaut suggests four different strategies that can discipline our imagination, and it is worth dwelling on them. (1) We should fit imagination with relevant evidence. When imagining that a specific situation is the case, we should check whether it fits any relevant evidence we may have. If we believe we would behave bravely in a given situation, we should check this possibility by confronting it with our actual behavior in a dangerous situation. Would I enjoy trekking in the Alps? To imagine the scenario I should recall my behavior and feelings in similar circumstances so to accurately foresee what my reaction would be. (2) We should avoid fantasy; following Gaut, we fantasize when we imagine something we take pleasure in imagining: as imagination depends on our volition, when we imagine about ourselves we run the risk of projecting our own desires and whishes onto the imagined scenario. For instance, we may enjoy the thought of having a vigorous confrontation with someone who has wronged us, yet sober reflection may convince us that we would actually behave differently. We run the same risk when we think of other persons' circumstances, as we run the risk of misrepresenting others' situations because we sentimentalize their circumstances, where Gaut uses 'sentimentality' with a negative acceptation as sentimental emotions are due to false or idealizing beliefs about their objects, so 'the avoidance of sentimentality is directly linked with the pursuit of truth' (p. 154).[3] (3) A resource for learning from imagination is experiential imagining. 'Experiential imagination, imagining what something is like, is a matter of entertaining a sensory or phenomenal thought without commitment to the thought-content's truth or instantiation' (p. 151). Experiential imagining involves particular attention to all the sensory and phenomenal details of a particular thought-content, and vividness is a key feature that enhances this type of imagining. To imagine something vividly is to imagine something in greater detail: 'the more vividly I imagine being tortured, the more intensely do I experientially imagine the situation in all relevant respects' (p. 151). Finally, (4) affective imagination is another resource that we can use to learn from imagination. Affective imagination does not amount to imagining what we would feel in a given situation: merely imagined state of affairs are capable of eliciting genuine emotions that we can use as checks for our imagined scenario;[4] indeed, the actual experience of the emotional state provides information about the scenario and ourselves, and the more vividly I can imagine the particular state of affairs, the more accurate will be my emotional experience. For instance, if I vividly imagine myself on a steep and dangerous path in the Alps, I can imagine the cold, the wind on my face, the physical difficulties I would have to endure and I may imagine what it is like to look below while walking through a narrow passage. Through the imagined state of affairs, I may come to feel fear and understand that I would not actually enjoy this kind of vacation. The emotional experience can tell us something about the scenario, or even about ourselves, as Gaut's example on torture shows: 'in imagining the instruments of torture with suitable vividness I may come to feel actual apprehension, disquiet and even fear, and so may come to learn through affective experience something about myself' (p. 155).[5]

1.2 *Imagination at play: thought experiments*

Let us return to the example of the vacation in the Alps. When I imagine myself on a steep and dangerous footpath, I try to figure out what it is like to be in that situation. I test the possibility that I may enjoy this kind of adventure, so I reason about this particular scenario, which is an imagined scenario, because I have never been trekking in the Alps before. I 'experiment-in-thought' what it would be like to be in that situation (see Gendler, 2004). Thought experiments are a tool used by scientists and philosophers alike to inquire into complex problems about the physical world or morality. Yet, the problem with these kinds of experiment is that they are not real: they are imagined, so they are not actually carried out. The question is, can we learn about the actual world by making up something? How is it possible that imagined scenarios can non-accidentally afford epistemic access to the real world?

These are questions about the epistemic reliability of thought experiments, but before I tackle such epistemological problems let me explain why we should be interested in their possible epistemic reliability. I contend that cinematic narratives can function like thought experiments and I will build a case for this analogy which requires a twofold argumentation: first we need to ascertain the epistemic reliability of thought experiments, and then we can verify whether the analogy between films and thought experiments can actually hold. If thought experiments are valuable tools to develop philosophical arguments and to justify beliefs, and cinematic fictional narratives can work as philosophical thought experiments inviting the audience to reason about specific sets of circumstances that are merely imagined, then we can conclude that cinematic fictional narratives can be epistemically valuable in virtue of their capacity to guide our imagination – they can serve to justify beliefs and develop arguments as they function just like thought experiments.

Before delving into the problem of the epistemic reliability of thought experiments, we need to grasp what they really are. Tamar Gendler holds that 'to perform a thought experiment is to reason about an imaginary scenario with the aim of confirming or disconfirming some hypothesis or theory' (2004, p. 1154).[6] When we perform a thought experiment we reason about a particular set of circumstances in great detail, but we can access this set of circumstances only via imagination, that is, the scenario cannot be properly observed. Moreover, we contemplate this scenario with a specific purpose, that of testing some hypothesis or theory. In my example, I aim to test the possibility that I may enjoy trekking in the Alps, hence, I consider this scenario in great detail: as I cannot actually observe it, I try to imagine it vividly.

Catherine Elgin (2014) marks a difference between actual scientific experiments and scientific thought experiments, and she holds that the difference lies simply in the fact that scientific thought experiments are not carried out. When we perform a scientific experiment we isolate the characteristics that we want to study and create a dedicated environment where a number of variables, which actually exist in nature, are completely left out, so that we can appreciate the behavior of the characteristics we are interested in. In the process of going from the field to the lab, the controls introduced may intervene in a significant way, like omitting something significant, so as to make the experiment incapable of explaining the real world. Hence, as Elgin has it, the trustworthiness of both a standard experiment and a thought experiment depends on the adequacy of the background assumptions and the obviousness with which they are designed (Elgin, 2014). Moreover, scientific experiments are dynamic events that unfold over time: they have a narrative structure, with a well-defined beginning, middle and end (Nersessian, 1992, 2007). In order to prepare the experiment, the scientist imagines how the events may unfold, and when he carries out the experiment the results need to be interpreted. Scientific thought experiments are very similar (Elgin, 2014). They also have a narrative structure, and they are to be interpreted; the difference is that the experiment does not actually take place. Scientific thought experiments are just imaginative exercises that aim to investigate what would happen if certain conditions were met. And the conditions they take into account need not even be realizable in the actual world. Standard experiments may begin as thought experiments with the scientist who has to design the experiment trying to foresee all possible scenarios and how the event will unravel. But thought experiments, contrary to standard experiments, are not actually implemented. They lack the actuality test.

However, even if we could say that scientific thought experiments have a clearer 'epistemological' position, as they are similar to actual scientific experiments, what about philosophical thought experiments? Philosophy makes extended use of thought experiments to articulate arguments, and the imagined scenarios that serve to test theories need not be framed within existing physical laws. For this reason, philosophical thought experiments are in an even more difficult position: what is it that makes them epistemically relevant?

To understand what makes a thought experiment epistemically relevant, we need to explain how they work. First we need to note that a thought experiment, per se, is not an argument (Häggqvist, 1998). Thought experiments cannot be considered arguments because they require interpretation and, as Gendler (2007) adds, because the reasoning they require is not based on deductive or inductive processes. Surely, thought experiments are related to arguments; indeed, both experiments and thought experiments work only through their connection with arguments (Häggqvist, 2009, p. 62). They both work in tight connection with arguments as they actually aim to prove the truth-value of a given theory or hypothesis, but they provide acceptance of the premises on which the arguments must depend. Let me explain these points with an example used by Gendler. She asks you to think of your neighbor's living room and to imagine painting the walls bright green. Would it clash with the current carpet or complement it? And then, if you were to remove all the furniture from the room, could you fit four elephants? Then if you remove all the elephants but one, could you ride a bike in the room without tipping as you turned? Reply to these questions and think of the process that leads to the relative beliefs. Did you apply deductive inferences moving from some known premises? Say, you have used your previously held beliefs about the size of elephants and of the living room, you also moved from 'a set of justified true beliefs concerning the solidity and limited malleability of elephants and living-room walls, a set of justified true beliefs concerning the possible configuration of objects in spaces governed by Euclidian geometry, and so on' (Gendler, 2004, p. 1158). Moving from these beliefs you may have come to deduce that four elephants, as a matter of fact, do not fit in the living room.

This is not what really happened in your mind, and this process seems even more unreasonable if you consider the other questions. How do you know whether the bright green paint will match the carpet? And how do you know whether you can ride a bike around the elephant in the living room? We come to form relative beliefs through manipulation of mental images. We have performed the 'experiment-in-thought' imagining our neighbor's living room in our head and then imagining it with bright green paint (the new information). And then again, we have imagined an elephant in the room, and we have imagined a certain experience, that of riding the bike in the room. Hence, following Gendler, we can say that we form these beliefs on a quasi-observational basis (see also Gendler, 1998, 2000).

How exactly do thought experiments work? Thought experiments are tools that 'pump' our intuitions – where intuitions are reactions to the *particularities* of individual cases, as opposed to more general reflective beliefs (Gaut, 2007) – recruiting representational schemas that were otherwise inactive.[7] They serve to frame, or reframe, problems and scenarios in ways that we may have not considered when reasoning in abstract and general terms, providing different perspectives on specific problems. Such framing, or reframing, activates different processing mechanisms that have been previously uninvolved. It is this capacity to activate different processing mechanisms that can foster the formation of beliefs that may be in disequilibrium with those already held, requiring revision to bring back equilibrium.

Let me start from an example to explain what I mean when I say that thought experiments activate 'different' processing mechanisms. Let us consider the trolley problem. This scenario was introduced by Philippa Foot, but it then became much debated, and the same moral problem the original scenario poses has been reframed with different scenarios. Foot (1978) asks you to imagine you are the driver of a trolley. The trolley rounds a bend and you see five workmen that are repairing the track. They cannot get off the track in time to save their lives, and the trolley's brakes do not work; so, if you want to save them you need to turn the trolley onto a parallel track. Unfortunately, on this track there is a workman who would not be able to save himself. Is it morally permissible to turn the trolley? You will kill one person to save five lives. This is one way of presenting the moral problem but not the only one. Judith Jarvis Thomson presents the same moral problem with a slightly different scenario:

> Consider a case – which I shall call *Fat Man* – in which you are standing on a footbridge over the trolley track. You can see a trolley hurtling down the track, out of control. You turn around to see where the trolley is headed, and there are five workmen on the track where it exits from under the footbridge. What to do? Being an expert on trolleys, you

> know of one certain way to stop an out-of-control trolley: Drop a really heavy weight in its path. But where to find one? It just so happens that standing next to you on the footbridge is a fat man, a really fat man. He is leaning over the railing, watching the trolley; all you have to do is give him a little shove, and over the railing he will go, onto the track in the path of the trolley. Would it be permissible for you to do this? Everyone to whom I have put this case says it would not be.
>
> (Thomson, 1985, p. 1409).

The moral problem remains the same: is it permissible to kill a person to save five? But the problem is presented is such a different way as to promote replies that can be different. As highlighted by Thomson, in the *Fat Man* scenario people seem less inclined to kill that one person in order to save five lives.

We need not dwell on the solution to the moral problem, as what we are interested in is the reason why there can be changes of beliefs from one formulation of the problem to the other. What happens in the *Fat Man* scenario that is so different from the first presentation of the problem? The problem has been presented differently, from another perspective, and this has activated different processing mechanisms that can bring forth a different appraisal of the situation.

Empirical investigations in cognitive and moral psychology have developed a broad literature on mental processing, showing, in particular, that presenting data differently, people find different ways to approach tasks or situations that would be otherwise identical. Such investigations have led to the elaboration of *dual processes* theories or *dual systems* accounts. These are theories about mental processing that stress how there are at least two different paths for the elaboration of information. One is automatic, implicit and unconscious, whereas the other is explicit and requires higher level cognitive capacities. Each path is activated by a different representational schema; here is where thought experiments can play a role: presenting a different scenario or perspective, thought experiments can activate a representational schema that may not have been active beforehand and that is elaborated by a different processing mechanism. This can potentially lead to the formation of beliefs that were previously disregarded or that can be in disequilibrium (inconsistent) with other already-held beliefs. The trolley problem is a case in point. Joshua Greene (2015), for instance, argues that characteristically consequentialist moral judgments are enabled by conscious reasoning and cognitive processes, whereas deontological judgments are driven by automatic, emotional responses. The abstract reasoning about the validity of consequentialism is based on high-level cognitive abilities, but when we imaginatively engage with the *Fat Man* scenario the automatic processing mechanism is activated, and this can lead to a different evaluation of the situation. The *Fat Man* scenario is a new representational schema that activates a processing mechanism that was not active in the abstract reasoning about consequentialism.

Greene and colleagues (2001, 2008, 2012) have conducted a number of experiments with fMRI proving that different areas of the brain are involved in deliberation when the moral dilemma is presented in a personal or an impersonal fashion. The first formulation of the trolley problem, where you just need to activate a switch to save the five lives, is an impersonal presentation of the problem as you are not 'directly' harming the one person that will die to save the other five. In the *Fat Man* scenario, you are asked to think of harming someone in a 'personal' and direct way. This personal formulation of the dilemma elicits an emotional response that is absent in the impersonal formulation. In the impersonal formulation of the dilemma, areas of the brain that are dedicated to the cognitive control (dorsolateral prefrontal cortex and inferior parietal lobe) are more involved in the elaboration of the judgment, and this results in the endorsement of the consequentialist standpoint. When a strong emotional, precognitive, response is elicited, different areas of the brain are activated – the amygdala (Greene, 2014; Greene, Sommerville, Nystrom, Darley, & Cohen, 2001; Greene, Morelli, Lowenberg, Nystrom, & Cohen, 2008) and the anterior cingulate cortex, which usually responds when two or more incompatible behavioral responses are activated (see Greene et al., 2008) – and the judgment elaborated tends to be typically deontological.

1.3 Thought experiments in moral philosophy

What the empirical investigations show is that there are at least two different processing mechanisms involved in our mental reasoning, and each of them can be activated with a different representational schema. This is clear in the case of the trolley problem. When we are presented with the first, impersonal, formulation of the problem, the cognitive and rational elaboration process is activated.[8] When we are presented with the second, more personal, formulation of the same dilemma, the automatic and emotional process kicks in.[9] The moral dilemma is the same but its different presentations serve to highlight the complexities of the dilemma. In the impersonal presentation you may come to think that it is morally permissible to kill one person to save five, but when you are confronted with the possibility to personally harm someone you may find that it is harder to give the same response. It is also worth noting that the presentations of the trolley problem can be even more complex, and similar examples are sometimes used to engage with the same dilemma; as in the case of the crying baby, where you are hiding with your baby and some other people from an army that wants to execute all of you. You hear the soldiers outside your door, and the baby starts crying. You must smother your child to death in order to save yourself and the others. Is this morally permissible? All the different formulations of the same problem show that thinking through imagined examples is epistemically relevant as such examples are capable of isolating and presenting different perspectives that complicate the scenario.

These thought experiments take the shape of fictional narratives and are particularly used in moral and political philosophy because imagining what it would be like in a certain situation is a central activity for moral thought; indeed, as moral judgments have bearings on other people, they are to pass the universalization test. This test requires that the judge, the proposer of the policy or the utterer of the judgment, would accept to be treated as the target of his proposed policy.[10] The difficulty of the universalization test is that it may not be straightforward for the judge to understand the target's situation properly. According to Berys Gaut (2007), the judge may have an improper understanding of the 'external' situation of the target – say, a proposer of the abolition of state-sponsored health care may believe that to be poor and sick may not be that bad after all – or an improper understanding of the target's psychology – what it means to be sick and unable to get treatment for a curable disease. Fiction can guide our imagination into the specific scenario of our target. So, guiding our imaginative practice, fictional narratives can provide vivid details of the situation and of the target's psychology. Such imaginative effort provides understanding of the situation and of the character's psychology in the given scenario. Thanks to such understanding we may come to realize that our beliefs were grounded on false premises or that we did not take into account all elements needed to utter a judgment on that particular case. In the previous chapter, I presented the case of Crialese's film *The Golden Door*, which aims to serve this very purpose: it tries to foster an understanding of what it means to be a migrant. When engaged with the film I confront my views on immigration with the particular perspective advanced by the film. I may have very restrictive views on immigration, but perhaps these views did not take into account an actual assessment of what it means to be a migrant and on what grounds we should forbid or allow migrants to enter the country.

There is another problem for the universalization test that is highlighted by Tamar Gendler (2007). The judge may not just misunderstand the target's situation, but he can also consider, perhaps unconsciously, himself as an exception: psychological studies have shown that people judge themselves with different eyes than when they are to judge other people. For instance,

> they consistently overestimate the likelihood that they will act generously or selflessly, while accurately predicting the ungenerosity and selfishness of others (whom they most likely turn out to resemble). Repeated studies have shown that people on average tend to think they are more charitable, cooperative, considerate, fair, kind, loyal, and sincere than the typical person but less belligerent, deceitful, gullible, lazy, impolite, mean, and unethical
>
> (Gendler, 2007, p. 81).

This means that persons may not be trustworthy judges of their own motives and behavior; they may be blind to their own possible deviance to the moral rule they claim to endorse. As an example, Gendler gives the biblical story of David and Bathsheba. David, King of Israel, is taken by Bathsheba's beauty and has her brought to the palace, where he lies with her, despite the fact that Bathsheba is married to Uriah, David's loyal soldier. Bathsheba becomes pregnant and David decides to send her husband to fight at the forefront of the hottest battle, so that he may be killed on the battlefield. David does not recognize the evil in his behavior and so God, displeased with David, sends Nathan to help David understand why his behavior is so problematic. Nathan tells David the following story:

> there were two men in one city; the one rich, and the other poor. The rich man had exceeding many flocks and herds: But the poor man had nothing, save one little ewe lamb, which . . . grew up together with him, and . . . was unto him as a daughter. And there came a traveller unto the rich man, and he spared to take of his own flock . . . but took the poor man's lamb, and dressed it for the man that was come to him
> (quoted in Gendler, 2007, p. 69).

Here David replies: 'as the Lord liveth, the man that hath done this thing shall surely die. And he shall restore the lamb fourfold, because he did this thing, and because he had no pity'. And Nathan then explains the story to David:

> Thou art the man . . . thou hast killed Uriah the Hittite with the sword, and hast taken his wife to be thy wife, and hast slain him with the sword of the children of Ammon. . .'. The story ends with David's recognition of his immoral behavior: 'I have sinned against the Lord.

David is unable to see how his own behavior is problematic, so Nathan has to reframe David's own story. Here we see how Nathan presents David with a thought experiment. He asks David to appraise the situation and the behavior of the rich man, but in doing so he also asks David to appraise his own behavior. The thought experiment here, reframing the events, allows for a judgment without David's first-person biases.

In light of these last considerations, we can once again appreciate the epistemic merits of reasoning through thought experiments. Abstract theoretical and moral knowledge is elaborated through specific processing mechanisms that require high-level cognitive skills. Thought experiments are capable of reframing the same abstract beliefs by testing them on fictional scenarios that are able to activate processing mechanisms that were otherwise inert. It is especially because of the affective imagination required to fully appreciate the scenarios presented that thought experiments are able to activate automatic processing mechanisms. Abstract knowledge is hardly capable of eliciting emotional response, but the imagined scenarios of thought experiments are so carefully designed as they aim to elicit also an emotional engagement.[11] By activating different processing mechanisms, thought experiments can bring new beliefs that may be in disequilibrium with the previously held beliefs on the issue at stake. So, following Gendler, we will say that the thought experiment is not just epistemically meritorious but it also succeeds as a device of persuasion if the evoked response becomes dominant, that is, in the process of reflecting on the consistency of our system of beliefs, we come to represent relevant non-thought experimental content in light of the thought experimental conclusion (see also Gendler, 2004).

1.4 Thought experiments in political philosophy

The epistemic merit of the thought experiment is that of presenting different and relevant perspectives that serve to test our beliefs. This process is of great importance for moral and political philosophy. So, let me focus the discussion more closely on problems of political philosophy. My view is that since political philosophy so often resorts to using thought experiments, then political films, when they are meant to work as thought experiments, can be conceived as argumentative tools for political philosophy, just as thought experiments are.

Rawls's argument (1964) supporting distributive justice is developed from the thought experiment of the original position, which is essential to understanding his theory. What are the principles of justice we would apply to our society? Rawls argues that these are the principles of liberty and equality, where the second is further divided into the fair opportunity principle and the difference principle (see Rawls, 1964). According to Rawls, our society should be organized following these principles because parties in the original position would choose such principles. The original position is an initial situation where parties are to make a choice about justice principles to apply in society. In order to avoid particularistic interest, Rawls posits that parties in the original position are behind a veil of ignorance:

> among the essential features of this situation is that no one knows his place in society, his class position or social status, nor does any one know his fortune in the distribution of natural assets and abilities, his intelligence, strength and the like. I shall even assume that the parties do not know their conceptions of the good or their special psychological propensities. The principles of justice are chosen behind a veil of ignorance
>
> (1964, p. 11).

Hence, parties lack knowledge of their own particular circumstances. They do not know their wealth, race, gender, skills, intelligence and education.

Yet, they have some general knowledge. In particular, despite the fact that they do not have particular interests, they have higher-order interests. They know that they will have a conception of the good, even if they do not know which one is going to be. So, they will want the best possible circumstances in order to be able to pursue such conception of the good, and they will want to be able to exercise their 'moral powers', entailing the capacity to reassess and change their conception of good. Hence, the parties in the original position have sufficient knowledge to understand that they will need social goods: rights and liberties, power and opportunities, income and wealth, and the social bases for self-respect. 'They assume that they normally prefer more primary social goods rather than less' (Rawls, 1964, p. 123). Since parties behind the veil of ignorance do not have any idea about their future position in society, among all various alternatives, they would choose the alternative whose worst outcome would leave them better off than the worst outcome of all other alternatives. There are other possible strategies of choice (e.g. the 'maximax' or the Bayesian maximization of expected utility), yet, following Rawls, parties in the original position would chose the 'maximin' rule, which aims to maximize the minimum outcome.

Rawls's theory of justice has been criticized from a number of angles: because of the implausibility of the maximin choice (Harsanyi, 1980), or due to a circularity of the argument (Bloom, 1975), or due to an alleged misconception of the self-implied by the theory (Sandel, 1998). For our purposes, however, the point is that Rawls developed an influential argument moving from a thought experiment, positing parties behind a veil of ignorance as if they were noumenical selves looking at the world.

Robert Nozick (1974) had a different conception of justice, as he advocated for an entitlement theory that could take into account changes in wealth distribution due to free transactions. To present his theory, Nozick invites us to reason about Chamberlain's example:

> It is not clear how those holding alternative conceptions of distributive justice can reject the entitlement conception of justice in holdings. For suppose a distribution favored by one of these non-entitlement conceptions is realized. Let us suppose it is your favorite one and let us call this distribution D1; perhaps everyone has an equal share, perhaps shares vary in accordance with some dimension you treasure. Now suppose that Wilt Chamberlain is greatly in demand by basketball teams, being a great gate attraction. (Also suppose contracts run for a year, with players being free agents.) He signs the following sort of contract with a team: In each home game, twenty-five cents from the price of each ticket of admission goes to him. (We ignore the question of whether he is 'gouging' the owners, letting them look for themselves.) The season starts, and people cheerfully attend his team's games; they buy their tickets, each time dropping a separate twenty-five cents of their admission price into a special box with Chamberlain's name on it. They are

> excited about seeing him play; it is worth the total admission price to them. Let us suppose that in one season one million persons attend his home games, and Wilt Chamberlain winds up with $250,000, a much larger sum than the average income and larger even than anyone else has. Is he entitled to this income? Is this new distribution D2 unjust? If so, why? . . . If D1 was a just distribution, and people voluntarily moved from it to D2, transferring parts of their shares they were given under D1 (what was it for if not to do something with?), isn't D2 also just?
> (1974, pp. 160–161).

Rawls and Nozick's thought experiments are clearly diverse, as diverse as all the other imaginative experiments deployed by philosophers in order to analyze counterfactuals or possible scenarios. Yet, these are prompts for intuitions that can direct our judgments about what is right or wrong, and I wanted to dwell on these examples to show how relevant these thought experiments are to the overall argument developed by the authors.

2 Film as thought experiment

2.1 Objections to the analogy

I defend the view that films have epistemic values, and such values can be justified through imagination: films can have an impact on the audience's system of beliefs because of the imaginative engagement they manage to elicit. Films guide our imagination into fictional worlds, and the epistemic gains they are capable of affording can be justified through our imaginative engagement. We have seen that imagination, with its constraints, is a reliable source of knowledge. So, guided imagination can also justify beliefs or more general epistemic gains. Indeed, thought experiments are an example of guided imagination that is capable of testing beliefs, theories and hypothesis. Now, I contend that films can be seen as thought experiments. However, I do not hold that all films are thought experiments; this seems implausible, especially if we consider nonfiction films, even though nonfiction films can also make use of thought experiments. I take it that this is the case of Joshua Oppenheim's *The Act of Killing* (2012) where the director asks the Indonesian *gangsters* to reenact the killings they perpetrated in their past. Moreover, I also do not hold that fiction films in order to be epistemically valuable necessarily need to be seen as thought experiments. This is one way, the one I defend here, of justifying the epistemic gains afforded by films. Films may not be intended to test theories or hypotheses and still have epistemic values – perhaps such values are justified through testimony.[12]

Do films function like thought experiments? In a general sense, all imaginative efforts, even assumptions, are thought experiments, as we entertain possibilities that are not the case in reality. But this is not the conception of thought experiments I have been using so far. I have been referring to a specific imaginative effort with a peculiar aim: that of testing (confirming or disconfirming) theories or hypotheses. So, thought experiments are designed to test beliefs. This is already quite relevant: this definition of a thought experiment implies that the experiment-in-thought is entertained for a reason. It has a specific purpose. So, to ask whether films can be seen as a thought experiment we need to ask whether films can be designed for that very purpose: to test beliefs.[13] Before I tackle this problem, let me take a step back to highlight something that may seem paradoxical.

Here I defend film's epistemic value by appealing to a specific epistemological tool: the thought experiment. Now, for my view (films are epistemically valuable since they can function as thought experiments) the problem is twofold. On the one hand, I need to defend the epistemic relevance of thought experiments (we can say this is a problem pertaining to the field of epistemology) while on the other I need to defend the view that films can function as thought experiments (and this is a problem in the philosophy of art). David Davies (2008) has noted that when films have been compared to thought experiments, the epistemological-side-of-the-fence has been rarely taken into account.[14] And in philosophy of art, the comparison between films and thought experiments serves to justify the epistemic capacities of artworks. This creates a paradoxical situation. In epistemology, the epistemic relevance of thought experiments is questioned as they are fictional; that is, for the same reason why, in philosophy of art, they are compared to films and narratives more generally. So, what grounds the comparison – their being fiction – may be the very reason why they are not epistemically valuable.

In the previous section of this chapter, I have defended thought experiments' capacity to be epistemically relevant. I endorse Tamar Gendler's conception of thought experiments, which can be labeled as a moderate inflationist view.[15] Inflationary views hold that thought experiments have a unique epistemic capacity that cannot be matched by the abstract reconstruction of arguments.[16] Thought experiments, for the moderate inflationist, mobilize already available cognitive resources in a new fashion, and despite being linked to arguments, they cannot be straightforwardly translated into deductive and inductive arguments. When they are translated into arguments, there is an epistemic loss. We can build up the inferential chain surrounding thought experiments and we can find out that we have valid arguments, but we will lose a specific path to knowledge: the capacity of thought experiments to activate different processing mechanisms that the abstract reasoning does not mobilize. This means that the value of thought experiments is not merely heuristic or rhetorical, but specifically epistemic.[17] Their epistemic value is not due to *what* they bring about – perhaps we could acquire the same beliefs from abstract reasoning or actual empirical tests – but rather to the '*how*' they are capable of mobilizing our cognitive stock.

With this conception of thought experiments at hand, we can cross the fence and compare thought experiments to films. This comparison is welcomed by philosophers who are in the business of defending film's capacity to philosophize.[18] I will clarify my position in the debate on Film as Philosophy (FaP) later on, but first I want to challenge Murray Smith's skeptical view on film's capacity to function as thought experiments (Smith, 2006).[19]

Smith's argument is not against films' capacity to bring epistemic contributions but more specifically against the comparison between film and thought experiments. So, Smith holds, films are not thought experiments, and the two, films and thought experiments, cannot be compared because they have different purposes. Thought experiments have an *epistemic role*, as they are designed to investigate the epistemic complexities of the actual world, whereas films have a different, entertaining role. To back up his argument, Smith brings two examples: Bernard Williams's thought experiment where a magician is capable of making an emperor and a peasant change places and Carl Reiner's romantic comedy *All of Me* (1984), whose premise is somewhat similar to that of the thought experiment, as the comedy plays on a case of 'cohabitation'; a case where the mind of two persons – that of Roger Cobb (played by Steve Martin) and of Edwina Cutwater (played by Lili Tomlin) – are simultaneously cohabiting the same body (that of Roger Cobb). The purpose of Williams's experiment is that of undermining dualism and bringing a contribution to problems in philosophy of mind. The purpose of *All of Me* has nothing to do with any philosophical project. Indeed, the film plays on the absurd consequences of having two minds in the same body, and its aim is to amuse and entertain the audience. I contend that the choice of examples is not ideal to elucidate the problem at stake. Smith is right when he says that *All of Me* has no epistemic role; after all, the film simply uses the absurd consequences of a thought experiment as the premise of the comedy, but it is not intended to 'function' as the thought experiment itself, that is, it does not aim at investigating the epistemic complexities of the mind/body distinction. However, that does not mean that there may not be films aiming to bring epistemic contributions. And, as a matter of fact, this is exactly the case with political films.[20] For instance, *Dead Man Walking* aimed to have an impact on the debate around the death penalty; Marco Bellocchio's film *The Sleeping Beauty* aims to elicit reflection on euthanasia, *4 Months 3 Weeks 2 Days* (Mungiu, 2007) on abortion and *The Golden Door* on immigration. In order to understand these films, we need to assess their capacity to bring an epistemic contribution.[21]

Smith, however, may still hold that films are not like thought experiments, and this is because films are replete with details that thought experiments do not use and that are useless from an epistemic perspective. Indeed, Smith argues that thought experiments require what Moran calls *hypothetical imagining*, whereas films require *dramatic imagining* (Moran, 1994). The latter kind of imagining involves a ramification of the counterfactual in specific ways: 'we might imagine experiencing the events "from the inside," that is, as a witness or as a participant, rather than imagining *that* the events occur' (2006, p. 39). On the other hand, hypothetical imagining simply requires that we imagine a counterfactual in a 'spare and abstract way' (p. 39). The problem, here, is that films provide details that, according to Smith, are useless for epistemic investigation, and thought experiments simply require that we imagine a counterfactual in *spare and abstract* fashion. Is this really the case, though? First, we may want to say that some thought experiments, especially those in moral philosophy, are quite detailed. Think of John Rawls's 'the original position', Elizabeth Anderson's 'mountain-climbing game' (2006), Ronald Dworkin's 'auction' (1981) or Judith Jarvis Thomson's 'violinist linked by the kidneys' (1976). Or, we could consider Bernard Williams's objection to consequentialism (2012), advanced through a thought experiment: Jim finds himself in a small town in South America, and he sees 20 Indians tied up against the wall. Jim finds out that the 'heavy man in a sweat-stained khaki shirt' is the captain in charge, who is about to tell Pedro to execute all the Indians. To analyze the problems for consequentialism, we would not need to focus on the literary details of the story written by Williams, and the scenario could be rewritten in a much drier fashion: 'X is about to execute twenty persons, Y can save nineteen of them by killing one'. My story describes the same moral problem, and it highlights the same difficulties for consequentialism. Yet, it is much less effective. Williams's story provides a clear set of circumstances that the reader is invited to imagine vividly. In so doing, fostering the imaginative participation of the reader, the person who may want to endorse utilitarian principles may find out clearly the consequences of such endorsement. For being a short story, one that we are to imagine abstractly and sparsely, Williams gives us quite a lot of detail; for instance, we do not need to know that we are in South America nor that the head of the military wears a khaki shirt. These seem to be details that are superfluous to *hypothetical imagining*.

However, and most importantly, the details that enable *dramatic imagining* are fundamental for moral reasoning. We have seen earlier that thought experiments are useful in moral reasoning, as when we utter moral judgments we think of them as universalizable. The difficulty with the universalization test is that we may fail to actually understand the situation of a person who finds himself in the target position. Here is where thought experiments' lushness of details become useful: we imagine what it would be like to be in that situation (that of the target position) and consider the possibility of endorsing the moral judgment. Our imaginative effort, however, cannot be spare and abstract, as we otherwise run the risk of misrepresenting the target position and make the test unreliable.

For instance, let us reconsider my analysis of Emanuele Crialese's film *The Golden Door*. When we discuss policies about immigration, we consider moral judgments related to the treatment and dignity of migrants. Would we accept the same policy were we in the migrants' position? We can entertain a thought experiment to see if we would endorse the same policy, but

I contend that the more detailed this thought experiment can be, the more reliable is the universalization test. If we entertain the experiment in a spare and abstract fashion, we run the risk of misrepresenting either the 'external' condition of being a migrant, that is, we may not understand the difficulties and struggles migrants have to face, or we risk misrepresenting the 'internal' condition of being a migrant, that is, what it is like to be in that situation.[22] This latter condition requires a psychological understanding that cannot be provided by spare and abstract imagination. Indeed, Crialese provides relevant details of the Mancuso family, which allow for a complete understanding of their mental states. For instance, the first part of the film narrative focuses on the Mancusos' life at their village. This part of the narrative is far from being irrelevant for the thought experiment itself. These details on the Mancusos' life provide valuable background knowledge that can help us frame and understand them: they are a poor family from rural Sicily; they are uneducated, religious, believe in supernatural forces and have an idealized image of the New World where chickens are as big as humans and money grows on trees. It is thanks to these details that we can better understand their feelings throughout the journey, and these details foster the dramatic imagining Smith is hinting at. But far from being counterproductive, they are what make the thought experiment successful. In particular, the final sequence, when Fortunata decides to leave the family and return to Sicily, is designed to elicit empathic engagement with the men of the family.[23] Crialese lingers with close-ups on the faces of each member of the family in order to foster emotional contagion and affective mimicry, but we actually feel the same sadness and the same fear the Mancusos are feeling, not just because we are drawn to simulate their mental states, but also because we have a sufficiently complex understanding of the characters' psychology, beliefs and desires. It is the combination of the sensory inputs (our capacity to see facial expressions and to simulate them) and the higher-level cognitive elaborations of the characters' psychology that leads to empathic engagement: our capacity to feel what the other feels, for the reasons why the other feels it. In Chapter 7, I provide a more detailed account of empathic engagement, which is based on Murray Smith's characterization of the concept, and that entails both elements of simulation theory and a sufficiently articulated knowledge of the other self's psychology. In other words, it is because I agree with Smith on what counts as empathic engagement and because I take empathy to be a relevant moral skill, that I cannot agree with the view that dramatic imagining is not necessary for thought experiments.

2.2 *Film as philosophy*

I take it that the first question that we should face is: why would we care about a film's capacity to philosophize? We want a film to be epistemically valuable, so that it can bring a contribution to knowledge.[24] I suspect that philosophy has a similar scope in this regard, that is, philosophical theories aim to make a contribution to knowledge. What if a film is epistemically valuable but it does not philosophize? I do not see much of a problem here; what counts is the epistemic value of the film and how, if, this is somehow linked to the aesthetic properties of the work. Now, suppose we say that a film can foster our moral education. We say that the film is epistemically valuable, and more specifically that it brings a contribution to the sphere of moral knowledge. As the film brings a contribution in a particular sphere that is usually a battlefield for philosophers, do we say that the film philosophizes? I am not sure about the answer here, but perhaps we need not worry too much about it: we care about the fact that the film brings an epistemic contribution. Why do we need to inquire about the method through which such a contribution is brought about? Is the film better off if we can say that it philosophizes? There are two reasons why we may want to hold that a film is better off if it philosophizes. The first is that we may see the act of philosophizing-as-a-value per se, independent of an epistemic contribution the film may bring. Or, and this is the second reason, what is of value is the possible contribution to a specifically 'philosophical' episteme. Let me analyze both possibilities in turn.

The case of 'philosophizing-as-a-value' treats the act of philosophizing as the valued end, independently of its outcome. In order to analyze this standpoint, we first need a definition of philosophy and of what counts as philosophizing. This is only the first difficulty that afflicts the FaP debate. Smith (2006) criticizes what he calls an 'expansive' strategy of authors who adopt an all-inclusive conception of philosophy.[25] The expansive strategy expands the definition of philosophy to the extent that it makes the idea that films can be philosophically relevant only trivially true. However, a strategy that aims to narrow the boundaries of philosophy runs a similar risk. If we count as philosophy only the scholarly lectures and publications in academic journals, then, again, it is only trivially true that films cannot philosophize. To define philosophy, we face a challenge that I am not sure can be met. A definition aims to establish clear boundaries but also to identify all instances of what is to be defined. A narrow definition of philosophy, as to entail only academic activities, identifies clear boundaries, but such boundaries seem artificial and fail to capture the 'essence' of philosophy. However, when we try to broaden the boundaries of philosophy, we run the risk of making such boundaries unclear. Paisley Livingston holds that

> philosophy refers to *more or less systematic* investigative, expressive, and communicative activities, at a *high level of generality and abstraction*, pertaining to the world and our knowledge of it; philosophers investigate, discuss, and pronounce upon a range of significant, general topics concerning the nature of reality, and, in particular, human action and value. The privileged, though not exclusive, methods that philosophers use in such investigations and communications include reasoning and argumentation *as well as attention to examples, whether*

> *actual or imagined*, that may be indicative of more general patterns and possibilities
>
> (2009, p. 12, italics mine).

The aim of this definition is clearly that of being broader than the narrow conception of philosophy and, according to Livingston, this definition has two virtues: it covers many items that are readily identified as philosophy and it is neutral with regard to the relation between cinema and philosophy (2009, p. 12). The virtues of this definition, however, do not really solve the problems of clarity: can we trace a clear distinction between what counts as philosophy and what does not? Livingston himself admits that the definition is vague, and I take it that it still leaves philosophy as an exceedingly broad concept. Indeed, activities that are investigative, expressive and communicative, be they *more or less systematic*, do count as philosophizing, and there is not a strict variety of topics that counts as 'typically' philosophical. But one thing seems to be clear: philosophy is a method and it is something done for something else – investigate, communicate or express. So, perhaps, we need not wrestle with the definition of philosophy as long as we agree on the idea that it is a method, a means to knowledge. We value philosophy as it can afford epistemic gains. But then, if philosophy is a means to knowledge or, more generally, epistemic gains, we can see that philosophizing is not a value per se. Hence, I take it, the debate on FaP is a subspecies of the debate concerning films' capacity to afford epistemic gains, but one that is uninformative, for the definition of philosophy, only adds to the difficulties instead of simplifying or clarifying, and the focus of our assessment should be the quality of the epistemic contribution and its relation to aesthetic properties.

Let me also entertain the second possibility listed previously: perhaps what we mean by 'film as philosophy' is that a film can bring a contribution to what can be labeled a 'specifically philosophical episteme'. It means that there is some knowledge that is specifically philosophical. But is there such a kind of knowledge? Smith (2006) seems to grant that this kind of knowledge exists, as he holds that there is a gap to be closed between knowledge in general and philosophical knowledge (p. 35). But what is philosophical knowledge?[26] One way to go could be that of pointing to the knowledge about 'philosophy' – that is, the discipline. So, this kind of knowledge would be either knowledge of the history of philosophy or some philosophy of philosophy – perhaps like what we are doing right now: a reflection on the methods of philosophy that could count as some kind of meta-philosophy. However, we would then need to say that we, or a film, philosophize *only* when engaged in these kinds of reflections, which seems implausible. Moreover, this is not the declination of 'philosophizing' implied by authors in the debate on FaP.

This was just to highlight the fact that the debate on FaP seems tainted by an unsolvable problem of definition: if we define philosophy too broadly, then we trivialize the problem. If we define it too narrowly, then we probably fail to identify philosophy tout court. But, and this is the most important thing I want to emphasize, I take it that no matter how one defines philosophy, this debate is of secondary importance: if a film affords epistemic gains, we are better off enquiring into the quality of the epistemic contribution and into the relation between such epistemic gains and the aesthetic properties of the film rather than debating what constitutes philosophizing, since the method (philosophical or not, if one can trace the difference) through which the epistemic contribution is achieved does not seem to add to the contribution itself.

Perhaps one way to distinguish the FaP debate from the general debate on films' epistemic values is to limit the topics that are unique to philosophical investigation. Livingston suggests that philosophers 'investigate, discuss, and pronounce upon a range of significant, general topics concerning the nature of reality, and, in particular, human action and value'. This sentence does not seem capable of tracing a clear line of demarcation for those topics that are typically or uniquely philosophical. Some of the examples that are typically discussed in the FaP debate clearly are about these topics – consider Wartenberg's analysis of *The Matrix*, or Livingston's own analysis of Ingmar Bergman's *Persona*.[27] However, the clause 'human action and value' is deliberately vague, so as to cover all possible spheres of knowledge in which philosophers have a say. For instance, reconsider the case of *The Golden Door*. Does the film philosophize? The film's theme may not strike one immediately as being philosophically relevant, but how we are to treat immigrants and whether they should be considered as citizens are important questions of political philosophy.

2.3 Cinematic features and epistemic gains

Here I want to linger on Livingston's position not only because it presents a challenge to those who want to hold that films can philosophize but also since it unveils problems that can be relevant in the general debate on art's epistemic values. Moreover, Livingston's analysis has the merit of focusing exclusively on films, whereas the debate on art's epistemic values is rarely framed in such specific terms.

Livingston holds that a thesis about FaP needs to entail two different claims. One about the film's capacity to make a philosophical contribution that can be seen as original and significant (this is what he calls the 'ends condition') and another about the exclusivity of the cinematographic means used to make such contributions (the 'means condition'). In other words, a thesis about FaP needs to provide an answer to two questions: (1) Can a film make an innovative contribution to philosophy? (2) Can it do so, can it contribute to philosophy, by means that are exclusively cinematographic? Proponents of films' capacity to philosophize can then disagree about the strength of the claims they are willing to endorse. Indeed, for each condition there is a strong and a more moderate claim. As for the 'ends' condition, there is a strong claim: cinema can make an innovative contribution to philosophy, and a moderate one: films can at best 'illustrate' or bring to mind philosophical views that have been introduced elsewhere (Livingston, 2009, p. 13). As for the means condition, there is a strong claim – there are exclusively cinematographic means that are able to articulate the philosophical contribution – and a moderate claim: the philosophical contribution can be translated (paraphrased) into linguistic terms. Hence, there are four possible theses about FaP that result from the combination of the different claims. The 'bold thesis' entails strong claims for both conditions, whereas what we may call the 'most-moderate thesis' entails the moderate claims for each condition. Other moderate theses can entail a strong claim for one condition but not for the other. Livingston advocates for the most-moderate thesis, and he holds that the bold thesis presents an unsolvable dilemma. The dilemma stems from an unclear definition of what counts as the 'specificities' of the cinematic medium. Livingston holds that if a film can make an innovative, independent and 'purely' filmic philosophical achievement, then the innovative insight cannot be paraphrased, and this inevitably casts doubts on its very existence. However, if we can paraphrase the insight, then, following Livingston, the linguistic mediation would be constitutive of the epistemic contribution. On the other hand, if we endorse a broad conception of cinema's exclusive capacities, it will only be trivially true that cinema can make philosophical contributions (even innovative contributions).[28] Indeed, suppose that we take cinema's 'recording and representational' capacity as 'exclusive' of the cinematic medium, then a recording of a philosophical lecture may also count as an exclusively cinematographic contribution to philosophy.

So, the problem for the bold thesis is that if it defines the 'exclusive' cinematographic capacities too broadly, it trivializes the problems, but if we take the purely filmic philosophical achievement as being impossible to translate, then we may doubt its very existence.

Livingston, though, is too drastic in his framing of the possibilities for supporters of the bold thesis. According to the author, the bold thesis cannot hold as it depends on the assumption that if there is a *purely cinematographic* way to make a philosophical contribution, *such a contribution* cannot be paraphrased. Therefore, if we can paraphrase a philosophical insight, then this is not 'purely' cinematographic. But what counts as 'purely' cinematographic? And what exactly is it that cannot be translated?

As David Davies notes (2008), cinema is a mixed art, and the specificity of the medium is to be related to the interplay of all the different features and tools at a director's disposal. The verbal medium counts as part of the 'cinematic' medium, which brings us to the problem of the recorded philosophical lecture: is this a valid example of a philosophical contribution brought through the cinematic medium? According to Davies, we need not have recourse to an extremely narrow conception of what is exclusive of the cinematic medium if we only need to make a distinction between the verbal and the cinematic medium. We just need a criterion that can help us differentiate between the two. Here is Davies's suggestion:

> suppose that *M2* is a verbal medium that can be used to articulate content of type *C*, and that *M1* is a mixed medium that incorporates *M2* as one of its elements. Then *M1* can be rightly viewed as a distinct medium for articulating this type of content iff, for some such content *Cn*, an 'utterance' *U* in *M1* articulates Cn and it is not the case that the utterance in *M2* contained in *U* articulates *Cn*
>
> (Davies, 2008, p. 14).

To explain the difference between the two mediums, Davies uses as an example the indication we give when we help someone maneuver his car into a parking space. We use a combination of verbal communication and hand gestures, and while the verbal communication contributes, the overall articulated content exceeds the contribution given by the verbal communication alone, as it is a combination of the verbal and gestural communication. So, M1, the mixed medium, can be seen as different from M2, the verbal medium, as the 'utterance' U in M1 exceeds the utterance in M2 contained in U.[29] So, with Davies, we can say that a film is able to make a philosophical contribution that is medium-exclusive to the verbal medium if there is a 'film *F* and some philosophically relevant content *PCa* such that F articulates *PCa* while it is not the case that *PCa* is articulated by the verbal content of *F*' (Davies, 2008, p. 14). This is an excellent criterion that can help us highlight how some contributions cannot be reduced to their verbal articulation. However, this criterion alone does not really tackle the dilemma of paraphrase.

Opponents of the bold thesis may still reply that the overall articulated content requires linguistic mediation to be brought into the philosophical arena. Indeed, Livingston's claim is that the philosophical contribution is only made possible through an interpretation (paraphrase) that is guided by linguistically articulated philosophical background assumptions. If this contribution cannot be paraphrased, then we may as well doubt its very existence. Here, I take it that we need to clarify what it is that cannot be paraphrased. I hold that there is a *purely cinematographic* way to make a philosophical contribution, and that *such contribution* cannot be paraphrased. However, we need to differentiate between the '*how*' (how is this contribution made?) and the '*what*' (what is this contribution about?). The '*what*' can be paraphrased, whereas the '*how*' cannot be paraphrased without an epistemic loss.

To explain what cannot be paraphrased of the epistemic contribution brought by films, I need to recall the epistemological view of thought experiments I have been advocating in this chapter. I hold that thought experiments are epistemically meritorious as they are capable of activating processing mechanisms that abstract reflection may not activate. So, thought experiments work with cognitive resources that are already available; they simply try a different route to activate such cognitive resources. Following Gendler, I also hold that thought experiments cannot be translated or paraphrased into arguments although they clearly are linked to and form part of arguments. They are not arguments though, as they do not depend on deductive and inductive inferences, and we cannot paraphrase a thought experiment into an argument without epistemic loss. What we lose when we paraphrase a thought experiment is exactly what makes it epistemically valuable: its capacity to activate different processing mechanisms. We can analyze the contribution of the thought experiment: when we talk about consequentialist and deontological theories, we import into the philosophical arena the intuitions prompted by the trolley problem. When we discuss the discomfort we would feel in choosing consequentialism, we can do that in abstract and general terms, perhaps discussing categorical imperatives. But if I want you to feel that very discomfort, I will have you work through the *Fat Man* scenario. We can surely paraphrase the message of this thought experiment: consequentialism brings unwelcomed consequences, as when you have to kill someone in order to save other people. But the paraphrase and the reasoning about such consequences requires high-level cognitive capacities. The actual thought experiment prompts the same considerations but by activating lower-level automatic reactions. We can paraphrase the message, but there is a specificity in the way the thought experiment activates automatic processing mechanisms that cannot be translated. The description and paraphrase of the experiment that activates automatic processing mechanisms does not activate those very mechanisms. So, the best way to conceive of the discomfort we feel when killing someone to save other lives is to perform the thought experiment and to imagine pushing the fat man from the bridge.

Let me focus the analysis on a single scene to show how films can use a wide array of features to guide an audience's imaginative engagement. All these features, which directors can utilize, contribute to the elicitation of affective automatic responses. By way of example, I will focus exclusively on the final scene of *The Golden Door*. In the final scene, the Mancuso family is summoned by the border police in a common room on Ellis Island; the police communicates to the family that Fortunata and Pietro cannot enter the New World, as she is feebleminded and Pietro is mute. Salvatore is asked what he intends to do. He can either enter the country with Angelo, leaving Pietro and Fortunata behind, or they can all return to Italy. Salvatore then makes a speech defending Pietro and Fortunata, as he does not want to go back to Italy but does not intend to leave his mother and son behind. The scene ends with Pietro speaking up for the first time in the film. Here Pietro does the talking on behalf of his grandmother, who remains silent throughout the scene. Pietro communicates Fortunata's decision to the family: she intends to go back to Sicily, but she wants them to continue their journey to the New World. The scene has a symbolic meaning, the males of the family are allowed into the New World with the new female figure (Luce – Charlotte Gainsbourg). Fortunata, the old woman of the family, represents the homeland (in Italian, homeland is a female noun: *la patria*), which needs to be left behind if the family is to enter the New World (with the new/young female character). The scene elicits empathy with the male characters: we feel the same sorrow and fear they are feeling as they must abandon their matriarch/homeland and enter the unknown New World. The empathic engagement is elicited through a number of cinematic features, including some details provided by the narrative structure (more on empathic engagement in the next chapter), but this scene in particular makes use of elements of the mise-en-scène together with some features of the cinematography that foster this kind of imaginative engagement.

The room to which the family is summoned is crowded, but Crialese wants to highlight the symbolic relevance of the scene, so the mise-en-scène aims to create a surreal atmosphere and to focus attention on the family. The camera frames the family with a medium shot. The composition of the shot is balanced: the two boys and the grandmother are placed on the right side of the shot, forming a triangle, whereas Salvatore, who does the main talking in the scene, is left alone on the left side of the shot. The lighting of the scene is characterized by the lack of a backlight to emphasize a two-dimensional perception of the scene, as if the family were painted on a black canvas. The lighting, the actors' performance, the composition and the stillness of the camera combine to provide a surreal character to the scene.

Other than in the very opening of the scene, we never see the police. The camera takes its vantage point, and it is as if the Mancuso family were put on trial in front of the spectator. The stillness of this surreal scene is only broken when Pietro lifts his head and suddenly starts to speak to his father. Salvatore and Angelo, surprised, turn their heads to Pietro, whereas Fortunata keeps on staring at the floor. While Pietro speaks of his grandmother's decision, Salvatore turns toward Fortunata. Pietro speaks for his grandmother, and Fortunata's facial expression mirrors the gravity of Pietro's words. Fortunata does not talk in the scene, but the actress's performance signals her melancholy and resignation. She lifts her hand on Salvatore's face first, then she caresses Angelo and finally she lifts Pietro's chin and smiles to her grandson. The camera lingers with close-ups on Salvatore, Angelo and then on Fortunata and Pietro's face to highlight their facial expression.

The sequence ends in an unreal silence. We return to the initial medium shot of the family, and the newly found stillness suggests that this shot is to be seen as a painting. Fortunata and Pietro have their faces looking down toward the left of the camera, whereas Angelo and Salvatore look toward the right where the police are supposed to sit. The shot then fades out to a white screen (in sharp contrast to the previous scene), which is the sea of milk in which the family swims with Luce and all the other migrants.

The verbal medium in this scene is doing minimal work; Pietro simply communicates Fortunata's decision, but he does not comment on it. It is the lighting, the composition of the shots, the actors' performance and the cinematography that all together contribute to elicit empathic engagement with the characters and that convey a sense of metaphorical relevance, where Fortunata symbolizes the old and beloved homeland that is to be left behind.

Note that I have described the scene and the kind of response it aims to elicit. Also, note that we are capable of talking of the symbolic relevance of the scene and of the value this scene has within the overall theme of the film. However, the description does not actually elicit the kind of affective response the film is designed to elicit! To feel that kind of engagement with the film, one must experience the film itself.

2.4 The bold thesis reassessed

These lower-level automatic activities do not happen in a vacuum. They happen at the subconscious level of a spectator who is engaged with the film. The spectator's experience, however, is not only made of automatic reactions to perceptual stimuli; the experience, rather, is the result of the interplay between the low-level automatic activities and the higher-level cognitive capacities.[30] The interplay between low-level automatic processing mechanisms and high-level cognitive activities allows us to develop complex reasoning about the issue at stake, integrating automatic reactions and reflection.[31] It means that the spectator is able to contextualize his or her automatic reactions and understand them in terms of general and abstract reflections.[32] What we feel for the Mancuso family is put in relation with complex questions about the dignity of a person and issues on immigration. Perhaps, Livingston would argue that it is the spectator's capacity to appraise their own automatic reactions in terms of more abstract reasoning that shifts the philosophical 'agency' from the film to the spectator, and to this extent it is not the film that can philosophize but the spectator. However, this conclusion fails to see the epistemic contribution brought by films and by thought experiments in general. Indeed, this view of philosophical activity has as its core abstract reasoning, but philosophy, and reasoning in general, is meant to be applied to, and to explain, particular cases.[33] As we have seen, in moral and political philosophy, thought experiments are an integral part of the argumentation, and they play a specific epistemic role, as they aim to elicit the activation of those mechanisms that are not activated through abstract reasoning.

Returning to the paraphrase dilemma, what we can paraphrase is the philosophical meaning of a thought experiment, and we can linguistically articulate its relation to the argument it is meant to develop (the thesis or hypothesis it is meant to confirm or disconfirm), but we cannot paraphrase its epistemic import in terms of efficiency. The same happens with cinema. We can paraphrase the meaning of a film, its message and its relation to philosophical arguments. But as the epistemic contribution depends on the activation of automatic processing mechanisms that are activated by the specific experience of the thought experiment, we cannot paraphrase the thought experiment, or the film, itself without an epistemic loss. This loss is a loss in efficiency, as to activate those very automatic low-level reactions we need to perform the thought experiments, or *experience* the film.

To be even more specific, there are two qualities that we cannot paraphrase: the *rhetorical efficiency* and the *epistemic efficiency*.[34] The film's *rhetorical efficiency* is due to the film's capacity to 'simplify' and make more concrete the abstract reasoning, so that it may also be understood by the layperson. The use of examples is one of the techniques more commonly accepted and encouraged for rhetorical purposes, not just because it makes the reasoning more accessible to the public, but also because it allows the rhetor to elicit emotions in the audience.[35] The *epistemic efficiency* consists in the film's capacity to activate those automatic, low-level, processing mechanisms that would have been otherwise inert. As in the case of a thought experiment, the description of the film/thought experiment does not activate those very mechanisms that are mobilized only through the experience of the film/thought experiment itself.

Both the rhetorical efficiency and the epistemic efficiency cannot be paraphrased; they are 'purely' cinematic. They cannot be paraphrased without epistemic and rhetorical loss, because the paraphrase does not achieve the same epistemic (activation of automatic processing mechanisms) and rhetorical (simplification and emotion engagement) merits. Moreover, we can say that rhetorical and epistemic efficiency are possible, thanks to means that are exclusively cinematic, to the extent that the filmic way of achieving rhetorical and epistemic values is not exclusively anchored to the verbal medium but instead depends on a combination of different features that are typical of cinematic representation and that combine to articulate contents in ways that the verbal medium alone cannot articulate.[36] As we have seen from the description of the final scene of *The Golden Door*, it is elements from the mise-en-scène, the editing, the cinematography and the soundtrack in combination with one another that guide the spectator's experience. How the combination of these features manages to bring the epistemic contribution is also proof of the interrelation between aesthetic and epistemic values. Indeed, the aesthetic properties (from the more formal properties like the color pallet or the type of shot used, its angle and length, to the more expressive properties like the capacity to move the audience or elicit emotion) combine to guide the imaginative engagement and to afford the epistemic gain.

The epistemic gain is driven by the affective automatic response. A film manages to have an impact on the spectator's system of belief as it triggers a reflection on complex issues starting from an automatic affective response that activates a process of examination and appraisal at a higher cognitive level. The automatic affective response is elicited through the combination of cinematographic features and their interplay with the narrative. Amy Coplan goes so far as to say that cinema has an advantage over literature when it comes to eliciting affective, noncognitive reactions due to some features being available to directors that writers cannot use; in particular she points to 'various forms of camera movement and shot composition, editing styles, lighting design, set design including the colour, placement, and relationship of various objects in the diegetic world, and sound design' (Coplan & Matravers, 2011, p. 121). Here Coplan aims to highlight how cinema can elicit affective responses through means that are typically cinematographic and that are not available to writers. In particular, she stresses the role of close-ups in favoring emotional contagion and that of sound design and music in establishing mood and eliciting affective responses. We need not endorse the argument that cinema is better placed than literature in eliciting affective responses; after all, literature may make use of different features to reach the same aim.[37] Coplan's attempt to defend the peculiarity of cinema is interesting to us as it registers how there are some typically cinematographic features that are apt to elicit affective responses.[38] However, we need not limit the list of such valuable features to those that are not available to writers; the combination of cinematographic features, including the verbal medium, 'scaffolds' the affective responses that can enable epistemic gains.

This process shows how aesthetic properties play a role in affording epistemic gains, and at the same time the epistemic gain afforded constitutes itself as an aesthetic property; indeed, we say that artworks can be intellectually challenging and compelling, and these qualities are essential components of the aesthetic experience afforded by political artworks, for these kinds of artworks are characterized by the aim of having an impact on the audience's system of beliefs. The epistemic value is both an outcome and a cause of aesthetic pleasure, and I do not take this to be inconsistent. We have seen that the epistemic contribution depends on the aesthetic properties that guide the imaginative engagement of the spectator, and at the same time the epistemic contribution enriches our experience.

To conclude this paragraph, we can now return to Livingston's thesis about FaP. It is my contention that we should re-evaluate the bold thesis. The paraphrase dilemma is actually a false dilemma. We can linguistically articulate the philosophical contribution made by films without the fear that such contribution may not be 'cinematic'. What we cannot paraphrase, without an epistemic loss, is the *modality* through which the contribution is brought. As is the case for thought experiments, we cannot paraphrase the film without losing its epistemic efficiency. We can articulate the philosophical contribution made by thought experiments, but their epistemic value lies in their capacity to trigger reflection through processing mechanisms that were not activated by abstract reasoning. If we want to activate those very mechanisms, we can only perform the thought experiment. Films are just the same. We can discuss and articulate the film's message and epistemic contribution, but we cannot, through the paraphrasing of the film, activate those processing mechanisms that enable the epistemic contribution.

In other words, as for thought experiments, the paraphrase brings a loss in epistemic efficiency. Nonetheless, the contribution can be articulated linguistically and related to a philosophical context. Indeed, in our experience of films our low-level and high-level cognitive capacities coexist. We can contextualize the intuitions 'pumped' by our affective responses to films, thanks to our top-down cognitive capacities: we are capable of inscribing our intuitions and affective responses within the wider context of a *problematique* that is relevant for the interpretation of the film's meaning.

Finally, can a film bring a *new* contribution to or perform cutting-edge philosophy? As Angela Curran notes (2011), we can say that a film philosophizes even if it does not do innovative or cutting-edge philosophy, so why add such a requirement? A film need not bring new contributions to do philosophy, although, in principle, I do not see any barrier to such possibility. According to Livingston, films cannot bring new philosophical contributions, since these would require a non-cinematic articulation of the relevant philosophical ideas. However, I hold that any philosophical contribution, even one that is not innovative, would require the articulation of the relevant philosophical ideas. Moreover, we have seen that the relevant *problematique* is necessarily mobilized by the natural, coexisting, activation of low-level affective reactions and the high-level cognitive capacities that interact to contextualize intuitions and affective responses within the wider philosophical problems (on this issue, see Smith, 2017). The interaction between low-level affective reactions and high-level cognitive capacities is typical of our experience of films, and while it allows for an accurate interpretation of the films – in light of complex philosophical questions – it also admits that the epistemic efficiency of the cinematic contribution cannot be paraphrased, as it is entirely dependent on cinematographic means.

As for the general debate on the epistemic values of films, this discussion proves that films can afford epistemic gains through cinematographic means. These means are what guide the imaginative engagement of the audience and the epistemic gains that films can afford interplay with cinema's aesthetic properties.

In the next chapter, I will investigate the different kinds of imaginative engagement films can elicit, but for the moment let me recapitulate what I have been doing so far. The aim of Chapters 4 and 5 has been to clarify whether cinema could afford epistemic gains and how epistemic and aesthetic value could interact. In Chapter 4, I argued that political cinema can convey empirical knowledge through testimony, but I was dissatisfied with the kind of justification we need to give to this kind of knowledge, not because testimony has a weak justificatory force, but rather because this kind of justification is to be located outside of the artwork itself: there are no aesthetic properties that grant the reliability of testimony. Testimony simply depends on the trustworthiness of the author. Hence, I hold, we could not establish a relation between epistemic and aesthetic value. To show the interaction between epistemic and aesthetic value, I argued for cinema's capacity to afford epistemic gains that are ultimately justified by imagination. As films guide (with cinematographic features) the imaginative engagement of the spectator, aesthetic properties play a role in bringing forth epistemic contributions.

In the first part of this chapter, I defended the justificatory role of imagination, bringing as an example the role of thought experiments, which are imaginative experiments (not actually carried out) designed to produce epistemic contributions in different fields of knowledge. The knowledge gathered by the performance of the thought experiment is justified by the imaginative effort. I have introduced a specific conception of thought experiments, which sees them as not only heuristically and rhetorically valuable but also epistemically so, due to their capacity to trigger reflections through processing mechanisms that abstract reasoning may not be able to mobilize. I have then developed an analogy between thought experiments and film, considering prominent objections to such an analogy. My contention is that films can afford epistemic gains just as thought experiments can, as they can activate low-level automatic processing mechanisms that would otherwise be left inactive by abstract reasoning. Moreover, I hold that cinema can afford epistemic gains through typically cinematographic means and that while we can paraphrase the film's message and inscribe its contribution within a general *problematique*, we cannot paraphrase the modality through which such an epistemic contribution is enabled. This means that if we paraphrase the film's contribution, we would lose epistemic efficiency in the process, as the contribution depends on the film's capacity to activate affective, noncognitive responses, and the only way to elicit such activation is to experience the film.

Before we move on to the next chapter, let me just highlight the coherence of the view that films can function as thought experiments with my overall framework for the analysis of political cinema. I have argued that we can use three criteria to analyze political cinema: the epistemic merit, the epistemic voice and the pedagogical method. Films can be more or less epistemically meritorious, and while the epistemic value can be justified through testimonial transmission, I have showed that when films function as thought experiments, their epistemic efficiency is strictly interrelated to their aesthetic properties, and it cannot be paraphrased (epistemic merit). Moreover, films can have an authoritative voice, when they aim to persuade their audience, or they may have a hesitant voice. We have seen that the thought experiment, per se, is not an argument, but it is naturally linked to one. So, a thought experiment can be used to persuade the audience, as the author of the work may manifest a specific attitude toward the experiment he or she presents. In *The Golden Door*, Crialese aims to elicit empathic engagement with the Mancuso family, and their story is used as an example to elicit reflection on the condition of being a migrant, which should involve a general reflection within the system of beliefs on standpoints about immigration. However, Crialese has a sympathetic attitude toward the Mancuso family, which tells us the director's position on matters of immigration. Other directors may choose to withdraw any judgment of the represented scenario or to illustrate different scenarios that may support contrasting theses to make use of a hesitant voice (see Bellocchio's *Sleeping Beauty*) (epistemic voice). When a film makes use of an authoritative voice, it may pedantically state the intended interpretation of the thought experiment, or it may leave it open to the spectator's engagement, making use of enthymematical reasoning (pedagogical method).

Hence, to see films functioning as thought experiments is coherent with the view that sees films as having rhetorical purposes as well as with the view that films can afford epistemic gains. The epistemic gains are granted by the films' capacity to activate automatic processing mechanisms, whereas the rhetorical value is granted by the use of examples to develop argumentations. Indeed, we have seen that for Aristotle, rhetoric requires simplicity, as the reasoning behind the argument is to be understood by the untrained public, and the use of examples is a rhetorical tool that serves to simplify complex abstract reasoning and bring it to its application to particular cases. In the previous chapter, I have shown how Conolly and Haydar trace an arbitrary distinction between political and personal morality, but such a distinction does not help clarify what counts as a political artwork. Conolly and Haydar overlook the possibility that artworks may focus on personal stories in order to test general judgments. Thought experiments can be about personal stories because personal stories provide different perspectives that are capable of 'pumping' intuitions and activating representational schemas that are not mobilized by abstract reasoning. The 'personal' in these stories is the specific perspective that allows us to better understand the target's position and psychology, which is crucial in testing the universalizability of moral judgments. Imagination is the source that allows us to conceive of and understand these different perspectives or that allows the understanding of scenarios that were previously unimagined or at least only superficially understood. Vivid imagination, together with its experiential and affective force, allows a deeper understanding of all these scenarios and possibilities, affording both epistemic and rhetorical gains.

Notes

1 For an in-depth analysis of the reliability of sources of knowledge, see Audi (2003).
2 We only need a 'working definition' (for an overview of the debates on imagination, see Kind, 2016). We can take Gaut's definition as a minimal definition, that entails different kinds of imagining, from those that require mental imagery to those that do not require it.
3 I expand on sentimentality and sentimental emotions in Chapter 7.
4 Gaut is a realist about emotions, so he holds, and I endorse his viewpoint, that the emotions we feel when we imagine a given scenario are not imagined emotions but actual ones. See also Chapter 7 of this book.

5 I will say more on the emotions epistemic relevance in Chapter 7 (see also Elgin, 2008).

6 We can perform different kinds of thought experiments: scientific, conceptual, mathematics, philosophical and so on (Gendler, 2004).

7 I endorse Tamar Gendler's view on thought experiments, which requires a dual-process account of mental reasoning (see Gendler, 2002, 2007, 2012). I expand on this later.

8 Clearly, that we are more likely to utter a consequentialist judgment when analyzing the impersonal formulation of the trolley problem is a generalization based on statistical tendencies. Empirical studies of Green and colleagues serve to support the idea that our discrepant judgments in the switch and the Fat Man cases are not the outcome of a single psychological system but rather the outcome of the competition between two distinct psychological systems.

9 In this chapter, I write that such 'automatic' process is also 'emotional'. This is not entirely accurate, but I leave it unspecified here, whereas in Chapter 7 I clarify what do I mean by 'emotions'.

10 Berys Gaut also notes that it is not a requirement of the universalization test that the target endorses the policy rather that the judge would accept the policy were he in the position of the target.

11 I provide an in-depth analysis of emotional response to fiction in Chapter 6.

12 Here I am restricting the focus of enquiry to narrative fiction, but some films may not have a narrative structure, so they would not count as thought experiments, and yet they may still afford epistemic gains. Nonetheless, I suppose that all the epistemic gains films can afford can be justified either through testimony or imagination. It may be worth noting that non-narrative films can also, in principle, afford epistemic gains through imagination. For instance, by making use of metaphors – these are going to be visual metaphors (Carroll, 1994, 1996c). For an account of metaphors as requiring a particular kind of imagining, see Elisabeth Camp (2009), and for a defense of metaphor's epistemic value, see again Camp (2006a, 2006b, 2007). She argues that metaphors, just like thought experiments, are epistemically efficient and that such efficiency cannot be paraphrased – while we can paraphrase the overall meaning and contribution of the metaphor.

13 This is coherent with the Intentionalist account of political cinema I have provided in Chapter 1.

14 The idea that films function as thought experiments has been entertained in the context of the Film as Philosophy (FaP) debate (see Wartenberg, 2006, 2007, 2011; Sinnerbrink, 2011).

15 For a full analysis of all the possible epistemological positions on thought experiments, see Davies (2007, 2010).

16 The extreme inflationist view is held by James Brown and implies a platonic conception of thought experiments, which are seen as 'telescopes into the abstract realm' (Brown, 2004). See also Brown (1991, 1992, 2011).

17 Deflationist views hold that thought experiments do not provide knowledge about the actual world (this is the extreme deflationary view, see Hempel, 1965) or that they are at best rhetorically valuable as thought experiments can be reduced to standard inferential arguments.

18 On the topic, the most relevant contributions in the analytic tradition are those of Wartenberg (2007) and Sinnebrink (2011). In the continental tradition of philosophy, the idea of film as philosophy is broadly accepted and there are a number of contributions from Jean Epstein (2014) to Daniel Frampton (2006).

19 Nowadays, Smith's position on film's capacity to philosophize and grant epistemic access to the actual world seems more permissive (2017). Nonetheless, a

confrontation with the argument articulated in *Film Art, Argument and Ambiguity* will allow me to introduce important clarifications on the idea that films can be compared to thought experiments

20 However, political films do not exhaust the category of films that may aim to bring epistemic contributions. See, for instance, Bergman's films analyzed by Paisley Livingston (2009).

21 I define political films as films aiming to have an impact on the audience's system of beliefs. To have an impact on the system of beliefs means to bring an epistemic contribution of some sort.

22 Berys Gaut refers to these as 'external' and 'internal' conditions of the target position (2007).

23 Here I am anticipating something that I clarified in Chapter 6, when I will delve into the concept of empathy at length.

24 When I use the term 'knowledge' I always imply a broad construction of it, as to entail epistemic gains more generally.

25 See, for instance, Mulhall (2002).

26 Smith (2006) only hints at the distinction between knowledge and philosophical knowledge, but he does not clarify how to trace the distinction.

27 Wartenberg (2011) sees *The Matrix* as a thought experiment inspired by Descartes, whereas Livingston holds that *Persona* can be explained in light of the Finnish psychologist and philosopher Enio Kaila's views of human actions and motives.

28 Livingston uses the expressions 'exclusive/specific of the cinematic medium' as well as 'purely cinematographic' interchangeably. I do the same here.

29 The 'utterance' in M1 is a compound of both the verbal medium and another medium (say, hand gestures), whereas the utterance in M2 only identifies the verbal utterance.

30 This will be analyzed in greater detail when I discuss the case of the spectators' emotional response in Chapter 6.

31 Murray Smith (2017) holds that the spectator's experience is characterized by the interplay of bottom-up perception and top-down cognition. These two different levels of processing mechanisms are not to be seen as isolated or independent from one another, as they are actually integrated.

32 This is just what happens when we engage with thought experiments, and in particular with personal formulations of thought experiments, as in the *Fat Man* scenario: automatic reactions are integrated into abstract reflections.

33 Also in his definition of philosophy, Livingston emphasizes how, among the methods of investigation available to the philosophers, there is that of considering specific examples and scenarios, whether actual or imagined. Thus, he admits the possibility of philosophical reasoning being carried out through examples.

34 Even deflationist accounts of thought experiments recognize thought experiments' rhetorical value.

35 We have seen in Chapter 2 that emotions can be used as tools to persuade the audience.

36 I take it that it suffices to show that cinema can articulate content in ways that are not reducible to the verbal articulation of the content itself to prove that that content is medium-exclusive. However, this version of medium-exclusivity is to be understood as a weak contention: one that simply aims to exclude the verbal medium. My claim – that cinema can afford epistemic gains – does not entail that such gains should be afforded through means that are 'essentially' cinematic. It is possible that other mixed medium art forms may articulate the same content with a different combination of features, say, for instance, mise-en-scène 'plus' soundtrack. We do not need a theory of medium-exclusivity that points to a

'uniqueness' of the cinematic experience. This would take us into the realm of those theories that try to identify what is distinctive of any art form. Noël Carroll labels these theories as medium-essentialists, as they aim to single out what distinguishes one art form from the others. For a thorough review of the limits of medium-essentialism, see the first four chapters of Carroll (1996c).

37 Derek Matravers, in the same essay (Coplan & Matravers, 2011), replies that literature can make use of different features that lead to the same result: the eliciting of affective, noncognitive responses.

38 I take it that Coplan is not in the business of defining what is 'essential' to cinema, but she just wants to highlight that there are cinematic features that are not available to writers. Hence, here I use the word 'typical' to qualify these features, as they may not be unique to cinema, but we usually find them in films.

7 Imaginative and emotional engagement with political cinema

In Chapter 6, I argued that imagination is a reliable source of knowledge and that films can afford epistemic gains guiding our imaginative engagement, as they can function like thought experiments. In this chapter, I want to expand on the possibility that imaginative engagement may actually trigger critical reflection. As I have shown in the first chapters, my definition of political cinema is indebted to Brecht's conceptualization of political theater. Yet the only contact point between my definition of political cinema and Brecht's theory of political art is limited to the idea that political artworks aim to elicit reflection about a political issue or issues. Brecht, however, held that some artworks, those fostering identification between characters and spectators, systematically 'block' critical thinking. This is a serious threat to my argument: if this were true, then these kinds of films – promoting identification between the characters and the spectators – would be doomed to fail as political films. In this chapter, I show that this is not the case and films that invite the spectator to feel with or to feel for a character can be just as effective as those works that make use of, what Brecht calls, the alienation effect.

The preliminary problem, though, is to understand what exactly Brecht had in mind when he argued that films promoting *Einfühlung* (literally, 'feeling into') impair critical thinking. This is itself a matter of contention. Paul Woodruff points out that Brecht used the concept to cover a host of different things: 'carrying the audience away emotionally, drawing them together into a collective entity, inducing them to feel sympathy with a character, making them share feelings with a character, or calling them to identify with a hero' (1988, p. 241).[1] This shows how difficult it is to calibrate criticism of Brecht's theory. In addition, recent debates in analytic aesthetics and cognitive film theory have brought forward new schemas to understand the spectator's engagement with characters that are not limited to a dichotomous contraposition of the kind 'identification/alienation'. Things are more complex than that. Some scholars have already highlighted how the Brechtian understanding of a spectator's emotional engagement fails to account for the cognitive dimension involved in emotional responses (Plantinga, 1997a, 1997b; Smith, 1995), but it is possible that rather than emotions per

DOI: 10.4324/9780367816872-8

se, what is problematic, for Brecht, is the mode of spectatorial engagement. That is to say, the problem may be empathic engagement or identification and not the very fact that spectators feel emotions. So, I divide this chapter into three different sections, made of two subsections each. In the first section, I focus on empathy, as this is perhaps the best candidate to translate Brecht's *Einfühlung*.[2] I introduce recent debates on the definition of empathy (Section 1.1) that I believe will also help to map different modes of character engagement, and I consider possible objections to empathic engagement with fiction (Section 1.2). In the second section of this chapter, I test Brecht's objection: does empathic engagement impair critical thinking? My answer is negative, and I analyze the Dardenne brothers' *Two Days, One Night* to back up my argument (Section 2.1), showing how empathy works with other modes of character engagement and how it can promote reflections on political issues. I also consider a related objection, the partial perspective objection (Section 2.2); this is an objection against the structure of a film rather than against a mode of imagining. I argue that the objection does not stand and that if we want to accurately analyze the epistemic contributions made by a film, we need to analyze its epistemic dimensions through the theoretical framework I propose in this book. In the third section of the chapter, I try to make sense of Brecht's objection by reconsidering the role of emotions in our engagement with fiction. I introduce Jenefer Robinson's definition of emotions (Section 3.1) and show how, despite their affective, precognitive component, emotions do not stymie our cognitive capacities. However, emotions can be used as a rhetorical tool (Section 3.2) and some narratives aim to elicit emotions that are not warranted by the presentation of the story. In particular, those works that aim to elicit 'tender' emotions concealing epistemic defects can be labeled as sentimental. Due to fact that sentimentality implies an epistemic defect, it can be an aesthetic flaw for political films.

1 Empathy and character engagement

1.1 What is empathy?

Defining empathy is not a simple task as its use in common language is quite vague and unclear, and academic debates have further amplified the difficulties of reaching a common definition. I introduce what I take to be the most relevant controversies about the definition of the concept and I argue that we should define empathy as an other-focused central imagining.[3]

We need to make a primary distinction between the idea of empathy as a process or the idea of empathy as an outcome. I hold with Peter Goldie (2011) that we should conceive of empathy as a process: this is a more refined conception of empathy as it distinguishes and characterizes the different processes that are at stake when we talk about empathy. Nonetheless, any process we may want to call 'empathic' cannot be disentangled from its outcome. If I say that I empathize with John, it means that we share a given affective state; the process through which I come to feel what John feels is not indifferent if we are to talk about empathic engagement, or so I hold, but what is necessary, although not sufficient, for empathy is that the outcome of any such process is my sharing (in a sense to be clarified) John's affective state. In other words, I share with Goldie a will to put an emphasis on the psychological process that underpins our empathic engagement, as long as the outcome of such a process is an affective state that is more congruent with someone else's situation than with our own.[4]

The starting point of this discussion is that empathy requires that an agent A comes to share agent B's affective state. What I want to look into is the kind of process that is needed for A to share B's state in order to have an instantiation of empathic engagement. In my discussion I imply that empathic engagement is always linked to the understanding of an affective state. It may be possible that the imaginative processes we undergo when we empathize with someone can be used in different contexts, as when we analyze decision-making mechanisms and try to predict behavior; but I am skeptical about whether this counts as empathy. For instance, let me consider an example discussed by Goldie, where agent B wants to buy some apples.[5] We know that B believes that English apples, in autumn, are the best apples. Agent A wants to predict which kind of apples B would buy, knowing that B believes that the current month is September, which, being in England, he believes to be autumn. The process through which A comes to co-cognize with B may be akin to what I define as 'empathy', but I do not hold that what A is doing is empathizing with B in the 'apple' case, primarily because the aim of the cognitive process implied here is not the understanding of an affective state. It may be held that empathy goes beyond the understanding of affective states but I do not consider such possibility here.[6]

Drawing from Wollheim's differentiation between central and acentral imagining (1980), Murray Smith (2011) argues that empathy is a kind of imagining, and specifically it is a personal, or central, form of imagining, which implies imagining experiencing events from the inside, that is, from a specific point of view. Central imagining requires that we imagine experiencing or perceiving an event. Apersonal, or acentral, imagining, instead, consists in imagining that certain events are happening or have happened, but we imagine the story from no specific point of view and we do not imagine perceiving or experiencing the events. Let me dwell on the difference in order to clarify possible terminological problems. When we imagine something 'centrally' we imagine perceiving or experiencing the event: I imagine swimming in the ocean. So, central imagining requires *de se* imagining, that is, imagining of one's own self, but not all *de se* imaginings are central imaginings. Indeed, to draw on an example from Langton, instead of imagining swimming in the ocean I could imagine *myself* swimming in the ocean.[7] In both cases, I self-ascribe the property of swimming in the water, so they are instances of *de se* imagining, but they differ due to the perspective provided in the act of imagining. In the first case, I imagine swimming in the ocean, so I imagine the cold water, the current dragging me and a cliff that I can see from the water. In the second case I imagine myself *from the outside* and I imagine myself being tossed about, shivering for the cold and staring at the cliff. This is still a case of *de se* imagining but from the outside. So, perhaps, the terminology *personal/apersonal* may be misleading, if we consider that in this second case I imagine from the outside, but I imagine myself. I will only use central and acentral imagining to refer to imagining from the inside and imagining from the outside, respectively. Also, with Smith, I hold that empathy requires central imagining but of a particular kind.

We have seen that acentral imagining can also be *de se* imagining, although it need not be. I can imagine myself swimming in the ocean or I can imagine *you* swimming in the ocean. In both cases I imagine from the outside *that* I am or you are performing the action of swimming in the ocean, say, for instance, that I picture the scene as watching it from the cliff, instead of being in the water. Central imagining can be *de se* imagining, but is it always so? Following Langton's examples, another instance of central imagining is when I imagine *being* you swimming in the ocean. Here it is not clear whether we can talk of imagining *de se*, and this is because the properties of the imagined subject – 'you' in this case – are not ascribed to myself.[8] I am aware of the fact that it is you swimming in the ocean, even though I imagine the event from the inside. When I engage in this kind of imagining I take up some of your psychological traits, beliefs and desires. For instance, as I am a timorous person, and not a great swimmer, I may be frightened by the idea of being in the open ocean, but I know that you are brave and a great athlete, so when I imagine being you in the ocean I imagine your graceful swimming, your composure and self-confidence. And I imagine all this from within the water, from your perspective. This is the kind of imagining process required by empathy.

Smith calls this kind of imagining 'other-focused central imagining'[9] as opposed to another kind of imagining which is self-focused.[10] With a self-focused central imagining you put yourself into someone else's shoes. I will call this kind of imaginative engagement also in-his-shoes imagining.[11] When we put ourselves into someone else's shoes we imagine the situation or events the subject is experiencing from our own perspective. We keep all our personal character traits, desires, goals and interests; we are just imagining ourselves in a given scenario. This kind of imagining plays an important role in our engagement with possible scenarios as it helps cognitive understanding of the situation, but in this kind of imagining, it is the *situation* itself that becomes the real focus of the imaginative process, whereas empathy requires a focus on the *other* and his feelings.[12]

Self-focused personal imagining can lead, only accidentally, to the same outcome empathic engagement would provide. That is to say, with in-his-shoes imagining we can come to share the same affective state of the agent who is in the situation we imagine, yet this is because some emotional responses to particular scenarios are almost universal or because they are accidentally the same. For instance, I can see Julie feeling scared because of being chased by a lion, and I can imagine myself in her situation and come to feel the same emotion. In this case, Julie and I share the same affective state, but this is because fear would be a universal response in this scenario; in-his-shoes imagining need not lead us to feel what the other is feeling. For instance, I can be a confident and extroverted person who is never scared to talk in front of an audience. If I imagine myself in John's shoes, who is introverted, shy and insecure, I will not share his discomfort and shame when he has to give a public speech.

In the literature on empathy, some authors seem to use the term, empathy, as an umbrella covering both kinds of imagining. For instance, Goldie, using as a framework Alvin Goldman's distinction between low-level and high-level empathy, argues that in-his-shoes imagining and other-focused central imagining are both kinds of higher-level empathy. On the contrary, when I speak of empathy, I refer exclusively to other-focused central imagining. It is a form of central imagining, insofar as we imagine experiencing and perceiving from the inside, but, contrary to in-his-shoes imagining, it is focused on another self, which means that we are to remove from the imaginative process – 'quarantine'[13] – some traits, beliefs, and desires that are typical of our own self. The outcome of the empathic engagement is an affective consonance between the empathizer and the empathized.[14] Through empathy we *actually feel with* someone else.

Empathy is just one of the possible kinds of emotional engagement with fictional characters. Berys Gaut provides a distinction between empathic engagement and imaginative identification that I find particularly useful, as it conceptually clarifies different possible ways in which we can feel with someone else. Following Gaut, identification requires that:

> I identify affectively with T in respect of emotion E just in case I imagine feeling E because I am aware that T is (fictionally) feeling E. The 'because' here is not purely causal but should be understood in terms of my imaginings being guided by my awareness of what is (fictionally) the case so as to rule out deviant causal chains
>
> (2010, p. 137),

whereas

> my empathizing with T in respect of some emotion E requires me actually to feel E because I imagine myself in T's (fictional) situation in which she feels E. The 'because' is again understood in the guidance sense, and imagining myself in T's situation is analyzed in terms of aspectual imaginative identification
>
> (2010, p. 138).

The difference is that in the case of identification, we *imagine* feeling an emotion, so we imagine what it is like to feel E, in virtue of being guided by the state in which T finds himself. The latter specification is necessary: we could imagine what it is like to feel fear, and we could just recall an occasion when we felt that emotion; in doing so, we would come to imagine what it is like to feel E, which is the same emotion T feels, but we would feel E for the wrong reasons. For instance, T may be anxious for he is on the verge of losing his job. Imagining his anxiety, I may recall the anxiety I used to feel before an exam. I may successfully imagine feeling E, where E is the emotion T feels, but I am not identifying with T because I do not imagine feeling anxious for the 'right' reasons, that is, for the reasons T feels anxious. Imagining feeling E, without imaginative identification, would imply a simple cognitive understanding of the emotion the character feels. Imaginative identification requires that we imagine feeling the emotion T feels in virtue of the reasons why T feels it.

In the case of empathic engagement, on Gaut's analysis, we *actually* feel the emotion E. The character is ashamed and I am as well.[15] And I am ashamed for the same reasons that the character feels ashamed. The difference implied is qualitative: when we empathize we actually experience the same, or a similar, affective state someone else experiences; I can be ashamed just as T is. When we identify with T, we imagine feeling what he is feeling, but we may actually feel something different; for instance, we can feel sorrow in virtue of our imagining feeling what T is feeling: shame. To wit, we can imagine feeling ashamed just as T is, and thereby come to feel actual sorrow for T's feeling that way. Our feeling differs from T's.

Empathy and identifications are kinds of imagining: these are mechanisms through which we come to feel with someone else. The other self is the subject of our imagining: we are to imagine what it is like to be T in order to feel with him; it means that we need to understand T's perspective, his main character traits, his beliefs and desires, as well as his goals and interests. This shows how complex this process is and how it requires the acquisition of a great deal of information about T, mental flexibility and the capacity to suppress one's perspective on the events in which T happens to be situated.

1.2 Can we actually feel with fictional characters?

Noël Carroll (2010b, 2013) and Carl Plantinga (2009b) have questioned the role of empathy and identification in our engagement with characters in fiction. Carroll argues that when the spectator's emotions matches those of the characters, this is not due to empathic engagement but due to what he calls 'criterial prefocusing'. Roughly, criterial prefocusing is the process through which authors frame events and situations. In foregrounding some aspects at the expense of others, authors are able to present situations as fitting into familiar schemas that are likely to elicit a predetermined emotional response. For instance, Carroll (2013) argues that Harriett Beecher Stowe managed to elicit concern and sympathy for the characters of her *Uncle Tom's Cabin* as she pressed onto the shared values between slaves' families and the audience: Christian devotion and the value of family unity. As the audience can positively relate to these values, it can also develop affection for those who share them. Hence, as Carroll has it, the reason behind the congruence of the emotional states is not the empathic engagement with another (fictional) self but the capacity to frame the events in terms that are meaningful and relevant to the audience. Plantinga argues that the concept of sympathy can entail both a concern for and a congruent emotion in response to the plight of another person, so we should not distinguish between empathy and sympathy. Any attempt to mark a difference between the terms is unhelpful for three reasons: it is stipulative rather than descriptive; it fails to correspond to actual usage of the terms and it tends to generate as much confusion as clarity (Plantinga, 2009b, p. 99). Undoubtedly, among scholars there is little agreement on the definition of empathy, but we should not throw in the towel, and even if the outcome of the philosophical debate were only stipulative distinctions, when conceptually conceivable, they can still be analytically meaningful.

However, Plantinga's objection to a possible distinction between empathy and sympathy is also based on the observation that our response to characters in fiction as well as in real life is neither solely empathetic nor sympathetic. Our responses are rather a mixture of shared feelings with, and feelings for, the other agent. When we feel with someone else, Plantinga holds, the emotions felt are never identical to but at most congruent with those felt by the agent, and such emotions are always mixed with 'feelings *for*' the agent we are responding to. In other words, our emotional response varies in degrees and quality from that of the agent with whom we supposedly empathize. For instance, when my friend loses her mother to an illness, I can share her sadness, although perhaps to a diminished degree, but together with the sadness I may also pity my friend. To a certain extent, my emotion is congruent as I also share a similar evaluative perspective, so that I feel sadness at the occurrence, but surely my sadness is not identical to that of my friend, and my emotional state is also affected by the fact that I pity her. Hence, my affective state is actually a complex one, which entails both congruent emotions and feelings for my friend. The same happens when we respond to fictional characters: our emotional response entails both (what is usually construed as) empathy and sympathy, so we should not try to distinguish between them, since such a distinction seems to hold only in seminar rooms (Plantinga, 2009b).

These objections advance some pointed insights, but I will insist on considering empathy and sympathy as distinct kinds of engagements. Indeed, the distinction is still conceivable and can be made conceptually clear, so we need not abandon terminological differentiations for fear of complexity. Plantinga's and Carroll's objections, rather than being conclusive in dismissing the role of empathic engagement, seem to point to the fact that our engagement with fictional characters is pluralistic. When we engage with fictional narratives, we do not exclusively empathize with characters, and empathy need not be the only mechanism through which we understand narratives nor the dominant one. During a narrative, we may switch from simple cognitive understanding to any other mode of engagement, and vice versa. Moreover, we may actually empathize with characters only in very few moments during the narrative, so that empathy may not be the major mode by which we engage with a story. Nonetheless, such empathic moments may be *qualitatively* relevant to our apprehension of the narrative.[16]

Even if we could not exclusively empathize with a character, as Plantinga seems to imply, it does not follow that empathy is not there. Empathy does not prevent other kinds of engagement and, as Smith (2011) argues, it is systematically connected with other lower-level, pre-reflexive, mental processes, like motor and affective mimicry and emotional contagion. Recent empirical findings in cognitive neuroscience have indeed backed up the claim that we respond to other selves by feeling what they actually feel. Studies of the mirror neurons system have suggested that in certain respects our brain activity is significantly similar when we perform an action and when we witness the same action being performed. These studies have provided the specification of the neural mechanisms underpinning such pre-reflective, lower level processes that, to use Smith's terminology, *scaffold* empathic engagement. Affective mimicry, for instance, allows us to recognize someone's affective state as we are able to simulate the feeling associated with his facial expression via the mechanism of facial feedback – that is, we mimic and reproduce both facial expression and the correlated emotion.[17] Witnessing a person expressing a given emotion activates the same brain areas that are activated when we actually experience that emotion (Gallese, 2009, 2011; Gallese & Guerra, 2015). The relevant implication of these new findings in neuroscience is that our body takes part in the comprehension of other individuals in ways that were unexplored by the classical mind-reading account where emotions and sensations were always represented with a propositional content. This is why Vittorio Gallese talks of 'embodied simulation', as we are capable of mapping others' actions, sensations and emotions, reusing mental states and processes involving representations that have a bodily format (and in that sense a non-propositional format) (Gallese, 2011). The process of simulation is triggered by perception, like seeing someone experiencing a particular emotion, although this can also be triggered by vivid imagination (Gallese, 2011).[18] The cinematic experience can be a prop for such simulation as we perceive the characters' emotions, and on the basis of this perception we can physically experience such emotions. Hence, the embodied simulation theory backs up the claim that we actually feel with the character.[19]

2 Does empathic engagement prevent critical reflection?

2.1 Empathy in political films

The first part of the chapter was devoted to the clarification of the concept of empathy. I follow Smith in defining empathy as an other-focused central imagining, and I have highlighted the differences between empathic imagining, in-his-shoes imagining and imaginative identification. I have also argued that empathy is only one of the possible modes of engagement with narratives; it is scaffolded by other pre-reflexive, lower-level kinds of mental processes and it does not prevent other kinds of engagement. Having clarified what it is meant by empathy, we can now turn to a possible Brechtian criticism of empathic engagement with narratives. With a better grasp of the term, and of its role in our engagement with narratives, we can tackle the Brechtian objection more accurately. In this section, I briefly summarize the objection and then I rebut it by showing that the objection misfires as it is grounded on an inaccurate understanding of empathy and of our engagement with narratives; empathy can foster, rather than hinder, critical reflection on political issues.

These preliminary remarks on empathy were necessary in assessing Brecht's stance on the role of empathy and its capacity to foster or hinder critical thinking. Philosophical research on fictional engagement has progressed and problematized the field. The next task is to look at fictional engagement with the conceptual schema we inherit from current debates. So, if it is unclear what exactly Brecht has in mind when he says that the audience of 'culinary theater' weeps when the character weeps, this is because processes of character engagement in fiction are complex and overlapping. Surely Brecht, in his criticism of 'culinary' theater, never uses the concept of central imagining. That concept comes from the debate in analytic aesthetics on the spectator's engagement with narratives, but I take it that the concept is apt to frame Brecht's criticism, which can be summed up with this famous quote:

> the dramatic theater's spectator says: Yes, I have felt like that too – Just like me – It's only natural – It'll never change – The sufferings of this man appall me, because they are inescapable – That's great art; it all seems the most obvious thing in the world – I weep when they weep, I laugh when they laugh
>
> (Brecht, 2014, p. 71).

Brecht's criticism is primarily aimed at what he calls dramatic, Aristotelian, theater, but it can be exported and made relevant to narrative fiction in general. He believed that art ought to play a central role in people's education and should promote critical thinking. Brecht held that dramatic theater was inapt to promote critical reflection on social and political structures, and, on the contrary, that it promoted critical numbness since it only focused on the character's thoughts and feelings. Following Brecht (2014), a spectator who shares the character's emotions is incapable of questioning and adopting a critical attitude toward the character's situation (pp. 394, 411).[20] Angela Curran summarizes Brecht's criticism of empathy as follows:

> (1) to facilitate a critical perspective on the social relations represented in drama, drama should go beyond revealing the thoughts and feelings of the protagonist to consider the larger social network in which the protagonist operates; (2) Aristotelian aesthetic practices do not enable the viewer to move from the individual perspective to the social perspective; (3) therefore, Aristotelian theater's use of empathy does not enable the audience to engage in reflection on the social relations represented in the drama
>
> (Curran, 2001, p. 175).

Let me analyze this argument. It seems too far-reaching to hold that every work should aim 'to facilitate a critical perspective on the social relations represented'; some artworks may have no intention to foster reflection on social relations or political problems.[21] So, I posit that this argument is directed toward political artworks. Even in this case, this argument does not really explain *why* empathic engagement should prevent reflection on political issues. The argument implicitly assumes that in being focused on the character's feelings and thoughts, the spectator is 'somehow' distracted and unable to adopt a critical attitude toward political problems presented in the work. There seems to be an irreparable divide: the spectator focuses either on the individual perspective or on the social perspective. Empathic imagination turns out to be something that blinds the spectator and confines him within the individual perspective.

In light of what we have said so far about empathy, we can say that this is incorrect. First, empathy requires some cognitive understanding of the character's situation, psychological traits, beliefs and desires, so the social and political framework within which the character is situated may be relevant to our understanding of the character's perspective; second, empathy is not an overwhelming mode of imagination: we do not empathize with a character throughout the narrative, and empathy does not prevent other forms of engagement with the narrative. Let me consider an example to further illustrate these points; I suggest we consider the Dardenne brothers' film *Two Days, One Night* (2014).

Sandra (Marion Cotillard) works in a solar-panel factory, but she has to stay away from work due to a nervous breakdown. After the illness, her job is in danger as the factory faces economic struggles. The workers of the factory will have a ballot in order to decide whether to take Sandra on board again or to take up a personal bonus of 1,000 euros. Sandra has two days to persuade her coworkers to renounce their bonus.

Instead of problematizing the typical social conflict in the Marxist dialectic – namely, the conflict between the bourgeoisie and the working class – in this film, the Dardenne brothers shift the locus of conflict to within the working class, as they aim to highlight the need for solidarity among the workers' community. They follow Sandra in her attempt to keep her job and the unfolding of the narrative provides relevant information about Sandra's situation and inner feelings. She is married to Manu (Frabrizio Rongione) who works as a chef, has two children and needs her job to help pay the mortgage. From the beginning of the film we are aligned to her, and our sympathy and support for her cause grow throughout the film.[22] We feel increasingly close to her not just because of her economic needs but also because of her psychological situation. Signs of her recent breakdown are evident from the beginning of the film, as she is locked in her room, curtains closed, during a sunny day, hiding under the bed sheets. She is also shown in her bathroom taking drugs and trying, unsuccessfully, not to cry. The Dardenne brothers highlight from the start her psychological weakness, which evokes pity, but it also reinforces her plea to keep the job. Fighting for her job becomes a matter of saving her own dignity as a person, and the psychological dimension of Sandra's fight is what drives us within the film.

Do we empathize with her? We do have empathic engagement in some moments of the narrative, but that does not mean that we constantly feel what she feels, or that such focus on her personal perspective diverts us from a broader understanding of her social situation. Sandra's psychological difficulties put her in a position of weakness that for most of the film elicits our pity. This initial sympathetic response can be explained through criterial prefocusing. Sandra's situation is framed in order to elicit our pity: she is weak but with a desire to come out of the difficulties, fighting resignation with the help of a loving husband who attracts our admiration for his unconditional love. She finds herself in such a complex situation without guilt, as she is on the verge of losing her job for reasons beyond her control. She then appears as the innocent who fights for her dignity; while her colleagues – unwilling to renounce their bonus in order to help her – are sometimes framed as greedy and heartless. Criterial prefocusing directs our sympathy, but it does not prevent empathy. On the contrary, cognitive understanding of Sandra's psychological troubles is necessary both for the unfolding of the narrative and for our empathic emotional involvement with Sandra. We understand Sandra's troubles, not just her economic troubles, but especially the psychological ones, and we understand her desire to save her job as it is something that can allow her to regain self-confidence. It is such understanding that allows us to feel with her in some moments of the narrative, particularly when she feels positive emotions like gratitude and happiness.

Her meeting with Timur provides an example of our empathic engagement with Sandra. The meeting is shot in a single long take: close to a football pitch, Sandra walks toward the camera that tracks back along the pitch. She stops and shouts Timur's name and then walks off camera while the camera lingers on the pitch where we see Timur walking toward the camera. Timur and Sandra are facing each other with a fence between them. The camera stays on Timur, framing the action in a medium close-up, so we can perceive Timur's distress. While Sandra speaks, the camera pans first on to Sandra and then back to Timur, lingering on their faces. When Sandra asks him if he would vote for her to stay, he bursts into tears leaning over Sandra's hands on the fence, with a consequent tilt of the camera. He agrees to vote for her and says that he is mad at himself for having voted for his bonus in a previous ballot. We are relieved by his outburst, as our alignment with Sandra makes us welcome his sorrow. Timur's reaction and shame reinforces the idea that Sandra has been treated unjustly, and the candor of his admission is moving as it shows bonding and solidarity with Sandra. The emotional intensity of the sequence is further emphasized by an anecdote recalled by Timur: when he had just been hired, he broke some cells at work but Sandra took responsibility for that mishap. Here the camera pans back to Sandra's face and we see her crying and smiling while commenting on Timur's story. The take ends with the camera tracking back along the football pitch and Sandra walking toward the camera, in a medium close-up, smiling in tears.

Aspects of cinematography, as well as elements of the narrative, contribute to our empathic engagement with Sandra. The use of close-up and medium close-up favors emotional contagion and affective mimicry. Moreover, the bodily engagement is backed up by our understanding of Sandra's difficulties. We have a rough (if limited) characterization of Sandra's self, and Timur's anecdote serves to reinforce our knowledge and puts us even closer to Sandra. The anecdote is instrumental as it allows us to know Sandra a little better. Not only does she deserve our sympathy, but she also deserves to be helped by her colleagues, as Timur's story has demonstrated her kind-hearted spirit. We know she also wants to save her job because this may help her overcome the state of depression she fears and which she is trying to fight. In light of our knowledge of Sandra, and our feelings *for* her, we share her gratitude and happiness – and so, we are enabled to feel *with* her.

The empathic engagement we have with Sandra, however, does not 'lock' us into her perspective, nor does it blind us. We do not constantly empathize with Sandra. We feel with her at the end of the sequence I have described, but we do not keep on sharing her feelings throughout the film.[23] Indeed, later in the film, after having received negative answers from some of her colleagues and finding out that Jean-Marc (the staff manager) says that she is no longer capable of working due to her psychological weaknesses, she feels unworthy and sorry for herself, to the extent that she tries to kill herself. In this case we do not share her feelings. We feel for her – we pity her – but we do not share her own feelings. Moreover, we are constantly aware of the social conditions that frame the story. The cognitive understanding of such conditions provides a framework for Sandra's situation and mental states. We are constantly aware of her family's economic difficulties, but we are also aware of the general economic and working conditions affecting the working class. Sandra's struggle to keep her job is inscribed in a context of economic instability. Her colleagues are unwilling to renounce their bonuses as the money is vital for their family economies and most of them also have second jobs on the side, mainly without regular contracts so that they can avoid paying taxes. Their economic security is further threatened by their precarious working conditions. One of Sandra's colleagues, Alphonse, has a fixed-term contract and is afraid to vote for Sandra as he fears repercussions from some of his colleagues, especially Jean-Marc, who may determine whether he can extend his contract. To understand Sandra's standpoint fully, we need to be aware of all the relevant conditions that affect her position.[24]

2.2 Partial perspectives and epistemic merit

An objection to my analysis may be that, despite the fact that it does not blind us to the social and political framing of the story, empathic engagement still requires that we immerse ourselves within an individual perspective, and such immersion may prevent critical thinking.[25] I call this objection 'the partial perspective objection' (PPO).[26] The idea of critical thinking is central to Brecht's theory of theater. He supported the idea that spectators should reach their own conclusions about the problems represented in the work (see, for instance, Brecht, 2014; Curran, 2011); empathic engagement, it may be held, requires that the spectator be immersed within a single character's perspective. Such immersion does not foster critical thinking since there is only a partial view – pertaining to the character – presented, so the spectator is induced to adhere to the presented perspective.[27] Such an objection shows little faith in the spectator's critical skills, but let me consider it.

We should distinguish the idea that empathy prevents critical thinking from the idea that critical thinking is hindered by the fact that the work focuses exclusively on a single perspective. The first is a claim about the nature of engagement with the work while the second is a claim about the structure of the work itself.[28] The argumentation I have previously provided suffices, I contend, to rebut the idea that empathy prevents critical thinking. PPO, as I have presented it, is not, strictly speaking, directed against empathy, but against the fact that a work may focus exclusively on a character's perspective, thereby providing only a partial account of a problem.[29]

So, PPO is restricted toward those kinds of works that only present a single perspective on an issue.[30] These works do not foster critical thinking (so they are not epistemically meritorious) because they do not provide sufficient inputs to the spectators. Probably, here, the main issue is related to Brecht's conception of 'critical thinking'. The kind of critical thinking implied by Brecht has two separable components (Curran, 2001). The first is, strictly speaking, cognitive and it requires a kind of 'freedom of thought' on the side of the audience. That is to say, the audience should be able to reach their own 'independently justified' conclusion in relation to the theme of the work (Curran, 2001, p. 175). The second component is a 'motivation' to action. This is related to Marxist ideology: Brecht held that theater should make the audience reflect on the fact that the social structure within which their life is inscribed is just transient and changeable, hence such reflections should also push the audience to change the unjust social arrangements. Curran writes that 'Brecht wanted to get people to question what they saw so that they would then be ready to go from the theater to work to change their situation in society' (2001, p. 176). Hence, for Brecht, fostering critical thinking means providing different inputs/perspectives in order to grant an ideal 'freedom of thought' and to instill in the audience the idea that their actions matter, as social organizations are transient and subject to change.

Now we have a better understanding of Brecht's conception of 'critical thinking' and we can assess the PPO objection. My contention is that the PPO does not hold, as it conflates different epistemic dimensions that need to be distinguished in order to appraise the epistemic value of a film. Hence, to explain the weakness of the PPO let me recall the three dimensions I have identified to appraise a political film: epistemic merit, epistemic voice and pedagogical method. A work has epistemic merit if it is able to analyze a problem paying due respect to all the relevant complexities that make that problem pressing. Marco Bellocchio's *Bella Addormentata (Sleeping Beauty)* manages to present, accurately, different standpoints on euthanasia, and Tim Robbins's *Dead Man Walking* battles against the death penalty presents insights and arguments of the opposing viewpoints. Analyzing a political problem, a work may have a more or less authoritative (or hesitant) voice: the author's stand on the problem can be more or less evident in the film. For instance, in *Sleeping Beauty*, Bellocchio has a hesitant voice: is euthanasia right or wrong? Bellocchio does not suggest the answer. Finally, a work uses a maieutic method if it invites the spectator to draw the conclusions about what has been presented, whereas it is pedantic if it overtly states its semantic meaning.

The problem with the PPO is that it does not differentiate between epistemic dimensions. Indeed, PPO implies that (1) works with a partial perspective are works with an authoritative voice as they do not consider 'other' possible alternative perspectives on the issue, as well as (2) works that do not consider 'other', different perspectives cannot foster critical thinking (i.e. be epistemically meritorious) because they do not allow the spectator's 'freedom of thought'. I contend that both implications are false and that the dimension of the epistemic merit is independent from other dimensions, so it is to be appraised on its own terms.

Is it the case that works adopting a single perspective on a problem have an authoritative voice? This can be the case, but it is not necessarily true. Authors may focus on a single perspective to show the flaws of this standpoint or may simply investigate that perspective without taking a stand on its appropriateness. Moreover, as we have seen in Chapter 2, the epistemic authority of a work comes in degrees. A work can be more or less authoritative/hesitant, and being aligned to a single perspective does not necessarily imply a strong authoritative position on the issue at stake. By way of example, think of Joshua Oppenheim's documentary *The Act of Killing* (2012). This is a documentary about the crimes perpetrated by a state-supported paramilitary organization in Indonesia during the mid-sixties. Oppenheim invites Anwar Congo, the main leader of the death squads that killed thousands of communists in Indonesia, to tell stories about those years and specifically to describe and even reenact the killings he committed. Nowadays, Anwar lives in impunity and he has been overly enthusiastic about the film project, as he thought this would have made him look like a movie star. The film is focused on a single perspective: that of Anwar and his collaborators. None of the families who have suffered a loss were involved in the project. Nonetheless, the film is far from being an apology for the Indonesian regime or of Anwar's crimes. *The Act of Killing* is an example of a work that focuses on a single, partial perspective. Yet, the film does not endorse that perspective. Moreover, the epistemic voice of the film is not markedly authoritative. The director, throughout the film, withdraws manifestations of a reprehensive attitude. Oppenheim follows Anwar's reconstructions and reenactments of the events, pressing him with questions. Any judgment of Anwar's stories and behavior is almost entirely left to the audience. I say 'almost entirely' because toward the end of the film Oppenheim steps in, revealing his position. In one of the reenactments, Anwar, playing the victim in an interrogation, feels extreme distress and has to stop the scene. Oppenheim, questioning Anwar after the scene and guiding him in the elaboration of his feelings, reminds him that for the actual victims the interrogations must have been much worse than what he has felt as they knew that it was not fiction. The film tracks Anwar's feelings as he reenacts and elaborates what he has done in his past. In the beginning he is arrogant and proud, whereas toward the end he starts to crack and feel remorse. He wonders whether he sinned, but the horrors he perpetrated are such that he cannot conceive of himself as guilty. This documentary shows how a film that focuses on a single, partial perspective need not endorse such a perspective nor must it have a markedly authoritative voice. Indeed, throughout the film the director does not overtly manifest his attitude toward Anwar, and the spectator is even moved to feel pity for him due to his psychological inability to recognize the immorality of his behavior.[31]

If the first implication – works that focus on a single perspective have an authoritative voice – is not necessarily true, the second – works that focus on a single perspective cannot foster critical reflection – is even more dubious. Something more needs to be said about the idea that the audience should reach its own conclusion when engaging with a work. It is not exactly clear whether, and how, an epistemically authoritative voice may actually prevent such 'freedom of thought'. After all, when we are in a dispute and we listen to someone else's argument, we are not bound to accept his standpoint. Our opponent may have an authoritative epistemic voice, but we need not endorse his argument just because he uttered it. What we do is assess the epistemic merits of his argument, and in order to be epistemically meritorious a standpoint need not be hesitant.

Curran acknowledges a danger of inconsistency in Brecht's thought: she sees that Brecht's political agenda may actually prevent what Brecht calls 'freedom of thought' in the audience. We have hints of Brecht's artistic intentions (about *Mother Courage*) from some extracts of a conversation he had with playwright Friedrich Wolf and that Curran herself quotes: Brecht's aim is that of arousing 'the audience to a clear recognition of the relationships in actual and possible situations (social conditions), and so lead it to *correct* conclusions and decisions' (2001, p. 179). The emphasis is mine as I want to emphasize how the very idea of there being some conclusions that are *correct* implies epistemic authority. Curran then argues that Brecht grants such liberty of thought as his goal 'is not to dictate but merely to suggest and to leave for the viewer's further justification which responses are appropriate to the injustices she or he has seen dramatized' (p. 179). Indeed, she argues, in *Mother Courage* Brecht does not provide positive directions for change as a more didactic play would have done (p. 179). And this is because, Curran holds:

> Brechtian drama enables or encourages a response, 'p,' from the audience when the basic premises for drawing the conclusion, 'p,' are presented as elements in the drama's story, but the conclusion, 'p,' is not required to make sense of the action of the play
>
> (p. 180).

Here she is exactly describing an enthymematical process, according to which we have a number of premises, but the conclusion is not overtly stated. Didactic, or let us say pedantic, works can provide this kind of conclusion, overtly stating the message of the work within the text. As we have seen in Chapter 2, this can be an aesthetic defect as well as being rhetorically less effective than an enthymeme. And indeed, *Mother Courage* can be seen, under this point of view, as a successful and maieutic play. However, it is clear that Brecht wants to show the aberration of war and of the capitalist system through the story of Mother Courage who aims to exploit war as a source of personal profit but in the end has to pay the price for such exploitation. The death of her three children and Brecht's overt intention to make Courage as unappealing and unsympathetic as possible show the overall negative appraisal of the capitalist system that leads people to consider all sorts of opportunities as sources of personal profit. As I have argued in the second chapter, epistemic authority comes in degrees, but overall Brecht offers a clear image of what he holds to be wrong. The very fact that he does not provide an alternative positive solution does not prove the epistemic hesitancy of the work. At best, this is just a clue of the work's maieutic method, and indeed the play invites the spectators to reason about Mother Courage and to judge her behavior.

Hence, we can say that Curran is conflating two epistemic dimensions: the epistemic voice and the pedagogical method of the work. Specifically, her argument (erroneously) implies that since the work uses a maieutic method, the work's voice is hesitant; and, as we have seen previously, the epistemically hesitant voice of a work is what provides the alleged 'freedom of thought' that is required by the Brechtian conception of critical thinking. Hence (if we were to follow this explanation), the work is epistemically meritorious because hesitant. But failure to distinguish between the epistemic dimensions of a work makes the reasoning here logically unsound. There is a problem with a premise: works that make use of a maieutic method need not have a hesitant voice (and *Mother Courage* is certainly not hesitant), but also other implications do not necessarily hold – for instance, it is not the case that maieutic works are always epistemically meritorious or that authoritative works cannot have epistemic merits. Curran's analysis of Brecht's *Mother Courage* highlights the confusion that stems from a lack of distinction between a work's epistemic dimensions. Hence, I contend that we are better off if we apply my theoretical framework to analyze political works, as the distinction between epistemic dimensions makes our judgments more nuanced and pointed.

The analytic framework I propose shows that epistemic dimensions are to be appraised separately and there is no necessary causation between the authoritativeness of the epistemic voice and the epistemic merits of a work. So PPO fails, because (1) not all works that focus on a partial perspective have an authoritative voice and (2) even if they do have an authoritative voice, this would not necessarily imply epistemic defectiveness. I have already shown (in Chapter 2) that this connection does not hold, as an authoritative voice can still be epistemically meritorious and, indeed, this is the case in *Two Days, One Night*.

The Dardenne brothers are not hesitant about what would be the right thing to do in Sandra's case. Their film wants to be a defense of altruism and communal belonging, and it reaches its purpose in two ways. First, it aligns us to Sandra; we see things from her perspective and we come to root for her. We hope she gets the job, also because we believe she deserves it. Second, when, at the end of the film, Sandra is confronted with the same dilemma with which she has been confronting her colleagues, she makes the 'consistent' choice: she chooses what she would have wanted her colleagues to choose, even when this goes against her self-interests. At the ballot, the pro-bonus party wins, and Sandra loses her job. Mr Doumont, the company manager, calls Sandra for a talk. As she managed to persuade half of the staff to give up their bonus, he decided to hire Sandra back despite the result of the ballot. This will happen, though, at the expense of Alphonse, who will not see his contract renewed. Here is where Sandra has to make her choice. If she accepts the job, Alphonse, who voted for her at the ballot, will be laid off. Sandra refuses to take up the job, making clear that the central point of the film is not to see Sandra winning her fight but rather to advocate for the need of solidarity within the working class.

The film has an authoritative stance as it clearly takes a position, but that does not mean that the film is pedantic or epistemically flawed. Quite the contrary. The film never states overtly what would be the right conclusion to draw, although Sandra's situation represents an example that makes a clear case for specific conclusions. Also, the work is epistemically meritorious. Throughout the film, the Dardenne brothers show negative reactions to Sandra's plea: some of her colleagues do not want to vote for her and articulate reasons to back up a vote for the bonus. More importantly, the film provides an example – Sandra's situation – and works like a thought experiment that engages the audience: what would it be like to be in Sandra's situation? What would you expect from your colleagues? And what would you do when you are offered a job at the expense of someone else who has just helped you?

The last scene acquires particular relevance, as it grants both the film's maieutic and epistemic merit. Indeed, as the film aligns us with Sandra, we end up rooting for her, hoping that she regains the job. After all, she manages to get it back, and this is when she gives it up. We are left with conflicting feelings. We should be happy that she got her job back, and yet she seems to self-sabotage her entire fight. Despite the sadness we feel for Sandra losing her job (even if by her choice), the final scene elicits a positive emotion, that of elevation. Elevation is a kind of admiration, but it occurs in response to actions that are perceived as morally superior (Haidt, 2000; Plantinga, 2009b). Such emotion signals the witnessing of an act of human beauty or virtue, and it is characterized by a 'distinctive feeling in the chest of warmth and expansion' (Haidt, 2003, p. 863). As a positive moral emotion, elevation marks the rightness of Sandra's decision. We understand the difficulty of the choice, one that we probably would be reluctant to make, but as an altruistic act we cannot but admire Sandra. We are emotionally moved by the beauty of her action while at the same time being sad for Sandra actually losing her fight to keep the job. This emotional conflict cannot be resolved and inevitably it invites reflection on the reasons that have led to such conflicting emotional engagement. It is worth noting that, as we have seen in Chapter 6, thought experiments are epistemically valuable for they are able to activate affective processing mechanisms that may have not been activated by abstract reasoning. These affective processing mechanisms 'pump' intuitions that may be in disequilibrium with other previously held beliefs and can therefore initiate the reassessment of such beliefs. This is what happens with *Two Days, One Night*. The film is epistemically valuable as it elicits a complex emotional response that drives our reflection about the issue at stake. We are pushed to confront the beliefs we form after general and abstract reasoning about Sandra's situation and the intuitions that are 'pumped' by our affective response to Sandra's situation and behavior. In the next section, I expand on the role of emotional response to fiction, so that the entire process through which we come to reflect on our beliefs can be more coherently explained.

In this second section, I have shown how the Brechtian argument about narrative art that aims to elicit reflection on political problems does not hold if it is grounded on the idea that empathy prevents reflection. In the first place empathy cannot impair reflection by 'locking' the spectator into the character's perspective because empathy is only one of the mechanisms through which we engage with narrative art, and it is not a phenomenon that binds us constantly throughout the work. Moreover, I have shown how the 'partial perspective objection' also does not hold as works with an authoritative voice need not be epistemically flawed and, furthermore, this objection proves to be inaccurate as it conflates judgments about different epistemic dimensions.

More generally, Brechtian criticism has constantly neglected the idea that in order to understand why certain social arrangements are unjust, we need to understand the perspectives of those who are in disadvantaged positions. As such perspectives are so inherently shaped by social conditions, I find the understanding of these perspectives inherently political. Understanding *what it is like to be* X can be seen as part of a thought experiment through which we try to understand not just what would be our perspective were we in that situation but rather what is the perspective of someone who actually *is* in that situation. This kind of imagining can shed light on *others'* perspectives. This kind of activity, understanding the other's perspective, is crucial for the 'political'. I have argued in the first chapter that the central criterion for the identification of something 'political' is the possible grouping of social forces along the continuum that identifies the dichotomous categories of friend and enemy. Reaching the actual contraposition, friend/enemy means the negation of the political: war. Hence, the aim of politics is that of keeping the tensions between groups within a certain range of control and avoiding war. As the contrapositions between groups are necessarily shaped around specific issues – those shaping social conflict – understanding the *other's* stand on something politically relevant will foster communication and comprehension; that is, this will help to keep groups' contraposition within the limits of the political.

3 Emotional engagement with fiction

3.1 Defining emotions

In this third section, I want to consider the possibility that narratives aiming to elicit emotional response may actually impair critical thinking. This is not exactly a position we could ascribe to Brecht, although the German playwright has repeatedly showed skepticism toward the use of emotion in fiction. Brecht believed that emotional engagement would have led viewers astray, having them overlook the political problems and the unjust social relations a work presumes. In the previous section, I questioned Brecht's position by analyzing the modes of character engagement and showing that there is nothing intrinsically worrying about empathy, or any other mode of imagining, that may prevent spectators from engaging critically with the social and political issues raised by the work. Here I pursue a different line of inquiry. I suppose that the problem with fiction's engagement is not the mode of imagining but rather the response it elicits: emotions. I need to note that Brecht himself did not subscribe overtly to the idea that any emotional response could impair critical judgment even though he clearly showed skepticism toward emotion.[32] Such skepticism is probably to be traced back to the Platonic divide between reason and passions, which saw the latter as subordinated and potentially threatening to the former. Scholars in the analytic tradition of aesthetics have already replied to Brechtian skepticism toward the use of emotions in fiction.[33] Brecht advocated a critical and attentive spectator response; emotions are deemed to distract the spectator. However, debates in the philosophy of emotions have been focused on the analysis of rational elements of emotional responses. In sheer contrast to the Platonic approach to emotions, many philosophers have advocated a judgment or evaluation-based definition of emotions, where these are mental states that can be seen as the outcome of a specific belief-desire structure. That is to say, my feeling a certain emotion is the result of my appraisal of a relevant belief related to my interests, goals and desires. Following this theory, emotions have a propositional content that is identified by the relevant belief, they have an object (are directed toward something) and are the result of a personal evaluation of that object. Robert Solomon holds that emotions are a 'personal evaluation of the significance of an incident' (1976, p. 187). Hence, emotions are rooted in cognitive appraisal; they have an object and they indicate our evaluative judgment about it. The classic example is fear. When I meet Fido, a barking pit bull, I may be paralyzed with fear. The dog is the object of my emotion and I judge him to be a threat to my safety. As the emotion is caused by my judgment, a change in such judgment will correspond to a change in the emotion. When I get to know that Fido is actually completely harmless, my fear no longer makes any sense. This approach to the definition of emotions implies that emotions are not to be conceived of as opposing or negating reason. Quite the contrary, emotions are rational and entail rational judgments of events. Certainly, we usually associate emotions with physiological changes but, so the cognitive approach holds, such physiological changes result from the individual's control and evaluation of a situation.[34] Consequently, any skepticism toward emotional responses to fiction based on the assumption that emotions undermine rational analysis of situations or events is ill-founded.

The cognitive approach to emotions, however, has difficulties explaining particular cases when we feel, at one and the same time, emotions related to judgments that are inconsistent with one other. Patricia Greenspan (1988) proposes the example of the person who is competing with a friend to win a prize. Suppose she loses. She ends up feeling both happiness and sadness. She is sad because she did not win the prize, but she is happy because her friend, who she adores, has won the prize. The two judgments (1. 'it is good that my friend won' and 2. 'it is not good that my friend won') are logically incoherent, and a rational person would need to either qualify them (she could be happy because in some respects it is good that her friend won, in some others it is not) or sum them up (either it is good – on the whole – that her friend won or it is not). According to Greenspan, emotions are different from judgments for judgments need to be made coherent, whereas emotions need not. Greenspan still holds that emotions have a propositional content, but as long as there are reasons backing up our feelings, these need not cohere with other feelings, no matter the reasons that count against one feeling an emotion. Hence, for Greenspan, emotions still have an evaluative component, even though the propositional attitude implied by them need not be a belief. For instance, I can still be afraid of Fido even after I have learned that he is harmless, and this may be due to some earlier trauma with dogs.

Greenspan's account of emotions opens up to evaluative content that is not necessarily grounded on beliefs, but I suggest that we go even further and take up Jenefer Robinson's position that surpasses the idea that evaluation is all that there is in emotions. Robinson (2005), developing her account from Williams James's psychological writings, argues that what is actually typical of emotions is their physiological occurrence, and cognitive approaches to emotions overlook the centrality that physiological states play when we feel emotions. In their attempt to explain the rationality of emotions they skip over physiological triggers. Robinson argues that we should consider emotions as a process, one that entails both pre-reflective, noncognitive appraisal as well as cognitive evaluations. This account of emotions seems to be heuristically apt to grasp the complexities of emotional responses and it is grounded on relevant empirical evidence, which has shown how evaluations need not be necessary for emotion and that affective appraisal can occur prior to cognition (Zajonc, 1984). In particular, some experiments conducted by neurophysiologist Joseph LeDoux have proven how the affective appraisal in cases of fear occurs automatically and prior to cognitive appraisal. LeDoux (1989, 1998) has been studying the fear system of rats, discovering how it operates very rapidly and without awareness: the stimulus perceived is processed emotionally without the organism being able to recognize or cognize about the stimulus itself. Scientists have proven that when a rat hears the sound of a buzzer, the auditory thalamus is activated; the thalamus functions as a station receiving inputs and sending them out to the relevant parts of the cortex. The auditory thalamus receives the buzzer input and sends it to the auditory cortex where the sound is processed cognitively, and the auditory cortex then sends signals to the amygdala, which is where the emotional significance of inputs is registered and the signal is assessed emotionally. However, as Robinson points out, this is the important part, the auditory thalamus sends signals not just to the auditory cortex but also to the amygdala itself, which then receives the signals before those signals are cognitively assessed by the cortex. Such processing highlights how the affective appraisal occurs before the cognitive one, but it also shows that the cognitive evaluation then kicks in to check on the previous automatic response.

From LeDoux's results, Robinson draws up a theory of emotions that entails both kinds of appraisals – affective and cognitive – interacting with one another. So, an emotion is a process where there is:

> 1) an initial affective appraisal of the situation that focuses attention on its significance to the organism and causes 2) physiological responses of various sort – especially ANS activity and change in the facial musculature – and motor responses which get the organism dealing with the situation as very broadly appraised by the affective appraisal and which gives way to 3) a further more discriminating cognitive appraisal or monitoring of the situation
>
> (Robinson, 2005, p. 55).

Robinson's account of emotions manages to integrate coherently both kinds of appraisals, affective and cognitive. The affective appraisal causes the physiological response and direct attention while the cognitive monitoring kicks in to check the appropriateness of the rough and ready, quick and dirty evaluations.

An apparent weakness in such a theory of emotions, especially if we are to apply it to our engagement with artworks, is that it seems to overshadow the role of cognitive evaluations. Affective, precognitive appraisal seems to be prominent for emotions like surprise or fear where the role of precognitive appraisal may have also served evolutionary purposes: the cognitive evaluation takes too much time in circumstances where prompt action is needed for survival. Nonetheless, humans are capable of complex cognitions and some emotions are the result of such cognitions. However, Robinson's view of emotions as a process can account also for these kinds of emotions – triggered by complex cognition. Indeed, affective appraisal, Robinson argues, can also occur after careful consideration and complex cognitive evaluation. The noncognitive appraisal can be a meta-response, that is, an evaluation, rough and ready, of an already existing cognitive evaluation. Robinson gives the example of the fear we feel when we realize how bad our financial portfolio is doing (2005, p. 74). To understand that the portfolio is doing so poorly requires careful consideration and study, and this implies complex cognitive evaluations. However, it is not due to such technical evaluations that we are frightened by our economic situation. Rather, it is the affective appraisal of these cognitive evaluations that causes physiological changes we associate to fear. The affective appraisal is a rough and ready, quick and dirty assessment of the existing cognitive evaluations. The cognitive evaluation entails propositions of the kind: 'stock market is dropping in light of recent political developments', and noncognitive appraisal gives a rough evaluation related to personal interests, goals, wishes, values and desires, of the kind – 'this is bad for me!' Hence, there can be emotional responses provoked by cognitively complex beliefs as well as by simple perceptions.

Moreover, the cognitive appraisal is always present for the monitoring of a situation. This is the process that is characteristic of fear:

> I hear the crackling sound; I jump; and I see that indeed there is a rattlesnake; I realize that effort is required to get me out of this situation, that the situation is unpredictable and that I am not in control of it
> (Robinson, 2005, p. 75).

Even though LeDoux has proven that cognitive appraisal occurs later than affective appraisal, it still occurs pretty fast (milliseconds) and it is not surprising that, together with affective appraisal, cognitive monitoring takes place below the level of consciousness; therefore, it is also quite complex to separate different levels of appraisal and reappraisal. What is clear is that cognitive monitoring happens, and it reacts with affective appraisal; this is why emotions can be seen as processes where these two levels of appraisal interact in sequences.[35]

If we apply this account of emotions to our engagement with artworks, we see how this works just as well as the judgment theory if we want to argue that emotions, per se, do not actually hobble or damage our cognitive capacities.[36] The very phenomenology of an emotion implies the activation of cognitive evaluations about the emotion itself and its causes. As I have shown with the Dardenne brothers' *Two Days, One Night*, we can feel pity for Sandra because we have cognitive understanding of the relevant conditions that define Sandra's situation; in particular, the final scene of the film fosters a careful, and conscious, reflection on our emotional response, as this is a complex mixture of conflicting feelings, like pity and admiration.

3.2 *Emotions and rhetorical purposes*

It is not a new discovery that emotions can be used for rhetorical purposes and that they can help develop or support arguments. But I want to stress again how the use of emotions need not imply a departure from argumentative soundness and coherence. Quite the contrary, as we have seen in the second chapter of this book, the rhetor, for Aristotle, can persuade his audience using proofs that are related to (1) ethos, (2) pathos and (3) logos. The first kind of proof, the ethical one, is related to the supposed credibility of the persuader. In terms that we have discussed in this book (specifically in Chapter 4), we can say that this aspect of argumentation is related to the trustworthiness of the testimony. The 'pathos' of the argumentation refers to the capacity of the rhetor to move her audience, and 'logos' refers to the actual logical cogency of the argument provided through the use of examples and data. The most persuasive argument will be one that scores highly in each dimension.

Transposing these ideas to our analysis of film's rhetoric, we can leave aside the first kind of proof, as that is strictly related to the trustworthiness of the author. In Chapter 4, I have shown how this kind of proof, as much as it is epistemically relevant, lies outside the work itself and so has little aesthetic relevance. Pathos and logos, on the other hand, are strictly related to the work itself. These two tools available to the 'rhetor' enhance their rhetorical capacity when they work together: when emotions are elicited to emphasize the main points of a sound argument. In these cases, pathos and logos resonate, and the epistemic merit of the work is enhanced.

Troubles, I hold, come when emotions are used to move the audience without being paired with a sound narrative that could articulate a justification for the emotions elicited. In other words, there can be rhetorical works whose only tool of persuasion is represented by the kinds of emotional responses they aim to elicit. Such rhetorical works can still serve their intended function – to persuade their audience – but they will manage to do so on a less solid ground. Such works are epistemically defective as their argument lacks the proof of 'logos'.[37] Among these works, I label as sentimental those that aim to elicit 'soft' or 'tender' emotions (like pity, sorrow, fondness, etc.) that are not justified by 'logos' embedded within the narrative.[38]

By now it should be clear that there is nothing pernicious in emotions per se. This also means that there is nothing wrong in films that aim to elicit tender or soft emotions (like pity, sorrow, fondness, etc.), even though these kinds of emotions have also been viewed with suspicion. Perhaps this is due to what Robert Solomon (2004) calls a 'general tendency in Western literature and philosophy' to treat the passions with contempt, where the traditional dominance of the role of reason and rationality has brought an attitude of disdain or at least discomfort even toward the display of emotions. Or perhaps, and somewhat related to this tendency, such downplaying of the role of emotions is again to be traced back to the Platonic divide between reason and passion, where the latter is subordinated to the former (again, see Solomon, 2004).

Yet, such mistrust of emotions needs to be clarified and reformulated.[39] As we have seen, emotions per se do not warrant intellectual mistrust. But I take it that they do so when they cover or when they are elicited in spite of epistemic defects of the narrative.[40] In these cases, I hold, such emotions make a work sentimental. Language can be tricky, so clarifications are in order. We say that emotions elicited in films are not necessarily something to be suspicious of, and yet we use the word 'sentimentality', implying some sort of negative judgment. I will use the term 'sentimentality' as well 'sentimental' to imply something warranting suspicion, and I will clarify this later. The term 'sentiment', per se, is a neutral term, and the clause 'sentimental emotion' is sometimes used in a neutral way as well, meaning just 'soft' or 'tender' emotions without any further negative connotation.[41] However, I will avoid this usage here, in order to simplify the terminological array, and I should also specify that my analysis of sentimentality is only partial, as it refers only to sentimentality in political films.

The reason why I am concerned with sentimentality is that it highlights a discrepant use of persuasive tools for films with rhetorical purposes. Specifically, a sentimental film is one that uses only emotions (pathos) with the aim to persuade its audience and does not provide a sound and epistemically complex narrative (logos) that could 'back up' the emotions elicited. The film may actually reach its intended aim – persuade its audience – but it does so with an epistemic defect. Moreover, the film will only persuade a particular kind of audience, one consisting of sentimentalists.[42]

The most famous definitions of sentimentality share the fact they make a reference to both an object and a subject. Mary Midgley, in one of the first philosophical explorations of the topic, argued that sentimentality implies a misrepresentation of the world in order to indulge our feeling (1979, p. 385). Mark Jefferson argued that such indulgence is of a specific kind, so the sentimentalist 'misrepresents the world in order to feel unconditionally warm-hearted about bits of it' (1983, p. 525). And Oscar Wilde famously stated that the typical sentimentalist is 'someone who wants to have the luxury of an emotion without having to pay for it' (2000, p. 501). These definitions point at the fact that sentimentality implies emotions that are unearned, false or unwarranted, and the subject who feels these emotions, the sentimentalist, indulges such feelings, where such indulgence implies either hypocrisy or superficiality in appraisal of the 'object' that elicited such emotions.

Any analysis of sentimentality seems bound to take into account the relation between the object that elicits sentimentality and the subject that is sentimental. The ancient Greeks had Gods to symbolize emotions, but if we were to choose a God to symbolize sentimentality, we would need to pick the Latin God of Janus. With one face, Janus looks at the subject of sentimentality who indulges in the emotions felt while being the kind of person who either values too much or too little those very emotions in real life. With the other face, Janus looks at the object, which is designed to elicit emotions in ways that are unwarranted.

We have cases of pure sentimentality when the object is sentimental, and the subject is sentimental as well. Paradoxically, in these cases, it is as if sentimentality were not there any longer, as there is no one to detect it: the sentimentalist indulging in those feelings does not see them as unwarranted. There can be cases of spurious sentimentality, when one of the two parts of the relation is not actually sentimental. The object may not be sentimental, but a sentimentalist may misuse it to indulge in emotions that warm his heart. Or contrarily, and this happens when we actually use the term to evaluate something negatively, there can be cases when the object aims to elicit unwarranted emotions but we detect the deception.[43]

We could analyze both sides of the relation, testing them for moral and aesthetic value: is it a moral defect to be a sentimentalist? And are sentimental films morally and aesthetically defective? Here, I am only interested in the second question. Primarily, the problem with sentimentality, when we analyze the characteristics of the object, is that it implies epistemic defects, and such defects can turn out to be aesthetically relevant. In the previous definitions of sentimentality there are recurrent terms like 'false', 'unearned' and 'unwarranted' – all terms that we have previously used to define epistemic defectiveness, which shows how sentimental films intend to elicit emotions without accounting for the epistemic complexities that shape the object of those emotions.

By way of example, we can think of Clint Eastwood's film *American Sniper* (2014), based on Chris Kyle's autobiography (2012). The film is about Chris Kyle, a Texan cowboy who enlists in the army, becoming a sniper in Iraq for the American Navy Seals team. Kyle has been one of the most 'efficient' snipers in the US army, with an incredible high number of 'kills'. Eastwood portrays Kyle as a selfless hero who goes to Iraq just because he 'needs' to protect everyone from the terrorist threat. *American Sniper* is intended as a work of *mythopoeia* ('the making of myths'), as the clear aim of the film is that of portraying Kyle as a hero and a symbol of the 'War on Terror'.

Why should we perceive Kyle as a hero? According to Eastwood, because he was fighting terrorists, was putting his life at risk to do that and his work as a sniper was crucial in protecting his fellow soldiers, as well as Americans in general.

The film is sentimental because it aims to elicit fondness and admiration for Kyle, as well as sorrow for his death, but it does not pause to reflect on what Kyle did – which is, after all, killing people. The lack of critical reflection about the moral implications of Kyle's actions and behavior makes the emotions the film aims to elicit unwarranted. The film simplistically distinguishes the good from evil. Kyle is the good guy, and everything he does is never morally questioned, whereas Iraqis are just shown as savages whose only intention is that of blowing up Americans; evidently, Kyle is doing us a service by taking them down one by one. Also, he never shows regret, even when he has to make tough calls, as when he shoots a child who is carrying a grenade. Throughout the film there are only a few moments when the narrative lingers on the moral problems related to the war in Iraq and to killing in general, but these moments are shallow and they are usually summed up by insights of the kind 'Do you want these fuckers to come to San Diego?' The film does not dwell on moral problems; Kyle has no doubts that what he is doing is right, and he has no remorse or regret. When he comes back from his last tour in Iraq he is distressed, but what may have been a serious PTSD is actually shaken off like a cold, because Eastwood's hero is actually flawless. Even when he is back home, he helps others; in particular, he devotes his time to helping Veterans who actually suffer from PTSD and, tragically, he is murdered by one them.

The film reshapes some actual facts of Kyle's life to emphasize positive traits and to sentimentalize his life. For instance, in his autobiography, Kyle only mentions a Syrian sniper named Mustafa who, in the film, becomes his anti-hero. Mustafa is described as a ruthless sniper, so he is hunted down and killed with a legendary shot from a long distance. What is paradoxical is that Mustafa is just like Kyle. They are actually doing the same job, and yet there is no problematizing or discussion of Kyle's killings and of the reasons that guide both Americans and Iraqis. In addition, the film overlooks some controversial aspects of the actual Kyle's character. Indeed, the real-life Kyle had repeatedly treated war and killings with superficiality, releasing statements that showed almost a pathological attitude toward war. In the prologue of his autobiography (2012), he writes about the number of his killings: 'The number is not important. I only wish I had killed more' (p. 15); or, commenting on being at war:

> I loved what I did. I still do. If circumstances were different – if my family didn't need me – I'd be back in a heartbeat. I'm not lying or exaggerating to say it was fun. I had the time of my life being a SEAL (p. 19).

The film skates over all the troublesome moral issues in order to depict the profile of a hero, but a hero is to be defined by the things that he did in his life, and as what he did is at least morally problematic, the shallowness of the film does not back up the admiration and fondness it intends to elicit.

American Sniper lacks the proof of 'logos', and it only tries to persuade the audience with 'pathos'. Indeed, the film uses an oversimplified narrative structure where characters have no nuance – they are either clearly good or clearly bad (like all the Iraqis, the 'Butcher' and Mustafa). With one-dimensional characters, and a shallow narrative that does not problematize a complex moral issue, the film simply wants the audience to admire Kyle and mourn his unjust death.

As we have seen previously, sentimentality is associated with an epistemic defect, and for this reason, we can say that when a political film is sentimental, such sentimentality is an aesthetic defect – as this is related to the film's epistemic value.

Notes

1 Evidence that may back up these interpretations can be found in Brecht's writing (2014, pp. 9, 15, 23, 25, 28, 37, 60, 71, 145, 171–173, 182, 187–188, 195, 270–271, 277).
2 The word 'empathy' entered the English language as a translation of the German *Einfühlung*. See Currie (2011).
3 For an overview on the distinction between the ordinary use of the term and the academic characterization of it, see Battaly (2011).
4 Martin Hoffman holds that 'the key requirement of an empathetic response . . . is the involvement of psychological processes that make a person have feelings that are more congruent with another's situation than with his own situation' (Hoffman, 2000, p. 30). As Goldie notes, such a definition does not clarify the psychological process involved, but it is focused on the outcome. However, the 'congruity' of one's affective state with the target of empathic engagement is a matter of degree.
5 Goldie borrows the example from Jane Heal (1998).
6 Both Goldie (2011) and Goldman (2011) seem to share this idea, but I hold that theory of mind, alone, does not qualify as empathy.
7 See Rae Langton (2012).
8 For a discussion of the possibility of imagining being Napoleon, see Williams (1972, pp. 26–45). When we imagine being someone else we somehow 'undress' our *self* of our own psychological traits, desires and beliefs to take up traits and beliefs of that someone else. This is why Francois Recanati (2009) calls this kind of imagining *quasi de se*. It is *quasi de se* imagining because I do not self-ascribe the properties of the subject I imagine being. The properties are ascribed to the imagined subject, so even if this kind of imagining can be seen as central imagining, the imagined properties are not ascribed to the self, as in proper *de se* imaginings.
9 It seems that Smith would use the labels '*personal* imagining' and '*central* imagining' interchangeably. As I have remarked previously, I prefer to use the label '*central* imagining' to highlight that we are talking about imagining from the inside, but that the focus of the imagining is another self (another person). So, in general, the labels 'personal' and 'apersonal' can be misleading: I can imagine something from the outside (apersonal), but the person that I imagine can be myself. And I can imagine something from the inside (personal), but the person I imagine may not be myself.
10 Let me highlight a terminological difference between Smith (2011) and Amy Coplan (2011), who uses different labels to identify the same kinds of imaginings; Smith's 'other-focused central imagining' becomes 'other-oriented perspective-taking', as opposed to a 'self-oriented perspective taking' which would correspond to Smith's 'self-focused central imagining'.
11 Following Goldie who calls this kind of imagining 'in-his-shoes-perspective-shifting' (2011).
12 'In-his-shoes imagining' provides cognitive understanding of the situation, but it can also promote understanding of our own self, as we may find out how we might react in a certain situation.
13 Alvin Goldman (2006).
14 The clause 'affective consonance' is deliberately vague, as it would be too strict to posit as a requirement of a perfect overlap between the affective states. This vagueness can accommodate the idea that empathic engagement does not occur in isolation, it is affected and it affects other modes of imagining and engagement (Smith, 2017), so the affective state of the empathizer can be relatively complex.

15 The process through which I come to feel ashamed is also important in empathy: I understand the target's situation as well as his main character traits, desires, beliefs and aspirations. I imagine from the inside, taking his perspective. So I feel ashamed for the same reasons that he feels ashamed. The emotion we feel is not accidentally the same as the target's emotion.

16 Smith (2011) distinguishes between qualitative and quantitative dimensions of the significance of empathy, arguing that there may be few (or many) moments inviting empathic imagining, and yet they may be more or less relevant to the full apprehension of the narrative and appreciation of the work.

17 See Zajonc (2000) for an overview of the theory of facial feedback and Alvin Goldman (2006) on recognizing and experiencing basic emotions. For implications in philosophical theories of emotions, see Jenefer Robinson (2005).

18 That embodied simulation is also triggered by imagination which may have relevant implications in other art forms where perceiving another person's emotion via the recognition of facial expression may not be possible, as in literature, for instance. Moreover, in *Musicophilia*, Oliver Sacks (2010) talks about the same phenomenon without using the label 'embodied simulation' when he explains that musicians can actively train their technical skills just by imagining, vividly, the movements they are to perform, as such imagination activates the same (visceromotor and somatosensory) brain areas activated when they actually perform the movements.

19 However, the simulation of a person's mental state does not amount to empathic engagement, as I define empathy as a form of imagining that also requires a higher-level cognitive state, involving consciousness and volition.

20 Brecht advocated an 'epic' theater which should 'renounce empathy' (Brecht, 2014, p. 434).

21 It may be possible to build a case for the possibility that Brecht might have held that all artworks had a political dimension to be appraised. Indeed, he says that 'certain developments have paved the way for a transformation that goes far beyond formal issues and is beginning to come to grips with the actual function of the theater – its social function' (Brecht, 2014, p. 188). It is not clear whether this implies that every play should be appraised in light of this alleged 'actual function'.

22 I use Smith's terminology describing how we engage with fictional characters (1995). Smith holds that narratives elicit three different levels of imaginative engagement with characters (and to these we should add phenomena of empathic engagement): recognition, alignment and allegiance. Recognition describes the spectator's construction of characters (p. 82), and alignment 'describes the process by which spectators are placed in relation to characters in terms of access to their actions, and to what they know and feel' (p. 83). Allegiance requires the spectator's moral judgment of the characters. So, in *Two Days, One Night*, we are aligned to Sandra as we have access to her actions and feelings, and we have the same knowledge of the events that she has.

23 Smith (2011) marks a difference between the *quantitative* and *qualitative* dimensions of the claim for the significance of empathy. Skeptics about empathy seem to imply that any claim about the relevance of empathy in the process of apprehending a narrative requires a 'quantitative' dominance of empathy as mode of engagement with the narrative – as if empathic engagement needed to occur 'most or much of the time when we watch a movie' (p. 113). But empathy can occupy a 'quantitatively' modest portion of time when we engage with fiction and yet be *qualitatively* relevant, making these moments significant in the narrative. In *Two Days, One Night*, there are few moments of empathic engagement, making empathy 'quantitatively' insignificant, but these are 'quality' moments,

relevant to the narrative, as these moments provide valuable insights into Sandra's psychology and state of mind.

24 To understand Sandra's standpoint and share her affective states, we need to understand all the aspects of her context of which she is aware and that she understands, as these can affect her mindset. Aspects of her context which are unbeknownst to her cannot affect her state of mind.

25 I take it that this is a Brechtian objection, or at least a declination, logically plausible, of Brecht's arguments (see Brecht, 2014; Curran, 2001).

26 The term 'immersion' as I use it here is meant to cover 'empathic engagement', but it also entails that the work is focused exclusively on a single perspective.

27 My aim in this chapter is to assess Brechtian criticism and show that empathy does not prevent critical reflection, so I do not need to assess contemporary philosophical standpoints that criticize empathy as being able, or even tending, to distort moral judgment (see Prinz, 2011a, 2011b; Bloom, 2014). However, I want to note that these critics use a different definition of empathy, treating it as 'constitutive' of morality – to use Prinz's expression, 'as a precondition on moral judgment' (2011a, p. 214). The definition of empathy I endorse, as other-focused central imagining, allows me to treat empathy not as a virtue, or as something constitutive of moral reasoning, but as a skill (see Battaly, 2011).

28 The PPO objection, as I present it here, is never been spelled out properly. I want to dwell on it anyway, as PPO seems implied in Brecht's criticism of the Aristotelian theater. Brecht's main concern is with the possibility that the viewer may be 'locked' into the character's perspective. It is not clear whether the spectator may be locked into the character's perspective only if he comes to share the character's emotions (because of empathic engagement) or also because the work is exclusively focused on a single character's perspective. These two possibilities are logically separable – this is why I analyze both of them – but it is hard to distinguish between them in Brecht's writings. Brecht's criticism is to be conceived as, primarily, a formal criticism of the Aristotelian theater: his epic theater required particular formal properties that could incentivize the audience's participation – like the *Verfremdungseffekt*. These formal properties are meant to be critically informative: Brecht held that all the different elements of the play/work should remain autonomous and comment on each other. Opposing what he calls a 'Wagnerian *Gesamtkunstwerk*', where all the aesthetic elements (mise-en-scène, words, and music) are fused together 'to engulf the spectator in the aesthetic totality' (Kellner, 1980, p. 33), Brecht believed that all the aesthetic elements should remain separate, providing different information that could foster the spectator's critical attitude. In addition, Laura Bradley (2006) remarks how in order to cultivate this critical attitude, 'Brecht's theater destroys the illusory "fourth wall" . . . It displays the stage apparatus, such as the lights, in full view of the audience and introduces narrative elements into the performance. Songs interrupt the dramatic action; projected images provide a visual commentary. . .; and captions summarize the play's political arguments and the content of individual scenes. The juxtaposition of these narrative or "epic" elements with the dramatic action forces the spectator to adopt an active, critical role by comparing and evaluating the different pieces of information' (p. 5). Also the acting style is meant to provide political awareness: 'by emphasizing the decisions that inform the actions of the characters, the performers encourage spectators to see how alternative courses of action could have provoked different outcomes' (p. 5). It is as if all these formal elements could provide inputs for critical reflection: inputs that are themselves to be conceived as different perspectives on the story presented and inputs that are not contemplated by the classical Aristotelian theater that presents only a character's perspective to the spectator. For

our purposes, it suffices to say that we can distinguish between a claim about the nature of engagement with the work and a claim about the structure of the work itself. Here I focus on the second to show how a work focused on a single perspective need not be epistemically flawed. Also, the PPO helps me to test the explanatory capacities of the theoretical framework I propose in the first chapter.

29 On a side note, let me remark that a film need not be focused on a single character's perspective to elicit empathy with the character. It is, in principle, possible that a work presents different perspectives and succeeds in eliciting empathic engagement with more than one of them, as in the case of complex or network narratives like Paul Haggis's *Crash* (2004). Moreover, it is also possible that a work may focus on a character's point of view and yet elicit empathic imagining with characters presenting an opposing perspective – as in *Dead Man Walking*, where Tim Robbins, protesting against the death penalty, still manages to elicit empathy with the parents of the victims who actually support the death penalty.

30 The objection overlooks the possibility that a work may present a character's perspective on a political problem with the aim of criticizing this very perspective. So, PPO oversimplifies matters of interpretation equating the character's perspective with the author's standpoint. I show that even if this were the case, PPO does not hold.

31 However, note how our pity toward Anwar does not amount to endorsing his own perspective.

32 I take it that Brecht's view of emotions is actually undertheorized. In parts of his writings, Brecht seems to emphasize the importance of emotions in response to art: 'it is a frequently recurring mistake to suppose that this – epic – kind of production simply does without all emotional effects: actually, emotions are only clarified in it, steering clear of subconscious origins and intoxicating no one' (Brecht, 2014, pp. 343–344). Brecht does not seem to condemn emotions tout court but emotions felt in specific cases. The problem is that he does not specify *when* emotions are 'intoxicating'. Surely, though, he manifested a certain skepticism against emotional engagement, as he claimed that 'the key thing about epic theater is perhaps that it appeals less to the spectators' emotions than to their reason' (Brecht, 2014, p. 119).

33 Plantinga (1997a); Smith (1996).

34 Lazarus (1991); Lyons (1980).

35 The interaction between affective and cognitive appraisal is constant throughout the development of the emotions. We have seen that the affective appraisal occurs immediately, but the cognitive monitoring steps in immediately after, below the level of consciousness; our affective state then reacts to the monitoring itself, adjusting to it. An emotion is a process as it requires the interrelation of these two different kinds of appraisals while the first instances of cognitive monitoring occur at a subconscious level, if the emotion is complex and unfolds over time we come to consciously monitor and reflect on it. Conscious reflection on our emotional response is crucial to our engagement with artworks.

36 Robinson's account also serves to tackle an important problem related to our emotional engagement with artworks, the so-called paradox of fiction: Do we feel real emotions when engaging with fiction, and why? Philosophers of art have tackled the problem in different ways. Most notably Kendall Walton (1990) has developed an 'irrealist' position arguing that we do not feel real emotions but 'quasi-emotions' in response to fiction, whereas other philosophers have contested this view while still endorsing a cognitive theory of emotions (Gaut, 2007). Central to this debate is the question: why do we feel X when we know that X is a response to something fictional? For instance, if we say that we feel pity for Anna Karenina, what is it that we feel pity for? (1) Do we imagine that a person

just like Anna actually exists in the world? (2) Do we pity Anna herself? (3) Do we pity a thought of Anna? (4) Do we pity a person who may undergo similar suffering? Jenefer Robinson poignantly replies to all these problems by showing that while philosophers can conceptually make up such fine-grained distinctions, our psychology cannot. 'Pre-cognitive affective appraisals do not discriminate between real and imagined scenarios: I respond emotionally to whatever seems to have a bearing on my interests and of those to whom I am close (my family, my group, my fellow humans). It does not matter to my emotion systems (fear, anger, sadness, etc. . .) whether I am responding to the real, the merely imagined, the possible or the impossible' (Robinson, 2005, p. 145).

37 Being epistemically flawed does not imply being incapable of persuading, as I have shown in Chapter 3.

38 Thus I regard sentimentality as a subcategory of a broader category of epistemic flaw, that of eliciting emotions that are not justified by the narrative. More specifically, a subcategory that entails all those works that aim to elicit 'tender' emotions. I consider sentimentality a subcategory of this flaw in order to differentiate sentimental works from other works that may aim to elicit different kinds of emotions. For instance, we can imagine a work that elicits strong emotions of racial hatred in its audience without (of course) building a good rational case for this. This kind of work suffers from the same type of epistemic flaw, but I refrain from labeling it as sentimental, as this label is more suited to identifying different, 'softer', kinds of emotions.

39 Brecht criticizes emotions that are 'unchecked' (2015, p. 345). He does not provide any further specification of what it means for an emotion to be 'unchecked', but I suggest that cases of sentimentality might be considered the appropriate target of Brechtian criticism.

40 What I mean is that we should not take the epistemic reliability of emotions for granted. Here I follow Catherine Elgin (2008), who holds that emotions can be epistemically reliable, but they are not infallible. Indeed, there can be cases where our emotions are not appropriate.

41 See Plantinga (2009b, p. 197).

42 This is true when we postulate a positive correlation between a film's epistemic merit and rhetorical value (see Chapter 3 of this book). Sentimentalists do not recognize the epistemic flaw in the work, so they can be persuaded in spite of the work's epistemic defect. I define sentimentality and sentimentalists later.

43 There can be cases when we actually feel the emotions the object wanted to elicit, and yet we are aware of their deceptiveness. This is what I mean when I say that sometimes emotions deserve our mistrust. Indeed, there can be cases where there is a discrepancy between our affective and cognitive appraisal. We may feel something while at the same time knowing we should not be feeling that. Just like when I am afraid of Fido despite knowing that he is completely harmless.

Conclusion

Political cinema can be conceived of as a genre. Political films are characterized by a specific purpose, and this very purpose can play a relevant role in our aesthetic appraisal. This means that the reasons why we take a film to be political can influence the film's aesthetic value. A film is political when its intended aim is to (1) persuade the audience about the validity of a political standpoint or (2) elicit reflection around a political issue. A political issue is an issue that shapes social conflict and grouping along the friend/enemy distinction, and a political standpoint is a specific position within the debate shaping the social conflict. The first function is a 'rhetorical' function, and the second is an 'explorational' function.

I have argued that in order to analyze and assess political films, we need to consider three criteria: (1) the epistemic voice, (2) the epistemic merit and (3) the pedagogical method. The criteria are related with one another and have bearings on the value of films *qua* art. The first criterion allows us to differentiate between political films with a rhetorical function and those with an explorational function. Films may have more or less authoritative or hesitant voices. Films with an authoritative epistemic voice have rhetorical purposes, whereas films that are epistemically hesitant have explorational purposes. The third criterion, the pedagogical method, has rhetorical, aesthetic and epistemic relevance. Films can make use of a maieutic method, or they can pedantically state their viewpoint and the lesson they want to impart. Following Aristotle, works that make use of maieutics tend to be rhetorically better off, as they invite the active participation of the audience. We have also seen that pedantry is often considered an aesthetic defect (see Lamarque, 2009), as it preempts the audience's intellectual engagement with the work. Instead, the maieutic method presupposes the audience's active intellectual engagement, and this is not only aesthetically valuable but also epistemically so – as Sosa (2009) points out, we are not just interested in *having* the truth; we also want to *discover* it. That is, we want to arrive at the truth through our own intelligent doings, relying on our own set of abilities, skills and faculties. The pedagogical criterion once again shows the interrelation between epistemic and aesthetic value.

DOI: 10.4324/9780367816872-9

Political films aim at either persuading the audience or eliciting reflection about specific (political) issues. More generally, we can say that political films aim to have an impact on the audience's system of beliefs, either because they want to change it, persuading the audience of the validity of a given standpoint, or because they want the audience to appreciate the epistemic difficulties of a specific issue, inviting reflection on one's own system of beliefs. The epistemic merits or demerits of a film determine its success as a political film. Indeed, I have argued that we can reasonably postulate a positive correlation between the epistemic merit and a film's capacity to persuade its audience or elicit reflection on a political issue. Furthermore, we have seen how films with a rhetorical purpose that are epistemically defective tend to belong to the subcategory of propaganda films.

Political films can afford epistemic gains. They can clarify already-held beliefs or make them more vivid. They can bring new knowledge that can be articulated in propositional terms. They can foster understanding of specific issues, characters, or situations, and they can foster empathic and sympathetic imaginings that are relevant skills for moral reasoning. A film's epistemic value determines the value of the film as a *political* film. However, a film's epistemic value does not necessarily affect its value *qua* art. The epistemic value is aesthetically relevant when it is expressed with artistic means. Hence, when the belief conveyed is exclusively justified by testimony, as in the case of the empirical knowledge conveyed by *Leviathan*, this epistemic gain is not aesthetically valuable for it is not expressed by artistic means.

However, political films can afford epistemic gains that are aesthetically relevant, for cinematographic features can guide our imaginative engagement, and imagination is a reliable source of knowledge. We can consider political films to be like thought experiments. Thought experiments are epistemically valuable tools because they are capable of activating processing mechanisms that are otherwise not mobilized by abstract and general reasoning. Films manage to have an impact on the spectator's system of belief as they can trigger reflection on complex issues starting from an automatic affective response that activates a process of examination and appraisal at a higher cognitive level. The automatic affective response is elicited through the combination of cinematographic features and their interplay with the narrative. Hence, films have a particular kind of *epistemic efficiency* – consisting in the film's capacity to activate those automatic, low-level processing mechanisms that would otherwise have been inert – that is realized through artistic means. As such, a film's epistemic efficiency is aesthetically relevant – it affects the value of a film *qua* art.

Finally, there is no specific mode of imagining that can impair the spectator's critical reflection. Empathic imagining is only one of a number of modes of imagining through which we engage with narrative art, and it does not bind us, constantly, throughout the film. Understanding *what it is like to be* X can be seen as part of a thought experiment where we try to understand not just what our perspective would be were we in a given situation but also the perspective of someone who actually *is* in that situation. This kind of imagining can shed light on *others'* perspectives and, hence, it can be morally and politically relevant. I have also shown that emotional engagement, in general, is not to be seen as pernicious for the spectator's critical engagement with the work, for emotional engagement implies an integration between low-level, automatic appraisals and high-level, cognitive faculties. However, I have also highlighted that emotions can be used for rhetorical purposes, and when they are not backed up by a sufficiently complex narrative – we can say that there is a discrepancy between 'logos' and 'pathos' – these emotions are unwarranted or unearned. Specifically, a sentimental film is one that elicits tender emotions that are unwarranted; so sentimentality, for a political film, is an aesthetic defect, to the extent that sentimentality implies an epistemic flaw, and sentimental films can be classed as a subcategory of propaganda.

It has been the ambition of this book to provide a theoretical framework that could help with the classification, analysis and assessment of political films. I wanted to provide the tools to differentiate between films with a political content and those that have nothing to do with the political realm. Moreover, I have suggested that we could consider the category of political cinema as one that actually plays a role in the aesthetic appreciation of artworks. That is to say, the features that determine a film's belonging to this category are also features that are crucial in the appreciation and assessment of artworks. To properly assess a political film, we need to appraise and interpret the film, paying attention to the features that make it political – that make it belong to the category of political cinema. There are two main elements that determine the film's belonging to the category: (1) the film's function (or aim) and (2) the kind of issue at stake in the film. So, we say that a film is political if: (1) it intends to serve either a rhetorical or an explorational function and (2) the issue at stake is a political issue – an issue that shapes social conflict around the friend/enemy distinction. To reach its aim (to persuade or elicit reflection), the film needs to be epistemically meritorious (although we have also contemplated cases where a film may manage to persuade the audience and yet be epistemically defective). Hence, the epistemic value of a political film is the crucial component for its assessment: it determines the work's belonging to the category – indeed, to have a rhetorical or explorational function means to aim to have an impact on the audience's system of beliefs – and it determines the overall value of the work. The film's epistemic value determines its value as a *political* film and its value *qua* art, as we have seen that a film's epistemic efficiency can be expressed via artistic means and, therefore, be aesthetically relevant.

References

Abell, C. (2015). Genre, interpretation and evaluation. *Proceedings of the Aristotelian Society*, *115*(1), 25–40.

Adler, J. (2008). *Epistemological problems of testimony*. Retrieved from https://stanford.library.sydney.edu.au/archives/fall2006/entries/testimony-episprob/

Allen, R., & Smith, M. (1997). *Film theory and philosophy: Aesthetics and the analytical tradition*. Oxford: Clarendon Press.

Altman, R. (2012). A semantic/syntactic approach to film genre. In B. K. Grant (Ed.), *Film genre reader IV* (p. 27). Austin: University of Texas Press.

Anderson, E. (2006). *What game would you rather play*. Retrieved from http://left2right.typepad.com/main/2006/02/what_game_would.html

Aristotle. (2015). *Retorica e poetica*. Novara: UTET.

Audi, R. (2003). *A contemporary introduction to the theory of knowledge*. New York: Routledge.

Battaly, H. D. (2011). Is empathy a virtue? In A. Coplan & P. Goldie (Eds.), *Empathy: Philosophical and psychological perspectives* (pp. 277–301). Oxford: Oxford University Press.

Benjamin, W. (2003). *Understanding Brecht* (new ed.). New York: Verso.

Bloom, A. (1975). Justice: John Rawls vs. the tradition of political philosophy. *American Political Science Review*, *69*(02), 648–662.

Bloom, P. (2014). Against empathy. *Boston Review*, *39*(5), 14. Retrieved from http://gateway.proquest.com/openurl?ctx_ver=Z39.88-2003&xri:pqil:res_ver=0.2&res_id=xri:ilcs-us&rft_id=xri:ilcs:rec:abell:R05075107

Böckenförde, E. W. (2010). *Diritto e secolarizzazione*. Roma: Laterza.

Bordwell, D. (1985). *Narration in the fiction film*. London: Methuen.

Bordwell, D. (1989). *Making meaning: Inference and rhetoric in the interpretation of cinema*. Cambridge: Harvard University Press.

Bordwell, D., & Carroll, N. (1996). *Post-theory*. Madison: The University of Wisconsin Press.

Bradley, L. (2006). *Brecht and political theatre: The mother on stage*. Oxford: Oxford University Press.

Brecht, B. (2014). *Brecht on theatre* (3rd ed.). London: Bloomsbury.

Brown, J. R. (1991). Thought experiments: A platonic account. In M. Frappier, L. Meynell, & J. R. Brown (Eds.), *Thought experiments in science and philosophy* (pp. 119–128). Lanham: Rowman & Littlefield Publishers.

Brown, J. R. (1992). Why empiricism won't work. *PSA: Proceedings of the Biennial Meeting of the Philosophy of Science Association*, 271–279.

Brown, J. R. (2004). Why thought experiments transcend empiricism. In C. Hitchcock (Ed.), *Contemporary debates in the philosophy of science* (pp. 23–43). Oxford: Blackwell.

Brown, J. R. (2011). *The laboratory of the mind: Thought experiments in the natural sciences*. New York: Routledge.

Buscombe, E. (2012). The idea of genre in American cinema. In B. K. Grant (Ed.), *Film genre reader IV* (p. 12). Austin: University of Texas Press.

Camp, E. (2006a). Metaphor and that certain 'je ne sais quoi'. *Philosophical Studies*, *129*(1), 1–25.

Camp, E. (2006b). Contextualism, metaphor, and what is said. *Mind & Language*, *21*(3), 280–309.

Camp, E. (2007). Thinking with maps. *Philosophical Perspectives*, *21*(1), 145–182.

Camp, E. (2009). Two varieties of literary imagination: Metaphor, fiction, and thought experiments. *Midwest Studies in Philosophy*, *33*(1), 107–130.

Carroll, N. (1993). Historical narratives and the philosophy of art. *The Journal of Aesthetics and Art Criticism*, *51*(3), 313–326.

Carroll, N. (1994). Visual metaphor. In J. Hintikka (Ed.), *Aspects of metaphor* (pp. 189–218). New York: Springer.

Carroll, N. (1996a). Prospects for film theory: A personal assessment. In D. Bordwell & N. Carroll (Eds.), *Post-theory. reconstructing film studies* (pp. 37–68). Madison: The University of Wisconsin Press.

Carroll, N. (1996b). *Theorizing the moving image*. Cambridge: Cambridge University Press.

Carroll, N. (1996c). A note on film metaphor. *Journal of Pragmatics*, *26*(6), 809–822.

Carroll, N. (1998). Art, narrative, and moral understanding. In J. Levinson (Ed.), *Aesthetics and ethics: Essays at the intersection* (pp. 126–160). Cambridge: Cambridge University Press.

Carroll, N. (2001). *Beyond aesthetics: Philosophical essays*. Cambridge: Cambridge University Press.

Carroll, N. (2002). The wheel of virtue: Art, literature, and moral knowledge. *The Journal of Aesthetics and Art Criticism*, *60*(1), 3–26.

Carroll, N. (2010a). Politics and aesthetics. In *Art in three dimensions* (pp. 272–282). Oxford: Oxford University Press.

Carroll, N. (2010b). Movies, the moral emotions, and sympathy. *Midwest Studies in Philosophy*, *34*(1), 1–19.

Carroll, N. (2013). Moral change: Fiction, film, and family. In J. Choi & M. Frey (Eds.), *Cine-ethics: Ethical dimensions of film theory, practice, and spectatorship* (pp. 43–56). New York: Routledge.

Cioffi, A. E. (2020). Aesthetics of Propaganda. *International Lexicon of Aesthetics*. Retrieved from https://lexicon.mimesisjournals.com/international_lexicon_of_aesthetics_item_detail.php?item_id=92

Conolly, O., & Haydar, B. (2001). Narrative art and moral knowledge. *The British Journal of Aesthetics*, *41*(2), 109–124.

Conolly, O., & Haydar, B. (2007). Literature, knowledge, and value. *Philosophy and Literature*, *31*(1), 111–124.

Conolly, O., & Haydar, B. (2008). Literature, politics, and character. *Philosophy and Literature*, *32*(1), 87–101.

Coplan, A. (2011). Understanding empathy. In A. Coplan & P. Goldie (Eds.), *Empathy: Philosophical and psychological perspectives* (pp. 3–18). Oxford: Oxford University Press.

Coplan, A., & Matravers, D. (2011). Film, literature and non-cognitive affect. In H. Carel & G. Tuck (Eds.), *New takes in film-philosophy* (pp. 117–134). London: Palgrave Macmillan.

Curran, A. (2001). Brecht's criticisms of Aristotle's aesthetics of tragedy. *Journal of Aesthetics and Art Criticism*, *59*(2), 167–184.

Curran, A. (2011). Review: Cinema, philosophy, Bergman: On film as philosophy by Livingston, Paisley. *Journal of Aesthetics and Art Criticism*, *69*(2), 253–255.

Currie, G. (2004). *Arts & minds*. Oxford: Oxford University Press.

Currie, G. (2011). Empathy for objects. In A. Coplan & P. Goldie (Eds.), *Empathy: Philosophical and psychological perspectives* (pp. 82–98). Oxford: Oxford University Press.

Danto, A. C. (1983). Art, philosophy, and the philosophy of art. *Humanities*, *4*(1), 1–2.

Davies, D. (2007). Thought experiments and fictional narratives. *Croatian Journal of Philosophy*, (19), 29–45.

Davies, D. (2008). Can film be a philosophical medium? *Postgraduate Journal of Aesthetics*, *5*(2), 1–20.

Davies, D. (2010). Learning through fictional narratives in art and science. In R. Frigg & M. Hunter (Eds.), *Beyond mimesis and convention* (pp. 51–69). New York: Springer.

Diffey, T. J. (1995). What can we learn from art? *Australasian Journal of Philosophy*, *73*(2), 204–211.

Dworkin, R. (1981). What is equality? part 2: Equality of resources. *Philosophy & Public Affairs*, 283–345.

Elgin, C. Z. (2008). Emotion and understanding. In G. Brun, U. Dogluoglu, & D. Kuenzle (Eds.), *Epistemology and emotions* (pp. 33–50). New York: Routledge.

Elgin, C. Z. (2014). Fiction as thought experiment. *Perspectives on Science*, *22*(2), 221–241.

Epstein, J. (2014). *The intelligence of a machine*. Minneapolis, MN: Univocal.

Fellowes, J. (2009). *How I put young Victoria on the throne*. Web-magazine interview. Retrieved from www.dailymail.co.uk/femail/article-1159788/Screenwriter-reveals-How-I-Young-Victoria-throne.html

Fenoglio, B. (1952). *I ventitre giorni della cittá di alba*. Torino: Einaudi.

Fenoglio, B. (1990). *Una questione privata. I ventitre giorni della città d'Alba*. Torino: Einaudi.

Fenoglio, B. (1992). *Romanzi e racconti*. Torino: Einaudi.

Flory, D. (2000). Black on white: Film noir and the epistemology of race in recent African American cinema. *Journal of Social Philosophy*, *31*(1), 82–116.

Flory, D. (2008). *Philosophy, black film, film noir*. University Park: Penn State University Press.

Foot, P. (1978). *Virtues and vices and other essays in moral philosophy*. Oxford: Oxford University Press.

Frampton, D. (2006). *Filmosophy*. New York: Columbia University Press.

Freeland, C. A. (1996). Feminist frameworks for horror films. In D. B. N. Carroll (Ed.), *Post-theory: Reconstructing film studies* (pp. 195–218). Madison: University of Wisconsin Press.

Friend, S. (2012). Fiction as a genre. *Proceedings of the Aristotelian Society, 112*(2pt2), 179–209.

Friend, S. (2014). Believing in stories. In G. Currie, M. Kieran, A. Meskin, & J. Robson (Eds.), *Aesthetics and the sciences of mind* (pp. 227–248). Oxford: Oxford University Press.

Gallese, V. (2009). The two sides of mimesis: Girards mimetic theory, embodied simulation and social identification. *Journal of Consciousness Studies, 16*(4), 21–44.

Gallese, V. (2011). Neuroscience and phenomenology. *Phenomenology and Mind, 1*, 34–47.

Gallese, V., & Guerra, M. (2015). *Lo schermo empatico. cinema e neuroscienze.* Milano: Cortina Editore.

Gaut, B. N. (2005). The cluster account of art defended. *The British Journal of Aesthetics, 45*(3), 273–288.

Gaut, B. N. (2007). *Art, emotion and ethics.* Oxford: Oxford University Press.

Gaut, B. N. (2010). Empathy and identification in cinema. *Midwest Studies in Philosophy, 34*(1), 136–157.

Gendler, T. S. (1998). Galileo and the indispensability of scientific thought experiment. *British Journal for the Philosophy of Science, 49*(3), 397–424.

Gendler, T. S. (2000). *Thought experiment: On the powers and limits of imaginary cases.* New York: Routledge.

Gendler, T. S. (2002). Personal identity and thought-experiments. *Philosophical Quarterly, 52*(206), 34–54.

Gendler, T. S. (2004). Thought experiments rethought – and reperceived. *Philosophy of Science, 71*(5), 1152–1163.

Gendler, T. S. (2007). Philosophical thought experiments, intuitions, and cognitive equilibrium. *Midwest Studies in Philosophy, 31*(1), 68–89.

Gendler, T. S. (2012). Between reason and reflex: Response to commentators. *Analysis, 72*(4), 799–811.

Goldie, P. (2011). Anti-empathy. In A. Coplan & P. Goldie (Eds.), *Empathy: Philosophical and psychological perspectives* (pp. 302–317). Oxford: Oxford University Press.

Goldman, A. H. (2006). The experiential account of aesthetic value. *The Journal of Aesthetics and Art Criticism, 64*(3), 333–342.

Goldman, A. H. (2011). Two routes to empathy. In A. Coplan & P. Goldie (Eds.), *Empathy: Philosophical and psychological perspectives* (pp. 31–44). Oxford: Oxford University Press.

Goldman, A. I. (2006). *Simulating minds: The philosophy, psychology, and neuroscience of mindreading.* New York: Oxford University Press.

Goodman, N. (1968). *Languages of art: An approach to a theory of symbols.* Camrbidge: Hackett Publishing.

Greene, J. D. (2014). *Moral tribes: Emotion, reason and the gap between us and them.* London: Atlantic Books Ltd.

Greene, J. D. (2015). Beyond point-and-shoot morality: Why cognitive (neuro) science matters for ethics. *The Law & Ethics of Human Rights, 9*(2), 141–172.

Greene, J. D., Morelli, S. A., Lowenberg, K., Nystrom, L. E., & Cohen, J. D. (2008). Cognitive load selectively interferes with utilitarian moral judgment. *Cognition, 107*(3), 1144–1154.

Greene, J. D., Sommerville, R. B., Nystrom, L. E., Darley, J. M., & Cohen, J. D. (2001). An fMRI investigation of emotional engagement in moral judgment. *Science, 293*(5537), 2105–2108.
Greenspan, P. S. (1988). *Emotions and reasons: An enquiry into emotional justification*. New York: Routledge.
Grimm, S. R. (2010). The goal of explanation. *Studies in History and Philosophy of Science Part A*, *41*(4), 337–344.
Grimm, S. R. (2012). The value of understanding. *Philosophy Compass*, *7*(2), 103–117.
Habermas, J. (2009). Modernity – an unfinished project. *Politicka Misao*, *46*(2), 96–114.
Habermas, J. (2013). A political constitution for the pluralist world society? *Journal of Chinese Philosophy*, *40*, 226–238. doi:10.1111/1540-6253.12074.
Häggqvist, S. (1998). Thought experiments in philosophy. *Australasian Journal of Philosophy*, *76*(1).
Häggqvist, S. (2009). A model for thought experiments. *Canadian Journal of Philosophy*, *39*(1), 55–76.
Haidt, J. (2000). The positive emotion of elevation. *Prevention and Treatment*, *3*(3), 1–5.
Haidt, J. (2003). Elevation and the positive psychology of morality. In C. L. M. Keyes & J. Haidt (Eds.), *Flourishing: Positive psychology and the life well-lived* (pp. 289–308). Washington, DC: APA.
Hanson, L. (2013). The reality of (Non-Aesthetic) artistic value. *The Philosophical Quarterly*, *63*(252), 492–508.
Harold, J. (2008). Immoralism and the valence constraint. *British Journal of Aesthetics*, *48*(1), 45–64.
Harold, J. (2011). Autonomism reconsidered. *British Journal of Aesthetics*, *51*(2), 137–147.
Harsanyi, J. C. (1980). Can the maximin principle serve as a basis for morality? A critique of john Rawls's theory. In *Essays on ethics, social behavior, and scientific explanation* (pp. 37–63). New York: Springer.
Heal, J. (1998). Co-cognition and off-line simulation: Two ways of understanding the simulation approach. *Mind and Language*, *13*(4), 477–498.
Hempel, C. (1965). *Aspects of scientific explanation and other essays in the philosophy of science*. New York: The Free Press.
Hills, A. (2016). Understanding why. *Noûs*, *50*(4), 661–688.
Hoffman, M. L. (2000). *Empathy and moral development: Implications for caring and justice*. Cambridge: Cambridge University Press.
Hummel, W. C., & Huntress, K. G. (1959). *The analysis of propaganda*. New York: Henry Holt.
Humphries, R. (2008). *Hollywood's blacklists: A political and cultural history*. Edinburgh: Edinburgh University Press.
Jefferson, M. (1983). What is wrong with sentimentality? *Mind*, *92*(368), 519–529.
Jowett, G., & O'Donnell, V. (1992). *Propaganda and persuasion* (2nd ed.). London: Sage Publications.
Kagan, S. (1989). *The limits of morality*. Oxford: Oxford University Press.
Kellner, D. (1980). Brecht's Marxist aesthetic: The Korsch connection. In B. N. Weber & H. Heinen (Eds.), *Bertolt Brecht* (pp. 29–42). Athens, GA: University of Georgia Press.

Kind, A. (2016). Imagining under constraints. In A. Kind & P. Kung (Eds.), *Knowledge through imagination* (pp. 145–159). Oxford: Oxford University Press.

Krutnik, F., Neale, S., Neve, B., Stanfield, P., & American Council of Learned Societies. (2007). *"Un-American" Hollywood politics and film in the blacklist era*. Brunswick, NJ: Rutgers University Press.

Kvanvig, J. L. (2003). *The value of knowledge and the pursuit of understanding*. Cambridge: Cambridge University Press.

Kyle, C., McEwen, S., DeFelice, J., & van den Berg, Gerrit Jan. (2012). *American sniper*. Surbiton: Nimrod.

Laetz, B., & Lopes, D. M. (2008). Genre. In P. Livingston & C. Plantinga (Eds.), *The Routledge companion to philosophy and film* (pp. 152–161). New York: Routledge.

Lamarque, P. (2009). *The philosophy of literature*. Oxford: Blackwell.

Langford, B. (2010). *Post-classical Hollywood: Film industry, style and ideology since 1945*. Edinburgh: Edinburgh University Press.

Langton, R. (2012). *Ethics and imagining de se*. Retrieved from http://people.duke.edu/~sb192/DKL/EthicsandImagining.pdf

Lasswell, H. D. (1927). The theory of political propaganda. *The American Political Science Review*, *21*(3), 627–631.

Lasswell, H. D. (1952). *Power and society: A framework for political inquiry*. London: Routledge & K. Paul.

Lazarus, R. S. (1991). *Emotion and adaptation*. New York: Oxford University Press.

LeDoux, J. E. (1989). Cognitive-emotional interactions in the brain. *Cognition and Emotion*, *3*(4), 267–289.

LeDoux, J. E. (1998). *The emotional brain: The mysterious underpinnings of emotional life*. New York: Simon and Schuster.

Lee, A. M., & Lee, E. B. (1939). *The fine art of propaganda: A study of father Coughlin's speeches*. San Diego: Harcourt Brace.

Levinson, J. (1996a). Intention and interpretation in literature. In *The pleasures of aesthetics* (pp. 175–213). Ithaca: Cornell University Press.

Levinson, J. (1996b). *The pleasures of aesthetics: Philosophical essays*. Ithaca: Cornell University Press.

Levinson, J. (2006). *Contemplating art. Essays in aesthetics*. Oxford: Clarendon Press.

Lippmann, W. (1927). *The phantom public*. New Jersey: Transaction Publishers.

Livingston, P. (2005). *Art and intention: A philosophical study*. Oxford: Clarendon Press

Livingston, P. (2009). *Cinema, philosophy, Bergman on film as philosophy*. Oxford: Oxford University Press.

Lopes, D. M. (2011). The myth of (Non-Aesthetic) artistic value. *The Philosophical Quarterly*, *61*(244), 518–536.

Lopes, D. M. (2014). *Beyond Art*. Oxford: Oxford University Press.

Lyons, W. E. (1980). *Emotion*. Cambridge: Cambridge University Press.

Maltby, R. (1983). *Harmless entertainment: Hollywood and the ideology of consensus*. Lanham: Scarecrow Press.

Midgley, M. (1979). Brutality and sentimentality. *Philosophy*, *54*(209), 385–389.

Moran, R. (1994). The expression of feeling in imagination. *The Philosophical Review*, *103*(1), 75–106.

Mulhall, S. (2002). *On film*. New York: Routledge.

Mulvey, L. (1989). Visual pleasure and narrative cinema. In *Visual and other pleasures* (pp. 14–26). New York: Springer.
Nersessian, N. J. (1992). In the theoretician's laboratory: Thought experimenting as mental modeling. *PSA: Proceedings of the Biennial Meeting of the Philosophy of Science Association*, 291–301.
Nersessian, N. J. (2007). Thought experimenting as mental modeling. *Croatian Journal of Philosophy*, *7*(2), 125–161.
Nevola, G. (2003). *Una patria per gli italiani. la questione nazionale oggi tra storia, cultura e politica*. Roma: Carocci.
Newman, M. (2014). EMU and inference: What the explanatory model of scientific understanding ignores. *European Journal for Philosophy of Science*, *4*(1), 55–74.
Nozick, R. (1973). Goodman, nelson, on merit, aesthetic. *The Journal of Philosophy*, *69*(21), 783–785.
Nozick, R. (1974). *Anarchy, state and utopia*. New York: Basic Books.
Nussbaum, M. C. (2013). *Political emotions*. Cambridge: Harvard University Press.
O'Shaughnessy, M. (2007). *The new face of political cinema: Commitment in French film since 1995*. Oxford: Berghahn Books.
Pareto, V. (1991). *The rise and fall of elites: An application of theoretical sociology*. New Brunswick, NJ: Transaction Publishers.
Parsons, G., & Carlson, A. (2008). *Functional beauty*. Oxford: Oxford University Press.
Pavese, C. (1948). *La casa in collina*. Turin: Einaudi.
Paxton, J. M., Ungar, L., & Greene, J. D. (2012). Reflection and reasoning in moral judgment. *Cognitive Science*, *36*(1), 163–177.
Plantinga, C. (1997a). Notes on spectator emotion and ideological film criticism. In R. Allen & M. Smith (Eds.), *Film theory and philosophy* (pp. 327–393). Oxford: Oxford University Press.
Plantinga, C. (1997b). *Rhetoric and representation in nonfiction film*. Cambridge: Cambridge University Press.
Plantinga, C. (2005). What a documentary is, after all. *The Journal of Aesthetics and Art Criticism*, *63*(2), 105–117.
Plantinga, C. (2009a). The philosophy of Errol Morris – Ten lessons. In W. Rothman (Ed.), *Three documentary filmmakers: Errol Morris, Ross McElwee, Jean Rouch* (pp. 43–60). Albany: SUNY Press.
Plantinga, C. (2009b). *Moving viewers: American film and the spectator's experience*. Berkeley: University of California Press.
Plantinga, C., & Smith, G. M. (1999). *Passionate views: Film, cognition, and emotion*. Baltimore: Johns Hopkins University Press.
Prinz, J. (2011a). Against empathy. *The Southern Journal of Philosophy*, *49*(s1), 214–233.
Prinz, J. (2011b). Is empathy necessary for morality. In A. Coplan & P. Goldie (Eds.), *Empathy: Philosophical and psychological perspectives* (pp. 211–229). Oxford: Oxford University Press.
Pritchard, D. (2009). Knowledge, understanding and epistemic value. *Royal Institute of Philosophy Supplement*, *64*, 19–43.
Rapp, C. (2009). The nature and goals of rhetoric. In G. Anagnostopoulos (Ed.), *A companion to Aristotle* (pp. 577–596) Oxford: Wiley-Blackwell.
Rawls, J. (1964). *A theory of justice*. Oxford: Clarendon Press.
Recanati, F. c. (2009). De re and de se. *Dialectica*, *63*(3), 249–269.

Robinson, J. (2005). *Deeper than reason: Emotion and its role in literature, music, and art*. Oxford: Clarendon Press.

Roiphe, A. R. (1970). *Up the sandbox!*. New York: Simon & Schuster.

Ross, S. T. (2002). Understanding propaganda: The epistemic merit model and its application to art. *Journal of Aesthetic Education*, *36*(1), 16–30.

Rusconi, G. E. (1993). *Se cessiamo di essere una nazione*. Bologna: Mulino.

Ryan, M., & Kellner, D. (Eds.). (1990). *Camera politica: The politics and ideology of contemporary Hollywood film*. Bloomington, IN: Indiana University Press.

Sacks, O. (2010). *Musicophilia: Tales of music and the brain*. New York: Vintage Canada.

Sandel, M. J. (1998). *Liberalism and the limits of justice*. Cambridge: Cambridge University Press.

Schmitt, C. (1996). *The concept of the political*. Chicago: University of Chicago Press.

Scott, I. (2000). *American politics in Hollywood film*. Edinburgh: Edinburgh University Press.

Sibley, F. (1959). Aesthetic concepts. *The Philosophical Review*, *68*(4), 421–450.

Sinnerbrink, R. (2011). *New philosophies of film: Thinking images*. London: Bloomsbury.

Smith, J. (2014). *Film criticism, the cold war, and the blacklist: Reading the Hollywood reds*. Berkeley: University of California Press.

Smith, M. (1995). *Engaging characters: Fiction, emotion, and the cinema*. New York: Oxford University Press.

Smith, M. (1996). The logic and legacy of Brechtianism. In D. B. N. Carroll (Ed.), *Post-theory: Reconstructing film studies* (pp. 130–148). Madison: University of Wisconsin Press.

Smith, M. (2006). Film art, argument, and ambiguity. *Journal of Aesthetics and Art Criticism*, *64*(1), 33–42.

Smith, M. (2011). Empathy, expansionism, and the extended mind. In A. Coplan & P. Goldie (Eds.), *Empathy: Philosophical and psychological perspectives* (pp. 99–117). Oxford: Oxford University Press.

Smith, M. (2017). Experience and explanation in the cinema. In B. Herzogenrath (Ed.), *Film and philosophy*. Minneapolis: University of Minnesota Press.

Solomon, R. C. (1976). *The passions*. University of Notre Dame Press.

Solomon, R. C. (2004). *In defense of sentimentality*. Oxford: Oxford University Press.

Sosa, E. (2007). *A virtue epistemology: Apt belief and reflective knowledge, volume I*. Oxford: Oxford University Press.

Sosa, E. (2009). *Reflective knowledge: Apt belief and reflective knowledge, volume II*. Oxford: Oxford University Press.

Stam, R. (2000). *Film theory: An introduction*. Oxford: Blackwell.

Stanley, J. (2015). *How propaganda works*. Princeton: Princeton University Press.

Stolnitz, J. (1992). On the cognitive triviality of art. *British Journal of Aesthetics*, *32*(3), 191–200.

Thompson, K., & Bordwell, D. (2010). *Film history* (3rd ed.). Boston: McGraw-Hill.

Thomson, J. J. (1976). A defense of abortion. In J. M. Humber & R. F. Almeder (Eds.), *Biomedical ethics and the law* (pp. 39–54). New York: Springer.

Thomson, J. J. (1985). Double effect, triple effect and the trolley problem: Squaring the circle in looping cases. *Yale Law Journal*, *94*(6), 1395–1415.

Vittorini, E. (1965). *Uomini e no*. Milano: Mondadori.
Walton, K. L. (1970). Categories of art. *The Philosophical Review*, *79*(3), 334–367.
Walton, K. L. (1990). *Mimesis as make-believe: On the foundations of the representational arts*. Cambridge: Harvard University Press.
Wartenberg, T. E. (2006). Beyond mere illustration: How films can be philosophy. *The Journal of Aesthetics and Art Criticism*, *64*(1), 19–32.
Wartenberg, T. E. (2007). *Thinking on screen: Film as philosophy*. New York: Routledge.
Wartenberg, T. E. (2011). On the possibility of cinematic philosophy. In H. Carel & G. Tuck (Eds.), *New takes in film-philosophy* (pp. 9–24). London: Palgrave Macmillan.
Welch, D. (2013). *Propaganda: Power and persuasion*. London: The British Library.
Wilcox, J. (1953). The beginnings of l'art pour l'art. *The Journal of Aesthetics and Art Criticism*, *11*(4), 360–377. doi:10.2307/426457
Wilde, O., Hart-Davis, R., & Holland, M. (2000). *The complete letters of Oscar Wilde*. London: Fourth Estate.
Williams, B. (2012). A critique of utilitarianism. In G. Scher (Ed.), *Ethics: Essential readings in moral theory* (pp. 253–261). New York: Routledge.
Williams, B. A. O. (1972). *Morality: An introduction to ethics*. New York: Harper & Row.
Wollheim, R. (1980). *Art and its objects: With six supplementary essays*. Cambridge: Cambridge University Press.
Woodruff, P. (1988). Engaging emotion in theater. *The Monist*, *71*(2), 235–257.
Zagzebski, L. (2001). Recovering understanding. In M. Steup (Ed.), *Knowledge, truth, and duty: Essays on epistemic justification, responsibility, and virtue* (pp. 235–252). Oxford: Oxford University Press.
Zajonc, R. B. (1984). On the primacy of affect. *American Psychologist*, *39*, 117–129.
Zajonc, R. B. (2000). Nonconscious and noncognitive affect. In J. P. Forgas (Ed.), *Feeling and thinking: The role of affect in social cognition* (pp. 31–58). Cambridge: Cambridge University Press.
Zangwill, N. (1998). Aesthetic/sensory dependence. *The British Journal of Aesthetics*, *38*(1), 66–81.

Filmography

Bechis, M. (1999). *Garage olimpo*. Argentina/France/Italy.
Bellocchio, M. (2012). *La Bella Addormentata*. Italy/France.
Comencini, L. (1960). *Tutti a casa*. Italy.
Crialese, E. (2006). *The golden door* (*Nuovomondo*). Italy.
Crialese, E. (2011). *Dry land*. (*Terraferma*). Italy.
Cuaròn, A. (2013). *Gravity*. United Kingdom/USA.
Curtis, R. (2003). *Love actually*. United Kingdom/USA/France.
Dardenne, L., & Dardenne, J. P. (2014). *Two days, one night*. Belgium/France/Italy.
Di Giacomo, F. (1980). *Men and not men*. (*Uomini e no*). Italy.
Dudow, S. (1932). *Kuhle Wampe*. Germany.
Eastwood, C. (2014). *American sniper*. USA.
Epstein, R. (1984). *The times of Harvey Milk*. USA.
Guggenheim, D. (2006). *An inconvenient truth*. USA.
Haggis, P. (2004). *Crash*. USA/Germany.
Koster, H. (1953). *The robe*. USA.
Lee, S. (1989). *Do the right thing*. USA.
Lizzani, C. (1951). *Achtung! Banditi*. Italy.
Mangiu, C. (2007). *4 months 3 weeks 2 days*. Romania.
Moore, M. (1998). *Roger and me*. USA.
Morris, E. (1999). *Mr. death: The rise and fall of Leuchter jr*. USA.
Oppenheimer, J. (2012). *The act of killing*. Norway/Denmark/United Kingdom.
Parkes, W., & Critchlow, K. F. (1975). *California Reich*. USA.
Petri, E. (1973). *Todo modo*. Italy.
Polanski, R. (1994). *Death and the maiden*. USA/United Kingdom/France.
Pontecorvo, G. (1959). *Kapò*. Italy/France/Yugoslavia.
Reiner, C. (1984). *All of me*. USA.
Robbins, T. (1995). *Dead man walking*. USA.
Rossellini, R. (1959). *Il generale Della Rovere*. Italy/France.
Scola, E. (1976). *Una giornata particolare*. Italy.
Stone, O. (1991). *JFK*. USA.
Valèe, J. M. (2009). *Young Victoria*. United Kingdom/USA.
Van Groeningen, F. (2012). *The broken circle breakdown*. Belgium.
Willimon, B. (2013–2016). *House of cards*. USA.
Zvyagintsev, A. (2014). *Leviathan*. Russia.

Index

Made in the USA
Las Vegas, NV
29 October 2024

fc984d5c-f029-475d-9863-173817d3ef80R01